Why We Write: Craft Essays on Writing War

A Military Writers Guild Anthology

Randy Brown &
Steve Leonard, editors

Middle West Press LLC
Johnston, Iowa

Language Arts & Disciplines / Writing / Authorship
Why We Write: Craft Essays on Writing War
ISBN (print): 978-0-9969317-8-6
ISBN (e-book): 978-0-9969317-9-3
Library of Congress Control Number: 2019953313

Middle West Press LLC
P.O. Box 31099
Johnston, Iowa 50131-9428
www.middlewestpress.com

Special thanks to James Burns of Aurora, Colo.
Your patronage helps publish great military-themed writing!
Learn more at: www.aimingcircle.com

Cover Design
Paul Hewitt / Battlefield Design
URL: www.battlefield-design.co.uk
E-mail: info@battlefield-design.co.uk

Other Military-themed Books from Middle West Press LLC

poetry

Welcome to FOB Haiku:
War Poems from Inside the Wire,
by Randy Brown, a.k.a. "Charlie Sherpa"

Hugging This Rock:
Poems of Earth & Sky, Love & War
by Eric Chandler

Permanent Change of Station
by Lisa Stice

non-fiction

Reporting for Duty:
U.S. Citizen-Soldier Journalism
from the Afghan Surge, 2010-2011
Edited by Randy Brown

Table of Contents

War Stories

Building Bridges & Platforms

The Arts of War & Writing

❖ ❖ ❖

Introduction

By Christopher G. Ingram

We each have a story to tell. Libraries, journals, songs, and social media are full of stories. Each story is as unique as the experience of the soul that spilled itself through ink or keys. Sharing them connects us all.

Building a mutually supportive community of storytellers has always been the heart of the Military Writers Guild. We began in 2014 as an informal group, with members mostly focused on discourse regarding the "profession of arms." We quickly expanded to include creators engaged in literature, history, scholarship, and more. The work continues: Recently, we announced the guild has achieved legal status as a 501(c)3 non-profit organization.

Through these efforts, our guild seeks to build an inclusive community of practice that elevates the discourse in military writing through collaboration, and the promotion of our craft.

The Military Writers Guild includes members of land, air, and maritime armed forces, those who have served or are currently serving in the defense of the United States, but also Australia, Canada, India, New Zealand, the United Kingdom, and more. And, because "military writing" is not limited to those who wear a uniform, our community of practice also includes "civilians"— journalists, think-tank analysts, historians, and other scholars who work and write in the military ecosphere.

Just as our backgrounds are unique, so too are our voices. Our members write and edit novels and memoirs, poems and podcasts, academic and literary journals, speculative fiction and hard-facts history, humor and tragedy. We each have a story. This anthology collects many perspectives and offers many insights—and serves as an example of what is possible, when our members engage in discourse with the world around them.

War is humanity under extreme conditions. We tell our war stories because we want others to remember our pain, our loss, our *esprit de corps*. We are witnesses to absurdities and heroics. The emotions from these experiences cut deep. Scars can remain unseen.

For some, telling stories can be therapeutic. Former U.S. Marine officer and memoirist Teresa Fazio, for example, describes how "words debrided my memories so scar tissue could form." Former U.S. Army Military Police soldier Jeremy Warneke tells how he used writing following a fellow soldier's non-combat death. Author of *We Meant Well: How I Helped Lose the*

Battle for the Hearts and Minds of the Iraqi People, former U.S. State Department officer Peter Van Buren writes about a memorial service he experienced while a Provincial Reconstruction Team (PRT) leader in Iraq.

Telling stories can involve challenging doctrine, dogma, or the institutions we cherish. Historian and U.S. Navy officer Benjamin "BJ" Armstrong writes about how sailor William Sims successfully argued for the reform of Navy targeting practices. When U.S. Marine officer Kate Germano retired from uniformed service, she continued to advocate for positive change on behalf of her fellow Marines. One result was her 2018 book, *Fight Like a Girl: The Truth Behind How Female Marines Are Trained*.

As journalist and historian Vanya Eftimova Bellinger, author of *Marie von Clausewitz: The Woman Behind the Making of "On War,"* points out, "conflict raises the profound and most unsettling questions about the human condition." In his essay, Australian Army officer Tom McDermott illuminates how writing enabled him to reflect on the moral ambiguities of his personal experiences in combat—and then helped create an institutional change to engage future leaders in such discussions.

Others face down bureaucratic absurdity with satire. With pithy novels such as *Fobbit* and *Brave Deeds*, former U.S. Army public affairs soldier David Abrams carries on in the tradition of Joseph Heller's *Catch-22*. As Abrams says in his essay: "humor on one page, horror on the next." After she left her role as a reports officer for U.S. Central Intelligence Agency's Directorate of Operations, Alex Finley proceeded to write two hilarious novels about life in a fictionalized organization called the "CYA."

As several contributors to *Why We Write* point out, a good story is rooted in the details. Vivid descriptions bring reality, depth, and a sense of immersion. Former U.S. Army officer Jocelyn Corbin, for example, takes readers along as she hands her ripcord to the jumpmaster. In a science-fiction short, former U.S. Navy officer Roger Misso places a discussion of professional development against a background of interstellar travel.

In the 1980s, Tom Clancy's *Red Storm Rising* realistically explored the effects of politics, strategy, and technology through speculative fiction. Today's writers, inspired by Clancy's work, similarly use science fiction to engage readers with innovative possibilities. Contributors P.W. Singer and August Cole's *Ghost Fleet: A Novel of the Next War*, and Max Brooks' *World War Z: An Oral History of the Zombie War*, enable us to consider how World War III or a zombie outbreak might "actually" happen.

Writing is the connective tissue between our individual past experiences and our collective futures. As former U.S. Army strategist, creator of the *Doctrine Man!!* web comic, and co-editor of this anthology Steve Leonard memorably puts it: Writing will be our legacy.

U.S. Army officer Joe Byerly, founder of the blog *From the Green Notebook*, writes about how he writes to collect and focus his thoughts, as well as to engage others in professional dialogue. Australian Army general officer Mick Ryan observes that writing is at the core of being part of a profession of arms. In his essay, U.S. Navy helicopter pilot John "Jack" McCain IV notes that "our stories become part of the living, breathing, heart of the service."

Many contributors to this anthology, some of whom are members of the Military Writers Guild, have created platforms for celebrating, empowering, or featuring military writing. Such resources include, but are not limited to: *The Field Grade Leader, The Cove, The Aiming Circle, The Dead Prussian* podcast, *Divergent Options, The Military Leader, Line of Advance, The Strategy Bridge* and more. Like the guild itself, these projects are motivated by a passion to help others tell their stories. We are a networked community that cares about both the experiences and the conduct of war, and the craft of writing about it.

This anthology is another platform, another resource, another opportunity to share stories. If you're reading this book, we know you have a story to tell. Our hope is that one of these writers will inspire you to tell that story, in your own way.

The Military Writers Guild can help.

Christopher G. Ingram is the current president of the Military Writers Guild. He serves as a U.S. Army infantry officer, and has successfully completed tours of duty in Afghanistan, Korea, and Kuwait. His first published work was a poem in high school, but he has also written legislation, policy white papers, and speeches as a U.S. Congressional staff member in House and Senate offices. He holds a graduate degree in international affairs from American University, Washington, D.C. He has taught international conflict courses at Louisiana State University, Baton Rouge, La., and has been published in the peer-reviewed Journal of Politics. *As a military writer, Chris is published in journals such as* The Strategy Bridge, Small Wars Journal, The Military Leader, From the Green Notebook, *and* Task & Purpose. *Follow him on Twitter: @ChrisGIngram*

Calls to Action, Calls to Arms

Get Your Legacy in Writing

By Steve Leonard

For a third-year engineering student, Technical Writing for Engineers was an obligatory, necessary evil. Most engineers can't write, and I was a typical engineer-in-waiting. Quite honestly, I'd never paid much attention in English class growing up, and typically used that time to either get a head start on other homework or to catch up on lost sleep. In high school, one of my friends actually tried to teach me how to sleep with my eyes open so I wouldn't be so obvious to our English teacher, Mrs. Thompson. Writing just wasn't my thing.

So, when I opened my class folder to find a note from the professor that simply said, "See me," I wasn't that surprised. To avoid spending too much time on my first paper, I'd regurgitated the text from one I wrote on Soviet missile design for a mechanical engineering class the previous semester. Well, I'd gambled and lost. It was a great way to start a new semester. Who knew that the English and Engineering departments actually shared notes?

Chuck Stratton was your stereotypical English professor: Rumpled, middle-aged, with a trademark cardigan sweater and shoes that were probably older than most of his students. Wire-rimmed bifocals perched atop a mop of unkempt graying hair. I sat down expecting to receive a lecture on student laziness, but what came next truly surprised me.

"I don't appreciate plagiarism," he said dryly, staring down at me over the top of his glasses. "You're either the best writer I've seen in 25 years of teaching, or you're a plagiarist. Which is it?"

Well, I wasn't a plagiarist, I assured him.

His stare turned into a frown, the skepticism stabbing into me. The tension in room was raw. A silence hung over us for what seemed hours. He took a long breath, then slowly exhaled with a sigh.

"Then you're in the wrong major," he replied. "You need to be developing this skill, putting it to use. You should be publishing already."

Great. Three years into becoming an engineer, I find this out. "It's a little late for me to switch majors," I said.

"It's never too late. You need to start writing now and keep after it. Assuming, of course, you're not a plagiarist."

It really was too late to change majors, but I did the next best thing, much to the chagrin of the cadre in my ROTC department: I delayed my graduation by nearly two years to hone a skill I never knew I possessed. I added English and history classes to my schedule, which forced me to write more and engineer less. I parked my Hewlett-Packard calculator, and pounded out my thoughts on the word processors in the computer lab. I wrote, and wrote a lot.

To this day, I struggle with the taxonomy of the grammar police. I still don't know the significance of a coordinating conjunction, and honestly can't tell you the three forms of verbs. Nor do I care, for that matter. I write the way I write, and apparently it comes out of my head in a relatively properly structured manner. But *why* I write is far more important than *how* I write. Chuck Stratton's last lesson to me still rings true today:

"Writing is our legacy."

You see, we are a storytelling people. We always have been. Whether we're telling someone about the drunk uncle who ruined every Thanksgiving dinner, or explaining the nuances of grand strategy to a colleague, we tell stories. Writing those stories down ensures that our thoughts, our very ideas, live beyond our short time in this life. Those stories help others see into your mind—how you think. And they ensure that others can learn from you—your stories, your thoughts, your ideas—long after you're gone. That magic is only possible, however, if you write things down.

So, I began to write my stories. I researched my subjects, and carefully crafted words around them. I approached every story as if I was sharing it over a cup of coffee, weaving a narrative that tied the facts together like a fireside chat. I set out to publish at least one article each year, and met with greater success the more I wrote. My writing style evolved. Eventually, I overcame all those days lost sleeping in Mrs. Thompson's high school English class.

Not every article was published. Some of my best work was rejected outright as either "too folksy" or "insufficiently academic." But I held true to the belief that scholarly writing doesn't necessarily have to be bland and dry. The only thing better than telling a good story is telling a good story well.

I revisited historical debates. I told stories about life and death. I revived the memories of people long since lost to the march of time, and introduced new players on the grand stage of humanity. I explored the future, the opportunities and threats that may lurk beyond the horizon. But I wrote, and kept on writing.

Along the way, I challenged others to write as well. In every counseling session, during those momentary lulls in action during long deployments, over a cold beer in the lobby of the Embassy Suites, I made my case for building a personal legacy of knowledge. "Tell your story" will probably be my epitaph. Most ignored my counsel, but those who accepted the challenge found a welcoming audience eager to hear their stories.

Why does a legacy matter? Because when the sun finally sets on your career, you want something lasting to mark your contribution to our profession, something that endures beyond your time in the rank and file. Most of us won't write memoirs—frankly, we're just not that interesting. But we all have experiences to share and lessons to pass on. We have stories that need to be told.

What you give back to our professional body of knowledge matters. It makes a difference. And if we're not here to make a difference, why are we here?

Steve Leonard is a former U.S. Army officer and senior military strategist, an award-winning faculty member at the University of Kansas School of Business, and the creative force behind the defense microblog Doctrine Man!! *A career writer and speaker with a passion for developing and mentoring the next generation of thought leaders, he is a senior fellow at the Modern War Institute at West Point; the co-founder of the national security blog* Divergent Options *and* The Smell of Victory *podcast; co-founder and board member of the Military Writers Guild; and a member of the editorial review board of the Arthur D. Simons Center's* InterAgency Journal (IAJ). *Published extensively, his writing focuses on issues of foreign policy, national security, strategy and planning, leadership and leader development. He also occasionally writes fiction. An alumnus of the U.S. Army's School of Advanced Military Studies, he led the interagency team that authored the Army's first stability operations doctrine, spearheaded the reintroduction of operational art into capstone doctrine, and wrote the guiding principles for the Army Design Methodology. He is the author of five books, numerous professional articles, countless blog posts, and is a prolific military cartoonist. Follow him on Twitter:* @Doctrine_Man

This Blog of Mine Goes Forth to War

By William Treadway

One Kansas winter night at the top of 2011, my unit boarded buses for Topeka, headed there to catch an eastbound plane for Afghanistan. I would deploy as a platoon leader in Alpha Troop as part of the "Second Surge." During our transit, I started writing an e-mail newsletter to family and friends back home. It wasn't meant to become a blog, but a friend suggested it as an alternative to blasting out e-mails. I called it *The Texan Who Would Be King*, cribbing the title from a Rudyard Kipling story about two ex-British soldiers who also travelled to Central Asia with expectations not met by reality. What would become our new reality stomped our own expectations flat, too.

We had trained for Iraq. We had planned for Iraq. We had expected to be closing Forward Operating Bases (FOB), and wrapping up the fight around the Tigris River. As a result, that first foot patrol in Afghanistan, amongst the grape rows on the banks of the Arghandab River, was a rude awakening for a passel of cavalry troopers. Many of us had spent more time than we'd have liked to admit dozing on a Bradley ramp.

As our operations entered full swing, so did my blog. Updates became longer, more regular, and included better pictures. It gained a small following amongst folks in our unit. I even got an e-mail telling me that the brass in Kandahar had eyes on the blog to better understand the incongruities between the war they planned, and the war we fought.

Our Squadron Commander (SCO) initially supported my writing. The blog had found its way to some of the families and wives of the men in my platoon, and the commander liked the compliments he received from the Family Readiness Group (FRG). He strived to be well-liked.

Around April, combat intensified. With it came casualties, including the first death in my platoon. The writing on the blog started to reflect these tensions and strains. As the stories grew heavier, I suspect that the compliments the commander once enjoyed were now becoming concerns.

I should point out that I was very careful. I did not use names of places that actually existed, and took steps to ensure I did not end up among the buffoons who posted graphics of their Combat Outposts (COP) on social media. Operational Security (OPSEC) was important to me, so most of what I wrote was not published until weeks after the events occurred.

That is, with one exception: the post that killed the blog.

The post was about an "Air Assault" on a town called Bur Muhammad.

It was truthfully an "Air Insertion," but the SCO didn't know much about military vocabulary and definitions. It was a circus, as these things often are when the commander is a clown. We were wheels up from FOB Pasab before sunrise. The plan had our Landing Zone (LZ) about 600 meters from the objective, meant to give us the opportunity to organize a deliberate approach and to seize it. However, when the Chinooks touched down and we stormed down the ramp to establish security, it did not take long to realize that they set us down directly adjacent to the objective.

I was pissed.

Thankfully, it turned out that the objective was not hostile, but downright hospitable. The compound would become the squadron's Command Post (CP) for the next couple of days. We secured it, brought in the headquarters element, and prepared to attack the next objective once dawn broke. It was then I witnessed the SCO take a unique approach to supervising his subordinate units. While combat operations were ongoing, with two of his three line units engaged, he decided to lay right down and go to sleep.

War, like they say, is just *exhausting*.

I wish I could say the rest of the mission passed as uneventfully as his nap, but Charlie Troop had a soldier killed-in-action (KIA) to precise enemy fire, and other platoons took casualties as well. All my platoon had to do was hold the center. While firefights occurred regularly, they seemed to be against the remnants of what Charlie Troop and the squadron's flex platoon had already chewed up and spat back out.

As dusk on the final day set in, both line troops began to consolidate and pull out of Bur Muhommad for extraction. When night came, I was on a knee with my soldiers in front of the most beautiful Pick-up Zone (PZ) I'd ever seen, compliments of Charlie Troop. Three immaculate NATO Y-shapes were laid out by infrared chemlight, exactly on the grid coordinates prescribed. The precision of these markings was critical, as just 100 meters to the south was a templated belt of Improvised Explosive Devices (IED). Charlie Troop's first sergeant was a Pathfinder-qualified former member of the 101st Airborne "Screaming Eagle" Division, so the fact that it was done perfectly came as no surprise.

What *did* come as a surprise was where the Chinooks chose to land instead of the PZ. I watched, champing at the bit for the sprint to come, as the three hulking birds appeared for a second as though they would land where they were supposed to. They didn't. Again. For the second time in the same mission.

Rather, all three popped flares simultaneously, bathing the field in light as though it were day, exposing the positions of a hundred soldiers. Remember that we were all in Pickup Zone posture, lined up ready to run to the helicopters, so the sudden illumination literally highlighted our moment of maximum vulnerability. And then it got worse: They decided to land in the templated IED belt.

Sometimes you've just got to embrace the Suck, so I told the men that we were going. We ran across the field like crazy people: no mine detectors, no enablers, shielded only by crossed fingers and my Forward Observer's magical Mormon underwear.

Upon arriving at the helicopter, I roared at the crew chief about my many grievances. About what a bunch of fuck-ups his unit was, about his mother's chosen profession and what diseases she'd contracted working it, about how every Shithook pilot in that lift squadron should be dragged from their bunks and shot. It was not my finest hour.

Regardless, and thankfully, he couldn't hear my misdirected anger over the din of the rotors. Only years later, while stationed at U.S. Army Aviation's home of Fort Rucker, Ala., would I realize that my true beef was with the air mission commander—the lead pilot.

When the mission was over, we had a day of recovery and After-Action Reviews (AAR). Having found some sleep and a little perspective, I raised my hand during the "sustains" and "improves" portion of the review. I mentioned I had a suggestion: We needed Chinook pilots to land where they were supposed to. This was met with strong resistance from the SCO (and everyone else) as unhelpful and unproductive. I did not take that well.

Within a day, I had posted a new blog entry, furious at the blasé attitude in response to what I considered to be real concerns. The post was not kind to the pilots of that lift squadron. I had gone back to the COP by this time, and didn't think much about it until a few weeks later at the FOB, when I ran into the SCO at the barber shop. With his usual craving for approval, he told me that it was a good post, and even agreed with me, laughing about taking the pilots to task.

I was stunned; I had expected an ass-chewing, at least. That, however, would come later.

Fast-forward two months, to when I'd left my platoon after a year-and-a-half to become the executive officer of Charlie Troop. In that role, I took a phone call from the SCO. "There's a motorcycle-borne IED threat against COP Kolk. All of your soldiers need to be in full kit when outside tents until further notice," he informed me. I confirmed, "Roger, Sir. The commander just walked in, would you like to talk to him?" He said yes, and that was the last I spoke to him about it.

After the call, I asked my troop commander if the SCO mentioned anything about wearing full kit outside the tent. He didn't, my immediate boss relayed. I shrugged it off and figured it wasn't terribly important since tent fabric will not save you from frag or blast. Additionally, COP Kolk had on its perimeter a K-rail chicane, two pneumatic steel gates, a 2-inch-thick iron swing gate (all at the only access point), and, of course, a complete wall of ubiquitous Hesco baskets, 14 feet tall and 7 feet thick. Good luck sneaking in and parking by the mess tent.

The fact is, despite all of that, I was wrong. My commander had given an order and I didn't follow it because it was stupid. This is obviously not the right answer for junior officers, but it was the course I took. Days later, the headquarters element arrived at our outpost. The SCO and his sergeant major were not happy to see folks outside the tents without full kit. My troop commander was also not super-pleased with me. No motorcycle-borne IEDs ever came.

I skated, with no material consequences for my insubordination. I was counseled on paper by the SCO and my troop commander (CO), though even that didn't impact future evaluations in the slightest. After the SCO got in his truck and left, my CO informed me I would no longer be writing my blog. When I asked why, he told me that the SCO was displeased with comments I made about Chinook pilots weeks prior, that we were all on the same team, and that my unprofessionalism towards fellow soldiers was unacceptable. The SCO lacked the fortitude to address this to my face.

Having just dodged the failure-to-follow-orders bullet, my position in this matter was not one of strength. If I kept publishing the blog, I might be putting myself back in the path of the danger I closely avoided. So, I shut it down and ceased writing my chronicle of the war.

I could object to the censorship, but it was at root self-imposed. Nothing could stop me from writing and publishing if I chose, but the consequence of disgrace would follow, and that I was not something I was willing to accept. Additionally, my attitude about and towards the Army deteriorated rapidly during the latter-half of the deployment. I no longer had anything constructive to provide, and mounting, meaningless casualties fueled a deep rage about the war.

At the end of the movie version of *The Man Who Would Be King*, the character played by Sean Connery sings a hymn. About to be executed for his crimes, he belts out while standing on a disintegrating rope bridge:

He bowed his head, his death to feel.
Who followed in his train?

The blog, too, was executed for its crimes, and rightly so, I must admit. But as it bowed, ready for death to feel, what would follow in its train? With the sails of blogging now without wind, I reserved myself to private poetry as an outlet for my thoughts and emotions. In the years since, I've written short stories and have made steady progress on a novel. I swore I wouldn't write again about my deployment, however, at least not for the public.

In my writing today, references to the war are always tangential, set apart, or couched in the tropes of science fiction. None of the writing is explicitly about Afghanistan—but, then again, maybe all of it is somehow about Afghanistan. Perhaps the truths contained within it hover below the text of every fictional interstellar battle, every costly error depicted in plot, and every toxic trait played out in fictional character.

After all, here I am, writing directly about Afghanistan.

Maybe you can't keep a good blog down.

William Treadway is a former tanker and U.S. 1st Armored Division alumnus. Born in Houston in the 1980s, he graduated from the U.S. Military Academy in 2009, and commissioned as an armor officer. In 2011, he took a platoon to Afghanistan to join the party. Upon completion of service, he returned to Houston, where he currently operates a computer hardware manufacturing business.

Pressing the Button

By Joe Byerly

In 2013, I sat nervously in front of my laptop with a 600-word idea on the screen. For the first time in my military career, I had created a short article that would be viewed by thousands of people, but only after I clicked the "Publish" button. It was my very first blog post on what would become *From the Green Notebook*, a website that I had created that same morning. I almost held back from "pushing the button." I was worried that it would be poorly received. I did not think people would read it. I thought my peers would look down on me.

In the end, however, I pushed the button. I published my ideas, and since then have done so more than a hundred more times.

I continue to "press the button," because it is my way to develop myself and contribute to the profession of arms. Writing helps me to collect and focus my thoughts. The blog serves as a catalyst for professional development. My writings help to start conversations, which may help others improve how they lead and develop themselves. It is also my chance to leave a legacy that will outlast my service.

One of my favorite quotes, attributed to E.M. Forster, is "How do I know what I think until I see what I say?" Seeing our thoughts in ink (or on the screen) can help us better grasp them. When I write, I challenge myself to be clearer in my thoughts and arguments. I find that I achieve a greater level of clarity in my ideas and convictions. Also, by considering a topic from the perspective of a person who might be unfamiliar with an idea, I improve my own fluency.

I carry a notebook with me everywhere, so that if an idea strikes me, I can immediately write it down. Those notes could remain random lines in my notebook, or develop into a 900-word blog post read by thousands. Whenever I get a few moments, I'll look over the notebook and reflect on its contents. I would have never started this practice, if I never "pressed the button."

Writing often helps start professional conversations, which may spark change throughout the military. A great example of this can be found during the Interwar Period. In the autumn of 1919, Maj. Dwight Eisenhower and Lt. Col. George Patton spent a considerable amount of time training, experimenting, and discussing new methods of tank warfare at Camp Meade, Md. They saw the possibility of using tanks to achieve rapid breakthroughs, rather than merely moving in support of the infantry. Eisenhower captured these ideas in writing and published them in a 1920 *Infantry Journal* article, titled "A Tank Discussion." At the time, he faced some pressure for publishing his thoughts. In the end, however, it contributed to a professional discussion that eventually led to better doctrine for the inclusion of armor in the fight.

There is also value in contributing to improvements on a smaller scale. Regarding my own blog, I've received e-mails from leaders all over the world, who have used my ideas to drive conversations and changes within their respective organizations.

Finally, I write because it allows me to create a legacy. By sharing my lessons, I can help future leaders not make the same stressful mistakes I did. In 2001, Tony Burgess and Nate Allen wrote the book *Taking the Guidon: Exceptional Leadership at the Company Level.* Even though the authors have since retired, their lessons continue to advise company-level leaders today.

When I "pressed the button" years ago, I had no idea that writing would eventually become part of who I am. I grow as a military professional with each post I write. I've started an untold number of conversations around the world that have positively influenced so many different types of leaders and organizations. Finally, I can leave something behind when I hang up the uniform, that future leaders can take and not make the same mistakes I did. I encourage you to do the same. You never know what will happen, once you "press the button."

Joe Byerly is a U.S. Army armor officer and recently served as a special advisor within the U.S. Special Operations Command. He received his undergraduate degree from the University of North Georgia and his graduate degree from the U.S. Naval War College. He is a non-resident fellow at the Modern War Institute at West Point and the founder of From the Green Notebook, *a blog emphasizing military leadership and professional development. His writings have been published in* War on the Rocks, Army Magazine, The Strategy Bridge, *and* Small Wars Journal.

How the World I Imagined Became Real

By Andrea N. Goldstein

I grew up in a house filled with books about war; as a teenager I wrote historical fiction. I imagined the daily lives of women during the Trojan War; I wrote about women who disguised themselves as men to fight in the American Civil War. I used fiction to tell stories of women forgotten by men who had written history.

One of my most influential high-school history teachers taught me that to truly understand history, we must understand women's lives. In order to understand their lives, we must look at the periphery of scholarship: letters, diaries, even recipes. Just because they are not in the canon does not mean they are not there.

I wrote fiction and poetry trying to imagine these realities, as much as I wrote to make sense of my own.

I did not go to college planning on joining the military, but that is what I did. And in the first few years of military indoctrination, I stopped writing. I thought my passion was gone, creativity suppressed entirely for who I needed to be as a naval officer.

But it was only dormant. The writer returned slowly, in waves.

First, I discovered a book by another military writer, U.S. Air Force veteran James Salter. I had recently returned from my first deployment, and was browsing in a bookstore near the University of Chicago while visiting for a former classmate's wedding. Salter's collection of short fiction *Dusk and Other Stories* was on a pile of "staff recommendations," and I purchased a copy.

His writing helped me make sense of my own world that frequently seemed diametrically opposed to itself, and find art in a world of discipline, to find the words to describe emotions and experiences that may barely even make sense to those who were there. Salter's writing changed my life.

And then, a year later, as I was getting ready to deploy again, I had my heart broken.

I have kept journals since I was 8, but I had not written in one since my senior year of college. As I tried to make sense of my loss, sitting in a hammock outside my parents' house on pre-deployment leave, I opened a blank page, and began to write. I found a poem that I had begun my senior year of college, before I had joined the Navy, and never finished. I finished it, and published it. During the deployment that followed, I went on to write 22 poems. I wrote in my journal every single day. I wrote about running on a warship as we transited the Straits of Malacca, about the world below as seen from a helicopter, about seeing meteor showers at sea, about my healing heart.

In putting pen to page, I became one of the women my teenaged self had imagined; I was not part of the canon, but I was at the periphery.

I did not publish any of it. It wasn't any good, but it was exercise to strengthen a muscle. A year later, a friend who remembered my high school writing connected me with the editorial team that began *Task & Purpose*.

They gave me a platform to write about what mattered to me. Personal essays at first. But then, the personal was also increasingly connected to culture, to policy. My articles began to go viral. Both friends and perfect strangers reached out to tell me that what I was writing resonated with them. Writing about what mattered to me began to mean writing about reforming the *institutions* that mattered to me. Why should more military women share their stories? Why did I leave active duty? How can gender perspectives improve the effectiveness of the military?

I began to write for other outlets. I began to make friends with other writers. I found a tribe within a tribe that not only remained, but grew after I left active-duty service for the reserves.

There's a pile of old journals on the bottom shelf of a bookcase in my house. It contains fragments of my life, days I lived, memories of war, scenarios I imagined, checklists and ideas for articles I may or may not have ever written.

In his last novel, James Salter wrote, "There comes a time when you realize that everything is a dream, and only those things preserved in writing have any possibility of being real."

I wrote to Salter a few years ago, thanking for him for writing and telling him what his work meant to me. He wrote back, and reflecting on his service in the Air Force, noted, "I think of them as great days and myself as having been lucky to have them."

He died a month later. I keep a copy of his note taped to my desk to remember that to be a military writer is to make reality of the often-unconscionable, not just for oneself, but for others. It is to continue a tradition. My journals and the articles I have published are evidence. It's all real. Perhaps, one day, it will emerge from the periphery.

Andrea N. Goldstein served in the U.S. Navy on active duty for seven years, and continues to serve as a reservist. A Pat Tillman Scholar and non-resident fellow at the Modern War Institute at West Point, she is a graduate of the University of Chicago, and The Fletcher School of Law and Diplomacy at Tufts University, Medford, Mass. She is widely published. She is a member of the Military Writers Guild, the Truman National Security Project, and the Council on Foreign Relations. Follow her on Twitter: @AN_Goldstein

Unraveling My Own Knowledge

By Phil Klay

I came home from Iraq with a lot of unquiet memories. Not traumatic memories, or even necessarily sad memories, but nevertheless unquiet. A year in Iraq means encountering some strange things.

There was the U.S. Marine flashing a "V for victory" sign as he and his buddy were brought in for surgery following an IED blast that would end up taking his friend's leg. The soldier who got an STD from a sex toy. The mortuary affairs specialist who described carefully uncurling the hands of a corpse to discover they clutched only rocks. The Nepalese chow hall workers who, a few days after Easter, repurposed a food sculpture of the Virgin Mary for a Hindu religious festival by sticking a third eye on her forehead. There were memories that were uplifting, memories that were deeply distressing, and memories that were simply odd. And then, of course, there was coming home.

America seemed so big, and so oblivious. Walking through Manhattan in the summer, seeing the people in elegant clothes, living their lives without seeming to have the least concern for what was happening overseas—it felt like being witness to a moral crime. There was such little public sense that we were a nation at war. I thought of a Navy doctor in Fallujah, who was interviewed by one of my Marines immediately after a mass casualty from a suicide bombing. He'd spent the last couple hours working feverishly on Iraqi civilians, and when my Marine requested an interview he'd taken him to the one place that was quiet—the morgue. There, the exhausted doctor wept, surrounded by the bodies of those they hadn't been able to save.

The disconnect between the two worlds was vast, and yet, we were only overseas because of the political decisions made at home. We were muddling through at the behest of an often distracted public who seemed poorly equipped to ensure accountability for the failures of our elected leaders, failures that had mortal consequences overseas. It was, I felt, disgusting. "We were at war while America was at the mall," I heard many veterans say. That felt right, even though my war, as a public affairs officer, hadn't been what most people imagine.

So I started writing about the war. Not about my experiences, but about people similar to those I'd known in the Corps. I wrote about the moral decisions soldiers face, decisions happening at a much lower level than the broad political debates most people think of—should we have gone in, did the Surge really work, what is victory supposed to look like in such a murky

PHIL KLAY

war—but decisions nonetheless of huge moral consequence. And I wrote about the experience of homecoming, of the ways in which the highly particular experiences of returning Marines clash with the expectations of the civilian population back home, a population that has nursed itself on stories of heroism and trauma and politically inflected understandings of what the war must mean. I wanted to sidestep the conventional narratives and give them something murkier and harder to categorize. We were at war, and they were at the mall—I wanted them to know what that felt like.

Except, of course, eventually I left the military. I moved back to New York. I settled back into a comfortable, New York existence. I even, occasionally, went to the mall, despite the fact that we were still very much at war. After all, a new pair of socks aren't going to purchase themselves.

Occasionally, though, the war would punch back into my consciousness in visceral ways. I'd learn a Marine I knew had died, or lost his vision in an IED blast. Once, I was in a bar in Greenpoint, writing, and a friend called and told me that a guy we'd both served with had been shot in Afghanistan. He was OK, but I might want to drop him a line, say hi.

So as time passed, my unquiet memories jostled uneasily with the fading sense of moral righteousness I'd experienced when I first came back, and even more uneasily with my difficulty reconciling the life I was living with the never-ending wars that so many of my fellow Marines were still fighting, but which I had left behind.

There is no form more perfect for expressing such conflicting feelings, ideas, moral sentiments, and experiences, than fiction. When working on a story, you take whatever nice, clean ideas you have about the world and you insert them into a situation where your characters have to grapple with those ideas. And as you set your characters in motion, navigating them around a situation you think you understand, and which you think has a clear moral to it, those characters inevitably end up taking a pickaxe to those nice, clean ideas. And then, midway through a story, I find out how thin my ideas about the world were, how simple and how false. And I have to work hard to do better.

There's a pervasive notion about war—the idea that only those who have been to war can truly understand what war is. In a large part because of the incredible difficulty and process of self-discovery that happens whenever I try and pin down the meaning of something in prose, I find this ridiculous. Just because you've been through an experience doesn't mean you understand anything about it. And often, the more intense the experience is, the more of a mystery it seems. As a father of two boys, this is certainly the way I feel about fatherhood, about which I can currently tell you little except exhaustion and joy. It's the way I feel about love, and the way I feel about suffering. In the grips of an intense experience, one which activates our emotional, aesthetic, moral and spiritual faculties, there is no

20

immediate understanding. Scraps of understanding only come with time, with conversation, with hard thinking. There is no question of what an experience *means,* but instead the question is what an individual *does* with that experience. How they choose to act, in relation to what they've been through.

This is what the fiction writer is forced to explore, time and again, as they create characters who must move through space and time, who must not simply intellectualize but also embody their experiences, and who must act. And when done well, this is what the reader must grapple with as well. If I have the sense that an experience is important—as I felt and still feel about the experience of Americans at war in a nation that seems unwilling to pay the least attention—then it is imperative for me not to deliver a message to a reader about that war, but to bring the reader in to ponder the questions and experiences I'm grappling with myself. And there is nothing better for this task than fiction.

Only in fiction can an author invite readers to imagine themselves inside the skulls of multiple people, to imagine experiences so seemingly foreign and yet so understandable articulated by a strong narrator. In his Nobel Prize Banquet Speech in 1952, the French writer Francois Mauriac said:

> We always believe in our uniqueness; we forget that the books which enchanted us, the novels of George Eliot or Dickens, of Tolstoy or Dostoevsky, or of Selma Lagerlöf, described countries very different from ours, human beings of another race and another religion. But nonetheless we loved them only because we recognized ourselves in them. The whole of mankind is revealed in the peasant of our birthplace.

And so ideally, in writing fiction, two things are happening: Instead of revealing to the reader what I know, I am slowly unraveling my own knowledge. And instead of taking in the revealed truth I have to offer, the reader instead is reacting to the text in ways I cannot imagine, supplying to the characters I have created—who are, after all, no more than constructions of words, blobs of ink upon a page—a human texture which they supply from their own lives. The reader is learning about a different world, yes, but also adding something to it, reacting with his own knowledge and wisdom. The text then serves as a bridge between me, that reader, and all the other readers creating their own versions of the characters I have supplied them. And in the best cases, the reader then starts to speak back, reacting to my stories by supplying something new.

It is for this exchange, this continuing conversation, that is the reason I write.

Phil Klay is a graduate of Dartmouth College and a veteran of the U.S. Marine Corps. He served in Iraq's Anbar Province from January 2007 to February 2008 as a Public Affairs Officer. After being discharged, he received an MFA from Hunter College of The City University of New York. In 2014, Klay's New York Times-*bestselling short-story collection* Redeployment *won the National Book Award for Fiction. The work also received the Marine Corps Heritage Foundation's James Webb award for fiction dealing with U.S. Marines or Marine Corps life; the National Book Critics' Circle John Leonard Award for best debut work in any genre; the American Library Association's W. Y. Boyd Literary Award for Excellence in Military Fiction; the Chautauqua Prize; and the Warwick Prize for Writing; and was short-listed for the Frank O'Connor Prize. He was also named a National Book Foundation "5 Under 35" honoree. Klay's writing has appeared in* The New York Times, Washington Post, Wall Street Journal, Newsweek, *and the Brookings Institution's Brookings Essay series.*

On Writing the Other Clausewitz

By Vanya Eftimova Bellinger

When people ask me about how I came to write a book on Marie von Clausewitz and the unknown history of Carl von Clausewitz's treatise *On War*, I usually answer that I owe everything to former U.S. President George W. Bush. It is a memorable line—and, in fact, true.

I was born in Bulgaria and spent years living in Germany. Yet just like many military writers from my generation, 9/11 and the Global War On Terrorism (GWOT) have marked my professional and personal life. The first time I heard about Carl von Clausewitz and his seminal work was in the tumultuous days preceding the U.S.-led invasion of Iraq in 2003. To convey the story of Marie and Carl von Clausewitz and the creation of *On War* became my obsession, but also an outlet for many of the pressing questions in my head.

The popular notion is that people write because they have something important to say. I, however, have always had more questions than answers about the world we live in. Writing about an issue helps me learn and discover more about it. In my first decade as a journalist, I have repeatedly volunteered, or even relentlessly petitioned, to work diverse assignments. The more unique the better. For example, I have written about hoarding (why do we need to keep every little scrap of paper from our messy life?); long-distance relationships (is this the new normal or a ruse for people who avoid true commitment?); Mitt Romney's election party in 2012 (how does it feel to see your greatest political dream die in one night, in the most public way?); the first ladies (why do American voters hesitate to elect a female president, but are eager to award an unelected woman so much visibility and informal power?); and the pets U.S. soldiers bring back home from war zones (does saving one innocent creature from war's hell really bring back a feeling of normalcy?).

War and organized violence evolved into my most enduring fascination, for conflict raises the profound and most unsettling questions about the human condition. As many others, I remember exactly where I was on Sept. 11, 2001. I spent the night after the terrorist attacks against the United States in the newsroom of the Bulgarian National Television, monitoring the wire for breaking news. Honestly, I was little help. That night, there were too many reporters like myself, helplessly pushing the refresh button and hoping for answers, any answers, about what had transpired.

I heard the name Carl von Clausewitz for the first time in 2003, as well as the famous phrase that "war is continuation of politics by other means." Pundits on the television and in the media frequently repeated it as reference to President George W. Bush's decision to invade Iraq — in the wake of 9/11, there was a political vision for the overhaul of the Middle East, and war was the instrument to be employed to achieve it. The concept about the political nature of war stuck in my head, because it vainly tried to explain Bush administration's insatiable rush to go to war when the rest of the world questioned the outcome of the invasion. At the same time, it impelled me to think what it means to develop realistic political goals for a military operation, and whether war as a political instrument had its limits. It should come as no surprise that around that period I bought my first copy of *On War* in German.

In 2003 in Berlin, I marched against the U.S.-led invasion in Iraq in what was called back then perhaps the largest demonstration in Germany after World War II. Today, as I teach U.S. officers in Professional Military Education (PME) programs, I like to show them the pictures from that day. I know that my gesture is often perceived as the proverbial thumb in the eye, especially since most of them had sacrificed so much during the long and hard deployments in Iraq. In this case, I don't shy away from debate, because we still need to wrestle with the issues surrounding the GWOT. We still have not even started to truly answer the questions the invasion, the "Surge," and the withdrawal have raised.

Meanwhile war became, literally, an inseparable part of my world, too. I married an American soldier. Being a military spouse was a lonely and tedious occupation, even for those like me who were lucky enough to preserve their previous career during reoccurring moves, singlehandedly taking care of the household, and the intense stress of having your loved one frequently deployed. Yet this experience was also a blessing in disguise, because when my intellectual interests and personal story converged, I gave *On War* a second look in depth.

It is a well-known fact that Carl von Clausewitz never published the seminal theory in his lifetime. When he suddenly died in November 1831, it had been left to Marie to release it to the public. In my mind, however, this personal detail raised many questions. During their 2-decades-long marriage and the prolonged courtship preceding it, Carl and Marie shared almost everything—ideas, political views, and experiences during the Napoleonic Wars. Still, Carl's decision to leave the manuscript with Marie constituted an unusual move.

In the early 19th century, women seldom played public roles, let alone edit important books. Marie had never served in uniform, nor fought a battle. Despite reading extensively, she was not even a writer in her own right—the few essays she composed were shared only with closest friends and family.

Despite his persistent health problems, Clausewitz never felt the urge to finish and publish *On War* prematurely. The military theorist could have instructed some of his friends, most of them decorated veterans from the Napoleonic Wars, to publish his lifework. The thoughtful and disciplined man, instead, left the manuscript of *On War* to his wife. In my mind, there was obviously more to Marie than simply a high-born and well-connected court lady. Why did Clausewitz feel completely comfortable to leave it to Marie to publish a book that was aimed at nothing less than an overhaul of all existing theory on war?

If I could answer some of these questions, then, perhaps, I could better understand the conditions from which *On War* emerged.

Apart from the fact that the treatise was an unfinished work written in early 19th century German, lack of knowledge about the times and context of its creation remains the greatest obstacle for readers. By taking a long and hard look at the tumultuous time following one of the greatest upheavals in human history—the French Revolution and the Napoleonic Era—I could, perhaps, study too the perpetual questions about how internal politics shape the course of war, and how the passion of the people fuels and escalates conflicts.

It was a curious line of questioning. There were, at first, few primary sources I could engage. Although most biographers admitted the unusual role Marie played in Clausewitz's life and legacy, none studied her in depth. There was a reason for that—although the majority of his correspondence to Marie was published, and serves as a crucial source of information about his life and ideas, only 16 of Marie's letters to him were known. The rest, together with Clausewitz's papers, was considered lost in the fires and destruction of World War II.

In this case, my questions brought me further than I have ever expected. I submitted enquiries to various German museums, asking whether they possessed any documents on Marie and Carl von Clausewitz. In December 2012, I received the incredible e-mail from the Prussian Privy State Archives in Berlin, notifying me that the complete correspondence between Carl and Marie von Clausewitz fortuitously resurfaced.

Military history often circumvents the role women played in it. To some extent, it is understandable, for women's lives on the home front, their existence in the military camps, and work in the hospitals lack the glorious rush of the battle and the excitement of great victories. In this regard, superficially, Marie's story was rather typical. Hers was the world of Berlin's salons and political intrigues. She spent brief periods in the military camp between battles and marches, and cared for the wounded in the 1815 campaign. And yet, this was an example of the genuine world and conditions surrounding conflict, for real war is more than glorious battles. Neither Marie nor Carl always understood the complexity of their worlds, or made the right calls every time. Indeed, quite the contrary: Their thoughts and deeds often sound ambiguous and uncomfortable for modern audience, even more so because the notion that someone would read and publish their intimate correspondence two centuries later never crossed the couple's minds.

Through Marie's eyes, Clausewitz was not a distant genius or a vexing philosopher of war, but a veteran staff officer striving to capture his enormous experience on paper. He was an imperfect man and a messy writer. He was a senior officer impatient with the political class and increasingly unhappy with the trajectory of his country, yet also intellectually defended the primacy of the political realm over the military. An original thinker, he struggled with a myriad of questions. In his time, the fusion of politics and war emerged. When the French Revolution declared every man a citizen, war, the old domain of kings and professional military, became the business of the people. After 1789, France could, in theory, mobilize every male and rely on enormous resources; yet the infusion of people's passion into the system also introduced a certain instability in it, creating conditions for escalation of violence close to nearly absolute proportions. This was a new and radical reality many of Clausewitz's contemporaries also struggled to understand. What distinguished him and ultimately turned him into the historical figure we know today, is the sophisticated analysis of these developments and the desire to describe war in its totality.

With this grand vision in mind, Clausewitz wrote and rewrote the manuscript several times, placed it aside, and then explored different ideas ranging from politics to aesthetics. He never succumbed to the desire to publish the treatise prematurely for the sake of publicity and recognition. In this, the story about the creation of *On War* is rather reassuring and relatable. The great philosopher of war, as it turns out, was actually someone just like us, a man struggling with the great questions of the time. When Clausewitz died, following the same logic, Marie decided to publish the treatise the way the husband had left the manuscripts, for a comprehensive editing might inadvertently redraft some of his ideas, especially the ones that ran against the prevailing attitudes of the day. Most of all, she wished to remind his readers that this was an unfinished work, an exploration of an endless subject, where no firm prescriptions could exist.

Contrary to Clausewitz, I do not hesitate from publishing my work, even if I know that it is far from the last word on the subject. My book *Marie von Clausewitz: The Woman Behind the Making of "On War"* brought me recognition beyond my expectations, but it did not come without cost: My marriage did not survive the pressures of deployments and a 2-career family. Yet I continually wrangle with the questions of our time—and I still cogitate over *On War's* dense and complex text. Struggling to capture difficult ideas on paper gives me much intellectual heartbreak, but also provides me access to places of knowledge and has introduced me to people I have yearned to meet. I write because it is the way I can deal with the world outside and the clashing worlds in my mind—just as the Clausewitzes once did.

Vanya Eftimova Bellinger is an assistant professor of Strategy and Security Studies at the Air University's eSchool of Graduate Professional Military Education and Air Command and Staff College in Montgomery, Ala. Previously, she taught as a visiting professor at the U.S. Army War College in Carlisle, Penn. Bellinger is a doctoral student at King's College, London. She is a graduate of Norwich University's Master of Arts Program in Military History. Follow her on Twitter: @vanyaef

A Tall Ship ... and a Story to Steer Her By

By John "Jack" McCain IV

I was 15 years old when my father gave me a copy of Nicholas Monsarrat's *The Cruel Sea*. I was beginning to contemplate what I wanted to do after high school. While there had always been an inexplicit expectation that I would attend the U.S. Naval Academy, the book was the first time he gave me a more formal introduction to what life could hold, were the Navy to become my profession. His father had given him the book, presumably with the same intent, when he was about the same age.

The book tells the story of a ship's crew in the Royal Navy during World War II, escorting convoys and conducting anti-submarine operations in the Atlantic Ocean. It is a story of fatigue, failure, and the fraying of men's lives. It describes the difficulty and danger of life at sea while being hunted by submarine wolfpacks. Friendships are wrecked, men die, and the mission seems, at many times, utterly hopeless. But it is also a story of heroism, and comradeship, and the ultimate victory of the British in the war. Underpinning the whole tale is the story of the sea itself, beautiful, horrible, and unforgiving. Neither my father or grandfather were surface sailors, nor am I, and the men in the book were not Americans. But my naval forebears felt this story offered truths so important they chose it as my very first introduction to my professional and personal future. It is in stories like these, told through literature, film, photography, anecdote, and others, where the human soul of our military resides. That is why it is so important to recount our experiences—to tell our stories.

Homer gave us the story of Achilles' rage in the *Iliad*. In the *Odyssey*, he recounted the difficult homecoming of a soldier, Odysseus, a stranger to all but his faithful dog, Argos—an apt metaphor for anyone returning from deployment. Through the poem "An Irish Airman Foresees His Death," W.B. Yeats—although not a veteran himself (he was writing about a friend)—showed us the death meditation of an aviator in World War I. More recently, Oliver Stone told his personal Vietnam War story in his postmodernist film *Platoon,* delving into the bitterness and violence of a war without perceived purpose. Even the sometimes humorous, sometimes odious film *Range 15*—one of the first uniquely veteran-produced films— speaks to stories of trials, of tribes, and of traditions.

These stories serve as three distinct tools, each of which are critical for the service and the members therein: They serve the individual, as a tool of self-reflection. They serve the unit and service at large, as a mnemonic of tribal traditions, culture, and history. Finally, they serve as a bridge between the service member and the society they serve.

I have kept a journal for as long as I can remember. Sometimes months go by in-between times when I put my thoughts on paper. Even then, my notes are often simply a recounting of events. The act serves as a way to collect my thoughts, however, and to begin to put the events I have experienced into perspective—even at those times clarity is nowhere to be found. In a similar way, I also make a habit of reviewing my military pilot's logbook. Even just listing the names, dates, hours flown, and locations is an excellent way to re-live and remember the past events.

I have also been introduced to the concept of a death meditation, a tool through which someone envisions the story of their own death. This can be done in many forms, but my own personal method has been to write a pre-deployment letter to my young son. The practice forces reflection on the most important aspects of one's life, and combines thoughts of mortality with remembrance. Self-reflection on the page can help us make sense of the often-confused world that the military can be. We can learn from our mistakes, and grow as individuals. As Plato admonished, "an unexamined life is not worth living." We must examine and re-examine our own stories, to understand their meanings.

Telling our own stories, the act of "contemplative storytelling," also serves to reinforce our internal convictions. Here is an example: While stationed in Guam, one of my good friends from the Naval Academy died tragically in an aviation accident. I was scheduled to fly just a few hours after I had received the heartbreaking news, and as I was in a pre-deployment phase, I needed to complete this required flight. So, I told myself a story: Just because it had happened to her, didn't mean I would be next. I told myself I couldn't be killed in an aircraft, at least not like that. Then I got in the helicopter, and flew.

This might sound heartless, but anyone who has experienced loss under similar circumstances will likely understand the utility of this type of self-storytelling. It is not self-delusion, but rather contemplation. Moments of fear or loss are part of the human condition. Sometimes, we must convince ourselves that we actually are as brave as we must be, or as strong as we must be, or that fate really is on our side—that we won't be next. These narratives can be a self-kindness, a comfort, a way of steeling ourselves for the fight.

Fastened to the walls of my first squadron building were wooden boards bearing small plaques. On each plaque was a date: the names of a crew, and the number of people who had been rescued on a particular flight. The lives saved totaled well over a thousand. This was a physical representation of the history of my tribe, something of which each member of the squadron was fiercely proud. Almost every military unit has some similar legacy to which they can point, and every individual member of that unit has stories that contribute to that collective identity. Whole cultures are formed through a tradition of "sea stories," lessons-learned, celebrated heroes, and official histories. Our stories become part of the living, breathing, heart of the service.

That applies as much to society, as it does to a unit or branch of military service. Filmmaking, books, photography, poetry, and other mediums are some of the only ways in which a civilian—including future recruits—may interact with the military. From Valley Forge to Pearl Harbor to the science-fictional Battle of Yavin, stories shape how civil society views and values its military.

Members of the military should continue to write, and share, and make movies, and take pictures, and tell the tales of their own experiences. The services should encourage the telling of these stories, and allow those serving to share their experiences. The power of a good story is as important as the sharpest policy paper, or most complicated engineering project, or even a parent's advice. My father knew that when he handed me *The Cruel Sea*. I have kept my eye on the horizon ever since.

John "Jack" McCain IV is a veteran U.S. Navy search-and-rescue helicopter pilot with service in Afghanistan, Guam, the Pacific, the Persian Gulf, and elsewhere. He is a graduate of the U.S. Naval Academy, and the Georgetown School of Foreign Service, and is the author of Angola, Clausewitz, and the American Way of War. *McCain is a member of the Military Writers Guild, and has written for the U.S. Naval Institute,* Best Defense, War on the Rocks, *and other media outlets.*

Bridging the Civil-Military Divide

By Marcia Byrom Hartwell

The U.S. Army in Iraq was probably as startled as I was to find myself embedded as a civilian advisor in its midst. Having researched, organized field interviews, and worked on international conflicts and development while based in the United Kingdom, I had earned first a master of science, then a doctorate, in International Development. I understood the intricacies of geopolitical violence, but knew next to nothing about the U.S. military. My relatives had fought in earlier wars and I had been living in the U.K. for 10 years, where the armed forces mingled casually with civilians in academic and daily life. As a social scientist analyzing dynamics in early post-conflict transitions, I was curious about how local and international security forces prevented violence. Numerous field trips had taken me to Northern Ireland, Serbia, and South Africa, to ask individuals living in divided communities for their opinions on forgiveness and revenge. This led to discussions about justice, and as to when processes were perceived as fair.

In short, I learned how easily people could be incited to fight their neighbors, and how difficult it was persuading them to stop.

This dilemma underscored an ambiguity I found beneath the surface of all conflicts: Victims can be perpetrators; perpetrators can be victims. Sometimes, they are the same person, feeding a vicious cycle that blurs the lines for outsiders trying to separate the difference. Police from these communities occasionally shared their informal opinions, but rarely ever on record. Their greatest loyalties lay with members of their force, with whom they shared their frontline danger. These security barriers were difficult for a civilian without an "in" to crack.

Then, I found myself holding a front-door pass.

Early on, I realized that my only hope for successfully negotiating this new military terrain was to pretend I had moved to a foreign country. In this, 10 years in England had given me plenty of practice. This time, however, I was dealing with my own country's citizens, albeit those who operated with unfamiliar customs, and spoke in a mostly indecipherable, acronym-based language.

I asked questions, listened, and stopped making assumptions. I applied answers to the complex relationships between Iraqi civilians and their protectors, and to the equally complicated negotiations between civilian and military organizations sharing operational space.

For my first year, from 2009 to 2010, my focus was reconciliation writ large. This included U.S.-led reintegration of former insurgents into legitimate security jobs; exploring tribal allegiances; and supporting Iraqi attempts to bridge their own divides. These formed an Iraqi version of a reconciliation "roadmap" I knew well. In 2010 and 2011, I began charting unfamiliar territory. As areas transferred from U.S. military to Iraqi civilian control, divisions and differences loomed large. Obvious differences included: skewed numbers of personnel (no organizations came close to matching the overwhelming military numbers); different timelines (short-term versus long-term goals); and unrealistic expectations by the well-funded U.S. military of civilian organizations with tiny budgets.

Delving deeper, I discovered other issues buried beneath the polite civil-military conversations. For example: The primary goal for unarmed civilians was to avoid violence whenever possible. They did so by closely monitoring and evaluating at all times the potential for physical danger. The military's mission is the opposite: Soldiers are trained to move toward violence, to engage, and to neutralize threats. This cultural rift caused misunderstandings and frustration, particularly in the context of military and civilian leaders jointly making decisions about when and how to move through unsafe areas.

Civil-military trust was an issue. Civilians worried about unintended consequences from military actions, which could turn them into targets. Soldiers worried that humanitarian workers might withhold information learned from locals, and leave soldiers open to surprise attacks.

For civilians, a less dangerous but no less frustrating problem was a lack of military self-awareness about how soldiers' presence, for example, could disadvantage civilian projects and operations. The very appearance of the U.S. military could marginalize an international civilian organization's relationship with their host government—and with the local people who benefited from their programs. That's because, distracted by power and weapons, government bureaucrats at all levels often shifted their focus away from civilians to the military.

Many U.S. and international civilian humanitarian and development organizations worked hard with coalition militaries to bridge these divides. Building civil-military trust could often be narrowed down to acknowledging the overriding importance leadership, personality, and experience play in achieving successful outcomes. A mix of the "right" credentials with the "wrong" personality and limited experience could be destructive to progress, regardless of whether civilian or military.

Conversely, both civilian and military leaders with the "wrong" credentials and the "right" personalities could make great strides when they focused on common ground and goals. Whenever civil-military relations became tense, civilians learned it was better to engage in dialogue sooner than later, given the military's tendency to prefer immediate actions.

Both communities shared a mix of hope and futility as they watched the limited effects of their efforts. In Iraq, the best-equipped army and the most well-intended civilian programs were unable to stop attacks against people trying to go about their daily lives. We could see their sad, weary expressions as our armored convoys rolled past.

I researched, wrote, and discussed these topics in numerous papers for civil-military practitioners, academics, and others. My desire to publicize these mostly ignored vital issues pushed me to write a book, which outlined ways to navigate and redefine civil-military roles past, present, and future in complex international environments. I've repeated these out loud to anyone willing to listen and been grateful for the opportunities to share. Now a different civil-military divide demands our attention.

The disconnect this time is between stateside U.S. civil society and the U.S. military. When I returned home to the United States in 2011, I was unprepared for the attitudes I encountered. These ranged from judgmental hyper-patriotism in some regions, to a less-engaged "spare me the details" attitudes regarding our nation's wars. Domestic race, class, politics and generational attitudes were playing out their corrosive roles. Similar shadows were cast on civilians who had worked alongside the military. None of this matched the complex diverse military I had come to know.

Civil-military operatives might have differences, but their shared tactical experiences often forged a mutual respect on the ground that their distant headquarters lacked. It began to look as if a similar gap existed between many Americans and their deployed citizens. Vietnam-era veterans blamed the lack of a draft for this out-of-touch attitude. The Vietnam War was divisive, but it certainly had every American's attention. With the exception of those who legally or illegally avoided the draft, it was their sons, brothers, fathers, lovers who were fighting and dying in a confusing war. Now, Americans look the other way as we engage in endless wars. The civil-military divide grows wider and the suicide rate for returning veterans stays high. Those of us who know a different truth write because we must. We explain why our lessons-learned are relevant to our current political and military decision-making processes. Our fellow citizens must be made to pay attention to the consequences of actions being taken in their name.

Marcia Byrom Hartwell is a researcher, practitioner, advisor, and author focusing on dynamics in early post-conflict transitions; past, present, future civil-military roles in complex crises. Her numerous publications include Negotiating Civil-Military Space: Redefining Roles in an Unpredictable World. *She holds degrees from Oxford University; London School of Economics; and Smith College, Northhampton, Mass. She is a former public policy scholar at the Wilson Center, Washington, D.C., and embedded as a civilian advisor with the U.S. Army in Iraq, 2009-2011. She recently joined the political science department at the University of Maine at Farmington.*

William Sims and Sailors as Scholars

By Benjamin "BJ" Armstrong

In November of 1900, Lt. William Sims joined the wardroom of USS Kentucky, the U.S. Navy's newest battleship. He had just come from a tour in the Paris embassy, studying and collecting intelligence on European battleship design and gunnery practices. As he sailed for China Station, Sims got his sea legs back and began getting to know his new ship. He started comparing what he had observed in Europe with what he found back at sea with his shipmates, and began to think that—despite new ships and a newfound global role following the victory in the Spanish-American War—the U.S. Navy still had a lot of room for improvement.

In the following years, Sims helped instigate a campaign of innovation and organizational reform. He discovered—more frankly, stole—ideas from Capt. Percy Scott of the Royal Navy regarding the methods of continuous-aim-fire. Based on those methods, he went on to revolutionize American naval gunnery. Eventually, William Sims became known throughout the American fleet as "the man who taught us how to shoot."

In the years leading up to World War I, Sims continued pushing boundaries, beyond his initial focus on gunnery tactics and techniques. He and his colleagues formed a group that called themselves The Society for the Repression of Ignorant Assumptions. They advocated for the all-big-gun battleship, developed torpedo boat and destroyer tactics, and supported the creation of the Office of the Chief of Naval Operations.

When the United States entered the World War I, Admiral Sims commanded American naval forces in European waters. During the war, he was central to the adoption of the convoy system that defeated the U-boats, which were strangling the British Isles. When he returned home at the end of the war, he was appointed to a second term as president of the U.S. Naval War College. There, he developed the curriculum and courses in Newport, and helped establish the system of study and war-gaming used to examine the advents of naval aviation and American submarines.

Sims had written his first article for publication at the start of the 20th century, shortly after the Navy promoted him to lieutenant commander. The success of that piece led him to realize the power of sharing innovations through professional writing. Throughout the remainder of his life, he wrote articles for the Naval Institute's professional naval journal *Proceedings,* and for popular magazines like *World's Work.* After returning from World War I, he collaborated with Burton Hendrick to write a book.

One part history and one part war memoir, *The Victory at Sea* won a Pulitzer Prize in 1921.

Throughout his career, Sims fought military bureaucracy, and instigated innovation. Beyond the details of how to reform military organizations, or the specifics of tactical innovation, however, perhaps the essential part of Sims' legacy is his example as a writer engaged in an evolving professional discourse.

In 1906, William Sims was a lieutenant commander, and serving in his role as Inspector of Target Practice with the U.S. Navy's Bureau of Ordnance, where he was finishing the implementation of his gunnery reforms. The Treaty of Portsmouth, brokered by President Theodore Roosevelt, had just ended the Russo-Japanese War. Navalists all over the world were combing through news reports of the Battle of Tsushima to analyze its lessons for modern naval warfare. One of these was the already-famous historian and eminent strategist Alfred Thayer Mahan.

In his day, Americans saw Mahan as one of the great thinkers on the subject of war and peace, perhaps comparable to how the public now views Brent Scrowcroft or James Stavridis. Mahan wrote an article for *Proceedings* that analyzed the battle between the Russian Imperial Navy and the Japanese in the Sea of Japan. At its end, Mahan concluded the battle demonstrated that a properly designed fleet required battleships of moderate size, with a varied battery of many different sized guns, which could be built in large numbers and were multi-mission capable. It was a conclusion in line with the thinking of most of the admirals in the U.S. Navy, and it encouraged the status quo.

Sims' own experience, however, gathering intelligence on battleships and in developing continuous-aim-fire, suggested something entirely different. He also had a friend with a first-hand account of the events in the Tsushima Strait on which to base his analysis. President Roosevelt, who was considering taking Sims on as his naval aide, encouraged the young officer to write down his thoughts and to submit them to *Proceedings*.

Sims wrote an article entitled "The Inherent Tactical Qualities of All-Big-Gun, One-Caliber Battleships" that directly contradicted Mahan. He demonstrated that the lesson of the Russo-Japanese War was that large battleships—with batteries full of the largest guns of all the same calibers—were the best way to construct a fleet. He concluded this was true, even if the expense meant a navy could only afford a smaller number of ships. As Sims wrote in the conclusion of his article, "I have attempted to show that Captain Mahan's conclusions are probably in error." Indeed, the development of the HMS Dreadnought that same year, seems to indicate Sims was far closer to understanding the future than was Mahan.

The text of Sims's essay offers contemporary readers something more than just an interesting sea story involving two great naval minds and an abandoned ship class. First, it demonstrates that healthy professional debate is good for national security. Without discussion generated by forward-thinking officers and creative civilian analysts, a military bureaucracy will stagnate and become reactionary.

The scholarly study evident in Sims' article also demonstrates the importance of developing real expertise through both study and experience. Reading the text of the original article, Sims' deep knowledge of battleship employment and design becomes clear. Today's military innovators and thinkers must be willing to similarly jump into the arena of ideas, but also to do the hard and sometimes tedious work of getting the facts right.

Sims knew that in order to challenge the world's leading navalist in a debate, his observations had to be correct, and his arguments convincing. In modern debates—regarding the future of the big-deck nuclear aircraft carriers, or questions of the military effectiveness of swarming, or the future implications of artificial intelligence in war—our arguments must be logical, informed by a mastery of the facts, and presented well.

Expertise may be developed upon the deck-plates or in cockpits, from service in the desert, or from working on staffs in the halls of power. Some may come from the study of tactics manuals, doctrine, or organizational publications. These sources, however, are insufficient. Here again, Sims provides a relevant role model, given his alignment of professional engagement with personal study.

In 1921, for example, Sims published a *Proceedings* article derived from his Newport lecture "The Practical Naval Officer." The title and subject were something like a jazz-like riff: He had taken the title and some of the inspiration from a lecture Alfred Thayer Mahan had given in Newport nearly 30 years earlier. Sims, who had locked horns with the great navalist on Tsushima, now came to embrace Mahan's view of how to prepare officers for command and policymaking.

Sims lamented the fact that, when he was a junior officer, he had spent his time reading subjects that had no real bearing on the military profession. He had read some philosophy and political economy, but had also avoided reading about military history, government, or international relations. Today, many officers suggest that the kind of knowledge Sims was missing would now come from mid-career professional military education. Sims's own perception of his student time at the Naval War College, however, was not that it taught him the things he needed to know, but that it highlighted all of the things he did not know and still needed to learn. That conclusion set him on a path of personal learning, rather than classroom-based credentialing. He wrote:

Specifically addressing the younger officers of the navy, let me say that you now have the opportunity that can never return. It lies with you to determine whether, when you become old, you will have to regret the wasted years of your youth; whether at that period of life you will find yourselves simply "practical men"—"beefeaters"—or really educated military naval officers.

It will depend largely upon self-instruction and self-discipline. But you must keep clearly in view the fact that, under modern naval conditions, an officer may be highly successful, and even brilliant, in all grades up to the responsible positions of high command, and then find his mind almost wholly unprepared to perform its vitally important functions in time of war.

Sims left a short reading list in his article as a place to start, which included Mahan, Corbett, Clausewitz, and others. As both a historian and military officer, I find it impressive how well the list still stands up today. Sims himself pointed out, however, a basic reading list of "classics" is just a start. That list may change from decade to decade, to reflect the shifting character of war. The value is not the titles on the list, but the pursuit of knowledge the list represents. Sims emphasized to graduating officers that they should consider themselves to be at the beginning of their education, rather than at an end.

In his book *Saltwater Leadership*, Rear Adm. Robert Wray conducted a survey of experienced naval officers, asking them to rank 76 leadership traits. In the results, the last two traits on the list—the factors judged least important things to teach young naval officers—were sensitivity and scholarship. A bit higher on that list, right in the middle, was writing ability.

Admiral Sims would probably take exception to the exercise. He would emphasize that professional writing should be about something; it must demonstrate mastery not only of the technical aspects of a problem, but also understanding of the context and history of the issues involved. It must be the result of experience and personal study, and that means scholarship.

The pursuit of professional writing and study has a long history in the maritime services, and across the military more widely. The sailors who really made a difference—names like Samuel Du Pont, William Sims, Ernest King, Chester Nimitz, Bull Halsey, Bud Zumwalt, James Stavridis— studied their profession and wrote articles to forward its development. They engaged in professional discourse well before they assumed the highest responsibilities of command. Our military and our nation are better for it.

William Sims' writings offer an opportunity to be mentored by an accomplished leader who lived more than a century ago. His essays, articles, and lectures might help professionals find 21st century solutions to 21st century challenges. His methods, after all, haven't changed: Asking questions, doing the challenging work of research and reflection, and exploring potential answers in writing and discourse, is at the heart of being a military professional.

Benjamin "BJ" Armstrong is a member of the Military Writers Guild. He is an active-duty U.S. naval officer who has served as a search-and-rescue helicopter pilot, and a staff officer and strategist in the Pentagon. A military professor at the U.S. Naval Academy, he earned his doctorate from King's College, London and has published widely on historical and military professional subjects.

I Write

By Andrew Steadman

I write.

Why?

I write to bring forth ideas.

I write to impact, influence, and inspire.

I write to join others in building community.

I write because not enough people do.

I write because I am thankful for the freedom to write.

I write because overcoming a blank page is an intellectual victory.

I write to be a conduit, not a roadblock.

I write when I feel like it, because that's when the best writing happens.

When I don't feel like writing, I think.

I write before sunrise, with coffee, listening to Zoë Keating.

I write slow and edit as I go, which is against most advice.

I write for the nervous rush I feel at the moment I press "publish."

I write about timeless principles, not the latest social drama.

I write to end the global epidemic of passive voice.

I write seeking the positive, because negativity is exceedingly abundant.

I write to incite action, personal growth, and meaningful change.

ANDREW STEADMAN

I write to ignite an "aha" in myself and others.

I write to create a platform through which others can also share their ideas.

I write because having an audience makes me more observant and engaging.

I write because writing transforms my opinions into beliefs.

I write because beliefs are no good if they remain in my head.

I write about leadership: growing oneself, and growing teams.

I write because too few leaders in my profession publicly share their ideas.

I write because I believe leaders must challenge their own boundaries.

I write because "leader development" rarely means people are learning the art of leadership.

I write because I believe people are in search of insight, inspiration, clarity, common sense, and intellectual engagement. I am, too.

I write to show thanks to those who have invested in my success.

I write to share my failures, so that others might avoid them.

I write because what I write will outlive what I say.

I write because I want my daughters to hear directly from me.

I write to become a better person.

I write to become a better leader.

I write for me.

I write for you.

I write.

Andrew Steadman is a husband, father, and U.S. Army infantry officer. He is also creator of The Military Leader, *a blog, book, and podcast dedicated to helping leaders grow themselves and their teams. He is a member of the Military Writers Guild.*

How I Fell in Love with AP Style, but Settled Down with Doctrine

By Miranda Summers Lowe

In 2009, I was not living my dream. I was 26, had a master's degree from an Ivy League school, a deployment to Iraq, and a fresh commission in the U.S. Army, but the throes of the economic meltdown had left me living with my parents and working at a clothing retailer folding sweaters. I spent my nights filling out "professional" job applications, and my days off driving to job interview after job interview in which I just barely didn't make the cut. It was demoralizing. I began to doubt myself and my abilities.

What free time I had left was spent volunteering for extra National Guard duty and networking. Providence came in a combination of the two. I met a fellow officer at a book release event. When he learned I had a background in developing history exhibits, he mentioned he needed such an installation at the District of Columbia National Guard armory. The only trouble? The position required an officer qualified in "public affairs." I didn't like the connotation of public affairs.

As a branch, Public Affairs is often lampooned as being a function best left to pretty boys and sweet talkers. But I needed a job, wanted to do the exhibit work, and figured that more education never hurt anyone.

I checked into the Defense Information School ("DINFOS") on a sweltering July day at Fort Meade, Md., and immediately fell in love with the place. The first thing I saw, stretched out across a vibrant green lawn in front of the modern glass building, were dozens of video cameras lined up with perfect military precision. It was set-up for a videography exercise. DINFOS was a place where creativity met discipline, talent met technique, and hard work clashed with fleeting inspiration. It was also there I met my next great love: *The Associated Press Stylebook*.

I should take a step back and say that I had always been a writer. I'd written journals and diaries; long notes written in gel pen and folded into paper footballs to be passed in classes; and school yearbook and newspaper content. I knew I'd rather write a paper than take a test any day. Writing came easily to me, but I hadn't yet realized it didn't come easily to everyone.

Still, throughout college, I allowed myself to become convinced that I wasn't good at writing. The more I worked at becoming a better writer, the worse I got. Well-meaning professors and peers picked at my writing, destroying any sense of bounce or narrative flow. I would leave peer-editing sessions feeling like I was bobbing along the surface, just getting by. Later, I came to the conclusion that most writers, when they work with other people's writing, will try to make everyone sound like themselves. Or, more accurately, an idealized sense of themselves that even they can't attain.

And then I met the *AP stylebook*—a dictionary-like reference that journalists and others use to make their stories clear and understandable. Our J-instructor, as they like to call journalism teachers at DINFOS, was a retired U.S. Marine who had managed to be enlisted, warrant, and officer by the time he retired. He doled out AP-infused writing instruction with a dry wit that is forever seared in my brain: *"Do you think commas are free?"* *"You never mess with, or abbreviate, Texas."*

As I got to know AP style, my *how to* and *why to* write became clear. In academic writing, people argued over what was grammatically right and wrong in brutal personal attacks. The placement of a comma was an invitation to almost religious debate. By contrast, in AP style, it was clear what was right and wrong: It's in the book. Facts were listed out in order of importance *to the audience*. Editors pick headlines. Quotes need attribution. Yes, one sentence can be a paragraph, but there's no Oxford comma. We'd take timed tests on copy editing, or writing press releases. As I nailed assignment after assignment, my confidence started to return.

I had arrived to DINFOS as a lieutenant, before I'd even been a platoon leader. Learning AP style set me up to revel in the glorious ambiguity of military leadership. We had all come from different backgrounds, with different beliefs and ways of processing ideas into action. As an officer, I felt my job was, in effect, to apply a style guide to the people with whom I served. The style guide was the Great Equalizer: You may have grown up with an Oxford comma, but that's not what we're doing. You may have grown up making split-second decisions and sticking to them through pure determination, but here we apply "Military Decision-Making Process."

Any stylebook, of course, evolves through community and practice. When I read Army regulations and pamphlets found on dusty shelves, I see shared wisdom and values. I see parallels in other Army guides: Doctrine brought clarity to command in the way that the *AP Stylebook* brought clarity to my writing.

Working in public affairs, much of my body of work is not published under my own name. I've written on behalf of many people, in many styles and voices. I've worked on glossy pamphlets, technical websites, and funny social media posts. I've whipped out quick news items and speeches that go out into the world without another look, and I've worked on larger team projects that are edited and updated and smoothed over with graphics and standardized fonts until they become official Army products.

In the process of writing, however, I remind myself that not everything is according to Associated Press style. Speeches can be written to reflect an accent or personal history, social-media content written in slang, and history articles written more in keeping with the *Chicago Manual of Style*. In all of this writing, I find myself back in the continuous ambiguity of leadership—finding (pardon the pun) the *write and wrong* in any given situation. Ultimately, these aren't questions that can be found in a book. In the way that doctrine combines the experience of many and values of many into a single best-practice, I've worked on projects where people with incredibly different viewpoints and experiences come together to find one voice: The "Army voice."

I've heard many people say that they write to structure their thoughts or to get their ideas into the world. I write because it's a thing I can do. I firmly believe that most of my written products are ephemeral and worthless. The teams we build, however—the stories we tell, the histories we preserve, as well as the doctrine we use—are the essential, enduring engine of what the Army is, and will be.

Infantry officers boast about how long they can ruck. Artillery officers take pride in fast and accurate plotting. As long as I'm an Army writer, I'll be with my soldiers, trying to find a disciplined voice in the chaos of ambiguity.

And I'll do it with style.

In her civilian career, Miranda Summers Lowe is a military history curator at the Smithsonian Institution. She served on the Chief of Staff of the U.S. Army's Operation Enduring Freedom Study Group writing Afghanistan history. She has been a member of the U.S. National Guard since 2003, serving as a historian, public affairs officer, military intelligence officer, supply sergeant, and Black Hawk helicopter doorgunner. She deployed to Iraq in 2006, and Djibouti in 2014. She holds a graduate degree from Brown University, Providence, R.I. and an undergraduate degree from the College of William and Mary, Williamsburg, Va.

Writing and Our Profession

By Mick Ryan

> "If you want to be a writer, then be a writer, for God's sake.
> It's not that hard, and it doesn't require that much effort
> on a day to day basis. Find the time or make the time. Sit down, shut up
> and put your words together. Work at it and keep working at it.
> And if you need inspiration, think of yourself on your deathbed saying
> 'Well, at least I watched a lot of TV.'"—John Scalzi

I don't believe I am a talented writer, or even a reasonably good writer. I am not particularly creative or imaginative in how I construct my prose. I use passive voice too much. I even use adverbs! For me, writing is a little more like a managing any project. I select an objective, derive the key strands of that project, and then build from there. Once the rough shape is complete, I chisel away until I see something I like. I do not find writing an easy task or something that comes naturally.

But, I also see writing—just like reading—as one of the core aspects of my being a member of the profession of arms. Over many years, even decades, I have come to appreciate the intellectual aspects of being a soldier. As Williamson Murray wrote in *Strategy and Military Effectiveness*, our profession is not only the most physically demanding of all the professions, but also the most demanding, intellectually and morally. Hand in hand with the pursuit of learning, a soldier must also develop communication skills. Writing, at least in my mind, is the bridge that connects intellectual development and building an effective capacity to communicate. Being able to communicate effectively, to provide purpose and to inspire our people, is what being a leader in this profession is all about.

That said, I also really do love to write. And I think being a better writer makes me a more thoughtful leader.

Writing is an act of creation. As an Australian Army combat engineer, I was brought up with the motto of *fracimus et frangimus*. This translates as "we make and we break." While I always enjoyed demolitions and destroying things, I have always gained most satisfaction from building something new. A bridge construction or mosque renovation in a tiny Afghan village, for example, is a source of personal and professional satisfaction. In this regard, I find writing to be similar. It might be a piece of analysis or opinion. It may be a short story. Each is an act of creation.

Writing is also a way to learn new things, and to challenge one's beliefs or knowledge with new facts, opinions, and analysis. Writing allows me to explore and develop ideas. Our world is changing so quickly. Demographics and technologies are shifting how we communicate, work, trade, entertain, and, of course, fight with each other. Changes in the geopolitical environment are shaping how we think about strategy, strategic competition, and conflict. This fertile field is perfect terrain for new ways of waging war, and new methods of preparing our people for it. I want to be part of that.

During 33 years in the Army, I have learned a few things. Writing is one of the best mediums that I can use to share what I have learned. I have always written down my experiences. Sometimes this is has been as simple as keeping a daily diary, as I did during my time on the East Timor-Indonesia border in 2000, or in Uruzgan Province in Afghanistan during our tour there in 2006-2007. Other times, it has taken the form of publishing articles about specific operational experiences, as I did on several occasions in the aftermath of my Afghanistan mission.

I have also gone "meta," summarizing and synthesizing many lived experiences into themes and lessons. In 2017, for example, I wrote a "Mastering the Profession of Arms" series for the *War on the Rocks* website. Regardless of the topic or the format, I hope my writing ensures that some of my hard-won knowledge remains part of my institutional legacy.

I want to be part of the wider discourse—fostered on social media, blogs, journals, unit Professional Military Education (PME) sessions and schools, and more. I started on Twitter in late 2014. It quickly became clear to me that social media was a means to connect those who care deeply about our profession, but who also want have our ideas tested and critiqued. Rather than something to be prohibited or feared, on-line discourse builds the healthy intellectual foundation that is critical to to our individual and collective successes.

Novelist Stephen King has written that "Writing isn't about making money, getting famous, getting dates […] it's about enriching the lives of those who will read your work, and enriching your own life as well." Writing enriches me. It is a source of comfort when I am frustrated, and a source of enlightenment when I am uninformed. Writing allows me to hone my leadership style, and to be better at providing meaning and purpose to our people. Writing is now part of who I am, wrapped up in my personality as tightly as my appreciation of family and friends. I hope I am a better soldier, a better leader, and a better person because of it.

Mick Ryan is a general officer in the Australian Army and a member of the Military Writers Guild. A graduate of Johns Hopkins University School of Advanced International Studies, the U.S. Marine Corps Command and Staff College, and School of Advanced Warfare, he is an avid reader and writer on military and national security topics. He has previously published book chapters in Strategy Strikes Back: How Star Wars Explains Modern Military Conflict *and* Winning Westeros: How Game of Thrones Explains Modern Military Conflict. *A passionate advocate of Professional Military Education and lifelong learning, he currently commands the Australian Defence College in Canberra. Follow him on Twitter: @WarInTheFuture*

War Stories

The Squeaky Wheel and The Expanded Universe

By Kate Germano

There is a certain power that comes from being able to communicate to an expanded universe of people though writing. So, you could say that the U.S. Marine Corps opened Pandora's Box when I was relieved of command. While I was mortified about the way I was portrayed in the media and by the Marine Corps, being fired allowed me the freedom I needed write about the many obstacles faced by women in the Marines.

The pressures faced by women Marines are enormous. No matter how senior or accomplished we are, we have to carefully walk a gender-stereotype tightrope, attempting to neither appear "too aggressive," and therefore "mean"; or "too nice," and therefore "weak." We daily encounter sexism, gender bias, and harassment, but resist the urge to speak out. We don't want to draw attention to ourselves. We wrongly assume that it will be easier for the next generation of female Marines simply because we served, so we stay quiet. We try not to stick out. We struggle for the unattainable goal of acceptance by the brotherhood.

That is exactly the way many senior Marine leaders want it. As the most conservative of the military branches, with a large portion of the male ranks drawn from the Bible Belt, the Marine Corps is not known for being progressive. And, more than any other service, the Corps places a premium on conformity. We possess a singular attachment to our history, and are the most resistant of all of the services to change.

Squeaky wheels about social justice issues are not welcome, especially when it comes to gender issues.

As the branch of armed service with the smallest percentage of women—less than 9 percent compared to more than 18 percent for the Navy and Air Force, and 17 percent for the Army—the Marine Corps has the highest rates of sexual assault and harassment of all of the services. You would think that with these statistics—and given our shared leadership traits and principles—Marine women would look out for and take care of one other. We don't do a good job of supporting each other, however, because we are afraid of the stigma that comes with being surrounded by other women Marines. In our quest to belong, we work overtime trying to be "one of the guys," never speaking out against the actions and inactions of our coworkers, our bosses, even our subordinate Marines.

And so the cycles of gender bias, sexism, harassment, and assault persist.

In this context, it should be no surprise that, when I took command in June 2014 of the only all-female unit in the entire U.S. Department of Defense, I wasn't exactly considered a bra-burner. After all, like most Marine women, I had long turned a blind eye to the existence of gender bias and discrimination in the Marine Corps. Until I got to the 4th Recruit Training Battalion—the only place enlisted women Marines are made—it never occurred to me to question why the Marine Corps is the only service to have maintained segregated bootcamp for men and women.

Yes, I am aware that this is the 21st century.

When I arrived to to my Parris Island, S.C. command, however, I observed female recruits (and Marines), who folded under pressure when performing timed physical fitness events. I watched women on the rifle range cry when they were unable to hit their targets on Qualification Day. I witnessed female recruits quitting on hikes at the first sign of pain or fatigue. I found a row of chairs placed behind the female formation at the emblem ceremony after their final hike in case any of the women were too tired or sore to stand. And I found decades of recruit graduation scores that demonstrated the women had underperformed in every graduation category compared to the male recruits.

Compounding these issues, on a daily basis, my female Marines and recruits faced disparaging remarks and treatment from some male drill instructors and staff on the recruit depot. I can't tell you the number of times, for example, I heard slow or emotional male recruits called "pussies" or "girls." I was told by a fellow battalion commander—one of my peers— that my recruits were a "distraction" when we conducted an integrated hike. Senior enlisted leaders on the recruit depot commonly referred to my battalion as the "Fourth Dimension." In other words, my command was derided and labeled a drama-filled, alternate universe instead of an integral part of the normal Marine Corps recruit training environment.

I began to suspect that there was a direct correlation between the cultural foundation laid in a segregated bootcamp, and the high rates of sexual assault and harassment in the Marines. In my view, creating a recruit training environment free of gender bias would ensure stronger, faster, and tougher women Marines—and create mutual respect between men and women at the very beginnings of their military careers. With everything I had witnessed firsthand at Parris Island, I could no longer ignore gender bias and sexism. It became a matter of principle to try to change things for women on the recruit depot.

Unfortunately, the more vocal I became with my chain of command about the issues, the more my boss regarded *me* as the problem. I trusted that a voice of reason would eventually prevail, and that senior Marine leaders would see that I hadn't been mean to my recruits when I upheld the standards. I expected recruits to shoot expert on the rifle range. I expected my drill instructors to adhere to recruit training regulations, and to stop abusing our recruits and each other. I expected to make the Marine Corps better by demanding more of women, and speaking out about the dangers of segregated bootcamp.

All of a sudden, I became a squeaky wheel.

In the investigation used to justify my relief of command in June 2015, the investigating officer wrote that I had an "obsession with equality," and that I had been too hard on my female recruits and Marines in my quest to improve their performance. When I read the report, I was humiliated. After all, there is no worse characterization for a commanding officer than to be called mean and abusive.

But I was also angry. So angry that rather than crawling away in shame, I punched back. To me, it was a matter of principle, and I began speaking out in the media and writing on the topic of inequality for service women. Suddenly, I was surrounded by a social media network of men and women from all over the country—military, veteran, and civilian alike—who shared my perspectives or were at least willing to have mutually respectful, professional conversations.

The Marine Corps labeled me a squeaky wheel. It ended up expanding my universe, and my influence. After years on active duty of maintaining my silence, I am now free to speak my mind. To try to make a difference for my fellow Marines.

It's been a long time coming.

Kate Germano is a former U.S. Marine Corps officer. Among other assignments, she commanded 4th Recruit Training Battalion, Parris Island, S.C. Germano made headlines in the media in June 2015 when she confronted systemic problems of gender bias in the Corps. After a 20-year career, she retired from uniformed service in July 2016. In 2018, along with U.S. Army veteran Kelly Kennedy, she wrote Fight Like a Girl: The Truth Behind How Female Marines are Trained. *Follow her on Twitter:* @kate_germano

How I Write

By Robert L. Bateman

OK, confession time: I have long thought that Tom Hanks was pretty cool.

I mean, yeah, I liked his screen persona in the rom-coms of the '90s. (When you wear a Ranger Tab and Airborne wings, you can confess to liking chick-flicks without giving up your dude-card.) And, as an episodic amateur actor (same rule applies), as well as a soldier and historian, I especially appreciated the depth he brought to his character in *Saving Private Ryan*. Then I saw that he directed/co-produced some of the *Band of Brothers* series and I thought that quite decent. When I learned that he also spent years in my hometown of Cleveland, Ohio, I was won over. Because, seriously, when you are from Cleveland you will reach for any little thing. (See also: Carey, Drew.)

And now he has written something I especially like (an ode to manual typewriters that appeared in *The New York Times Sunday Review* Aug. 3, 2013), because it gets you to a place that I can really appreciate: the act, art, and emotion of writing. Hanks wrote about the tactile sensation of writing on a typewriter. You know, those clunky beasts that used to get ink all over us ... or maybe you do not. That depends. Mostly it depends, I think, upon how old you are, because it does not work for me, though I get it.

Mr. Hanks is about a decade older than me. I suspect this gap makes sense of our relative feelings about typewriters, because it sort of defines about how we feel about the act of writing. For him, the typewriter is an active element in the process, an almost living and breathing element of the effort to communicate. For me, not so much, because typewriters were a barrier to writing when I was growing up and so I never really liked them. But I appreciate what he is talking about when he gets into the almost spiritual aspect of putting words on paper.

In part this is because I have a similar ... well, fetish. I write most everything I ever publish in longhand first. Yes, it is ugly, scrawled, nearly unrecognizable-to-any-but-me print, but it is there, on paper. For me, it is the feeling of the pen in my hand, committing ideas on to paper, well before I hit a keyboard, which defines the act. Mr. Hanks made me think about that, about the process of writing, which made me think that some of you might be interested as well.

So, here is my advice about writing. It is simple:

1. Become Obsessed
2. Love Words

There, you see? I told you it was simple.

OK, that is not quite fair. Further, I accept that at almost any point a more accomplished writer may leap in and disagree. At this point in my life, however, I have finally accepted that I can honestly say, "I am a writer."

True, usually I do so in a self-help group, ("Hi, my name is Bob, and I am a writer." "Hi, Bob!") but, after a couple of books with my name on the spine, co-authoring or contributing to 13 others, and about 900 by-lines in print and on-line, I have finally owned up. This may be wrong, but I leave it to somebody else to tell me that. Please note, that is all writing I did outside of my military duties.

Soooo ... about writing.

See, the thing is that Mr. Hanks's typewriter essay hit a chord. A lot of the letters I have received during the time I have written things for *Esquire* magazine and others have asked me about writing, the art and method. I suspect that I got these questions because I seem approachable, because technically I was not a "professional" writer until I retired, but more of a normal-Joe who also happened to tell stories or histories, or raised questions of military doctrine or theory in a way that was easy for many to understand. But maybe all writers get these questions. Either way, I feel moderately guilty because, for the most part, I did not give a sufficient response to those folks about the writing bit. And I always write back to everyone. This sort of made me think about who, or perhaps what, I am.

Yes, I put a lot of words on paper, and in pixels, but really, was I a writer? Mr. Hanks made me face up to the fact with his essay. This naturally ennobles me to the point where I can now dictate how, "YOU TWO KIN BE A RITER!" Oh, the arrogance. Whatever. So, what follows will answer, once and for all, what I do as a writer.

Here is my "secret":

1. Have An Idea.

2. Write an outline in pen, in a college-ruled notebook.

3. Write a draft, again in pen, in the same notebook. This is the 80-percent solution.

4. Type that draft. During this step, I am inevitably editing what I wrote.

5. Immediately print out a copy of what was just typed. Set it aside for 14 to 30 days, depending upon the length. The key here for me is that it has to be long enough for me to forget most of what I wrote.

6. Edit the paper print-out, with a red pen.

7. Humbly submit the mass to my wife, accept 80 percent of her edits, and re-edit again.

8. Send.

That is brief. You can stop here. But for those who want to know more, here is a little more explanation:

STEP 1. IDEA: You have an idea, cool. It is too much. Believe me.

Right now you need to cut it to a single sentence. In fact, if you can, cut it to a single word before you even start writing.

STEP 2. OUTLINE: My technique is to be angry, or sad, about something before I even start. Use the tool that your 7th grade teacher gave you. I do. Write an outline. Be simple. Roman numeral I: Intro; II: Evidence; III. More evidence, etc.; IIV: Conclusion/Heartbreaker. Yeah, you are right, this is so simple that only a fool would need this step. Guilty. But if I go back and look at the things I have written for publication, I have to admit that, even with my clumsy and hardly artful grasp of the language, some of them made my readers cry. When I dissect them, I can see the structure, in hindsight.

STEP 3. WRITE: Do not f*ck about. Write. Fix it later. This is my phase with pen in hand and a notebook. Usually there is a beer involved as well. But the salient element is that you sit down and put words, literally, on paper.

STEP 4: TYPE: For me, this is usually the next morning. I tend to be "creative" in the evening, and "critical" in the early hours of the morning. For me, this means roughly 4:30 to 7 a.m. Yes, I understand, these may not be your hours, and I am not dictating my method, I am only explaining the sequence. While I type up the material from my initial handwritten draft, I usually correct or modify about 5 to 10 percent of the material.

STEP 5: FERMENT. Yes, that is what I call this part. The fermentation process is critical, at least for me. I need to forget the specifics of what I wrote so that when I look at them again, it is "new," and I can live up to the next step.

STEP 6: EDIT: (For me this is 3 to 10 days later—your mileage will vary): You suck. Convince yourself of that fact. You suck, you suck, you suck. Look at what you wrote. It sucks. Now take that initial draft, WHICH YOU PRINTED OUT IN PAPER IN STEP 5, and dissect. Have a cup of coffee. Hell, have a scotch. Take a deep breath. Edit, in your own (red) pen during the next 2 hours, and remove the suck. Then take that marked-up copy and sit it next to your computer. Make the fixes.

STEP 7: HUMBLE YOURSELF: OK, most of you will not have the luxury that I do in my personal editor. When she is not wow-ing the folks on Capitol Hill, or dazzling the people in the Office of the Secretary of Defense, or dissecting intelligence at Main State, or bringing peace in Colombo, Sri Lanka, or trying to do the same at USEMB Kabul, my wife graciously accedes to looking at my stuff. Given that she has a degree in English from Middlebury, and attended Breadloaf, I cede that I am quite lucky in the editor that I sleep beside. But you must have somebody who scares you intellectually ... ask them. I do.

STEP 7.5: INCORPORATE: The mother of my daughter is brilliant, but I have my own voice. I usually use about 80 percent of what she tells me. Sometimes, however, she misses the point and "corrects" something which is actually my "voice." These bits I ignore. You should, too. Think about it. We all have our ways. I suggest that you should not let your editor remove your personality.

STEP 8: SEND. Good luck.

See? It is not that hard. All you have to do is completely abase yourself, to yourself.

Regarding the equipment: I use an ultrafine pen, .05 mm, for my writing. One black, one red. That seems to help. Mr. Hanks may disagree due to his obsession with the mechanical. That is his opinion. It may be yours. Either way, write. And as Mr. Hanks suggests, do it on paper.

Robert L. Bateman is a former U.S. Army infantry officer, and a former military fellow with Center for Strategic and International Studies (CSIS). He has taught at Georgetown University in the School of Foreign Service Security Studies Program, George Mason University, and the U.S. Military Academy at West Point, N.Y. A prolific writer of essays and articles, he is also the author of two books, including No Gun Ri, A Military History of the Korean War Incident *and* Digital War: A View from the Front Lines. *Additionally, he has edited, co-authored, or contributed to 13 other works of military history. He lives in Washington, D.C.*

The Proof is in the Jump

By Jocelyn Corbin

"Are you going to vomit, cadet? Are you going to pass out, cadet? Cadet, are you all right?"

My eyes meet hers and I feel color creeping into my cheeks as the words "Ready to board, Sgt. Airborne!" spill out of my dry mouth. I am surprised by the confidence in my voice. My stomach cramps with nausea again, and my head throbs to a slow beat. I can't tell if it is nerves or dehydration. She lifts her black baseball cap from her head, and reveals a leathery forehead and slicked back blonde hair that looks hard and plastic. It's perfectly tied tight behind her head. *Is she even sweating?* It must be at least 95 degrees in this June, Georgia sun. I imagine that I must smell so bad, but I can't tell. I'm wearing the same uniform for the third day in a row. I'm used to my own stink.

She remains quiet, returns her hat firmly back to its home and places her hands casually on the belt line of her camouflage pants. I stand staring at her, not knowing if there is something else I'm supposed to say or do. I have felt like a failure for nearly three weeks in front of her, missing my cues, using the wrong form in my landings, and forgetting the names of equipment. She saw it all and now she wants me to fail, or quit. I'm not sure yet which one. Too scared to react, I wait for her next move.

"Safety check," she says, tapping her fingers on her belt after a long moment of awkward silence. She begins walking me through a basic safety screening of equipment, which I have already completed numerous times that day. It must be the 100th safety check this week. She tugs hard at all of my straps. I feel as though I am pulled and jerked in every direction by her, and I try hard not to trip as my weight shifts behind me. My hip aches from all of the falls I have experienced that week. I wonder if the bruises will show all summer. I picture the colors of my hip changing over the months, like seasons in a children's flip book. A sudden jerk at the top of my pack sends my shoulders back. My knees struggle to lock back into place. The inspection is complete. I look again to my Sgt. Airborne and focus on the brim of her black hat, trying to avoid her piercing eyes. I brace myself for an insult. *What would it be this time? "Princess?" "Cadidiot?"* She has many names for me. I've never felt so bullied in my 19 years of existence. *How can an adult talk to me like this? I'm trying my best!*

Her voice begins to soften. Astonishingly, for the first time in two weeks, she sounds more like a mom than a scary drill sergeant: "What do you do if your parachute gets tangled in jump?" *Is this the same insulting beast that has been in my grill all week?* I take a step back before answering. "I bicycle kick!" I say, correctly, trying not to beam. Her lips turn up just the slightest in each corner, although she doesn't dare to break a real smile.

"What if it doesn't open?" she challenges back to me in a harsher tone.

"I pull the reserve!" I say with even more enthusiasm. I look down and place my hand on the large metal handle from the parachute's front casing. Doubt begins to sink in and jabs me one more time in the gut. *Am I really strong enough to pull that thing?* Droplets form at the center of my shoulder blades and trickle down to the small of my back.

"Are you ready for this?" She asks in an almost whisper, looking me directly in the eye now with such intensity, I force myself to hold my eyes to hers. Does *she* think I'm ready?

"I want to be Airborne!" I declare. My hands tingle with excitement. This is it. This is everything I've been training for. It's Jump Day. I am the chosen one, after all, and I can't come home empty-handed. I will earn my silver wings. Kent State University only had two Airborne slots for the school, and I had earned my spot. Two weeks before, I had flown down to Fort Benning. Ga. and was immediately thrown into this sweaty hell. Two weeks of running, pull-ups, and rolling around in the dirt have led me to this day. All that is left now is to voluntarily jump out of a massive military aircraft, suspended 1,250 feet in the air. And then to do it again, another four times.

"Then get to it! Stay alert and stay alive," she nudges her head to the right indicating I should move to the C-141. "Remember," she warns, taking hold of my right strap, "If you don't jump, they'll push you." She lets go of my strap, turns on her heel and walks away.

They'll push me? I wonder if I heard her right. I take my first heavy steps on the sandy path toward the roaring aircraft. Looking up, I see soldiers in front of me slowly hobbling up the ramp, like wounded Frankenstein monsters. *These are America's heroes?* I try hard to clear my mind and focus on the inevitable act before me. I step onto the plane and take my position. *I will not be pushed.*

The high-pitched whine of the engines drowns out all else. I strap into my seat with an oversized lap belt and metal buckle. The whole plane is a giant waiting room in the sky; all waiting for our number to be called. I look around to others. I feel a little reassured that I am not the only cadet. The cadet across from me is from West Point. They have many more Airborne slots than my school's annual allotment. I wonder if he feels any less pressure to succeed. His eyes are closed now and he's mouthing something. Perhaps it's a prayer. *Why does he have to look so nervous?* I reach for my barf bag, and try to read the directions on the back. The words blur together and I close my eyes tight. I breathe in, hold it, and blow out hard.

How did I even get myself into this plane in the first place? All I wanted to do was go to college. I was determined, even if it meant I was joining the Army. I truly didn't know what I was getting myself into. No one else in my family had joined the military. I only knew what I saw in movies.

"Stand UP!" the jumpmaster yells, as he stands next to the open door of the aircraft and motions to my row.

"Stand UP," my row echoes and rises in unison. My call to destiny.

"Hook up!" he commands.

Again, we echo his words. I do my best to follow the motions of the soldier in front of me. I think of the warning my Black Hat gave me: "If you don't jump, they will push you." *Was it a warning, or was it advice? Did she say that to anyone else, or just me?*

"Check equipment!"

I quickly test the tension of my straps. Thanks to my Black Hat, I am secure. I'm close enough to the door now that I spy the ground below. It looks more like a map than real land. The surreality comforts me. *I will not be pushed.*

"Sound off for equipment check."

One by one, we call back.

"10 OK!"

"9 OK," someone confirms. "8 OK." I'm No. 7.

"7 OK," I strain my voice to be sure I'm heard. The plane bounces a little and my nausea begins to show again. I inch forward, knowing my turn is about to come. *I will not be pushed. I will not be pushed.*

"Jump!" he commands my row. One after another, the jumpers disappear out the door, swept away into the blue abyss. The green light flickers next to the open door, daring me to go. My feet fight for balance as I make my way closer.

There is only one jumper ahead of me. My hand is sweaty and shaking as I hand over my zip cord to the jumpmaster. I am sure to look him straight in the eye. I'm placing my future in his hand as I commit to the moment.

Everything is happening too quickly. I need more time to get ready. My boots are close to the edge of the plane now and it's actually my turn. All of the training, all of the bruises, all of the insults has led to this moment. *I will not be pushed.*

I know from training that you don't really leap out of the door. It's more of a big step than an actual jump. It's a step I know I can take. I lift up my right boot, close my eyes, put my chin down, and lean into the wind.

The airstream sucks the breath out of my lungs and I twist violently in the air. *Is this what's supposed to happen?* A hard yank of the ripcord heaves my body upright, and I try to gather my bearings. I touch my head and grab hold of my straps. *OK, my Kevlar is still on. My parachute is open. I'm OK. I* wonder, for a moment, why I feel like I am being pulled up instead of falling. I soon realize that it's just my parachute catching air above me and I take a deep breath. There's a sudden sense of peace and relief as I float down in slow motion. Besides the light whistling of the wind, it's quiet. I look up to the green, fluttering silk above me in a beautiful half balloon, and for the first time in weeks, I smile.

Hours later, after my fifth jump of the day, I stand on the top row of aluminum bleachers, thankful for the cool breeze. It's the only thing keeping me from leaning against the tall man next to me after the longest day of my life. I place my right hand for a moment on the metal badge on my chest to make sure it is real. I rub my thumb over the ridges of the wings and look out into the faces of the small crowd that has formed in front of us.

In our audience, it's easy to spot the Black Hats. I see my Sgt. Airborne, statuesque and terrifying. My hand drops to my side and I wonder why she felt compassion for me in those moments before that first flight. She wanted me to commit to the jump, and I did. Maybe her motherly instincts took over, or she saw a younger version of herself in me. She must have seen how much I wanted this. I guess I'll never know the true reason, but she helped me regain the confidence needed to take those first steps toward the plane. I would not throw up, or pass out, and I certainly wouldn't quit.

I long to shout to her, "I wasn't pushed. I jumped." I want her to be proud of me. But I know I can't yell out.

I gaze at her with gratitude, and I hope in that moment that she knows how much it means to me to be in those bleachers. But her stern face does not crack, and no acknowledgement is given. She is once again just a Black Hat, but I am now a paratrooper.

Jocelyn Corbin is U.S. Army veteran and teacher. From 2001 to 2006, Corbin served as a U.S. Army communications officer. Since 2010, she has taught high school English Language Arts and Reading Intervention in Kentucky public schools. She is married to an active-duty Army officer, and together they have four children. Her writing has been featured in the books Beyond the Uniform; Confessions of a Military Wife; Proud to Be: Writing by American Warriors, Vol. 7; *and* D is for Deployment.

Basic Training Teaches More than Marching and Maneuvers

By Ben Wilbert

The U.S. Army issues every Basic Training recruit a copy of the Blue Book. When I enlisted in the infantry just over 30 years ago, the inch-thick, stapled-across-the-top, tablet-sized book fit nicely into a cargo pocket of our Battle Dress Uniforms (BDU). We carried it everywhere, all the time. Drill sergeants said this historic scripture, thrust upon us along with new clothes and hairstyle, created accountability to our duties as soldiers, most immediately our three General Orders. They demanded we memorize them. Punchy, sleep-deprived, and stressed-out recruits were called upon, without notice, to recite any one of these orders. Failure to do so—itself a frequent occurrence—was rewarded with group punishment, fulfilled by a series of push-ups, squat-thrusts, or flutter-kicks.

For many of us, it became the most extended and intimate acquaintance with any book we'd ever had. Kids—many of whom skated through high school English classes—were smacked with the realities of reading for understanding, reading for purpose, and reading for mission. For some, these habits, formed through forced consumption, awoke a latent interest in the written word, reading, and even for writing.

One of the "luxuries" allowed during our initial training was the old-fashioned paper notepad. Excited letters flowed from our pens to share experiences with loved ones at home. Moms and girlfriends got the most, usually one a day, especially at the beginning of Basic Training, when separation anxiety was best assuaged by a return note from home. I'm sure my cohorts wrote more letters during our summer at Fort Benning, Ga. than any of their pals back home would write for years—if ever. Think about it: Even in the days before social media, e-mails, or texts, the ability to communicate with family was virtually unimpeded. In Basic, however, things were different. Our unit had two pay phones for about a hundred guys. Permitted phone time rarely occurred. Usually, it was only on Sundays for about two hours for the entire group. Further trouble came in financing the call. You either had enough change to feed the damn thing, used one of those rare phone cards, or called "collect"—reversing the changes to the people you called. You waited in line forever (at parade rest, no doubt), only to be limited to 10 minutes total usage. That was barely enough time to talk in separate calls to your mom, dad, and girlfriend!

Writing optimized your time if nothing else. And your money. Fortunately, for new young privates, the tools for writing are uniquely portable, easy to find, and best of all: cheap. Nothing special required. Just a pen or pencil, some paper, and time. Despite a schedule that started at 0400 hours—assuming all other obligations were met in preparation for the following day—guys worked to write letters in the dedicated "troop personal time" the hour before lights out. We also filched time during the hour-long fireguard duty at night, writing by the faint light of the street lamps, while sitting on the steps of Harmony Church barracks.

As pen pals sometimes discover after a few letters, however, it's hard to come up with fresh material that sounds original, relevant, or interesting, even when you're shooting rifles, setting Claymores, and throwing grenades. After all, moms don't typically get excited by details of such things. So the respectable letter writer would vary his material to make it at least palatable. Battle buddies would ask one another what to say, and exchanged topic ideas and anecdotes freely. Practice fostered growth as a writer. It allowed success and greater satisfaction in expression. One soldier, with the zealotry of a newfound freedom convert, made a show of his prolificacy by stacking his finished pages upon one another, and then shuffling them together while wondering aloud if it would require extra postage.

For many, the military experience represents a highpoint of excitement. What they see and do—where they go—during time in uniform achieves levels seldom repeated in later civilian life. Studs Terkel, the famed Pulitzer Prize-winning author, observed that many World War II veterans felt they were simply "marking time" after participating in the war. Service members and veterans sometimes turn to writing as a natural cathartic response to capture, process, or purge feelings related to the experience. As probably first written in personal journals, or letters home, they want to express more fully than what a picture or oral recitation can do.

A common thread amongst military writers is one of remembrance. They write because they don't want to forget, or to be forgotten themselves. For many, writing is followed by an act of getting published— whether it be print and paper, or bytes and blog posts. Writers preserve their experiences for posterity, and gain a small degree of credibility— maybe even immortality.

Writing is a solitary and often independent activity. The writer, alone with a keyboard and Internet connection, is utterly in control to fulfill the urge for permanency. Some of the best military-related writing I've read came in epistolary form—forwarded via e-mail (with all its quirky formatting) from a co-worker—by a former major who wrote heart-wrenching accounts of what he experienced during deployments ranging from Haiti to the Middle East. Straight from the author, unfiltered by editors or publicists, the sheer rawness gave it compelling force.

Military order and discipline depend on recognition. Service members are trained to respect those who have a particular patch or badge, symbols of rank and status. Three stripes are better than two. A silver oak leaf is better than a gold one. (I always thought that was backwards, too.) Writing allows veterans to show themselves and others what they did. Arthur Miller once wrote, "Sacrifice is the essence of commitment," and he was right. Whether they enjoyed it or not, each service member sacrificed. Everyone who writes wants some sort of recognition, and they gain it through a finished piece of writing.

Writing is its own commitment, and its own sacrifice. Achievements made in the military are often rewarded—a promotion, certificate, or ribbon—and help advancement through the ranks. Writing articles or books may add to a person's list of accomplishments, but for the most part, these are intangibles. There is no marksmanship or driver's badge for military writers.

Perhaps it's better to focus on the function of service, then, that is inherent within the practice of writing. To focus on helping others, and in passing knowledge to future readers. Like those informal letter-writing workshops we conducted back in the barracks, we hope something we share becomes useful to others—whether to our fellow soldiers, or to our fellow citizens.

Just as in Basic Training, the people who practice and persist become the ones who graduate. Everything is a test. All of us learn we can do more than survive, even if not everyone is destined to join the canons of great literature. No one quits. We are in this together.

Put that in your cargo pocket.

Ben Wilbert is originally from Iowa. He initially enlisted into the infantry and served full-time in the U.S. Army for six years in the late 1980s and early 1990s. In his first three years, he was part of the 7th Infantry Division (Light) at Fort Ord, Calif. Later, he was a medic stationed at Fort Sheridan, Ill. Today, he lives near Chicago and is a marketing executive for an industrial safety company.

We Write Alone, but We Are Not Alone

By Jessica Scott

Writing is a lonely endeavor, one where people look at you like you're a special kind of weird, somewhere between stockpiling canned goods and shotgun shells, and eating snozberries. When you're unpublished, writing lacks the validation of being published. When you're published, writing lacks the validation of enough sales. Non-writers think writing is easy, that anyone can do it.

But finding the right words is hard. Finding the words to describe the thousands of squeezing, burning needles gripping your chest when your 3-year-old doesn't think you love her because you left her to deploy to Iraq is hard. Finding the words to describe the desolating fear that your husband may not make it home from Iraq isn't the easiest stuff. Describing how it feels to hear your 5-year-old cry over the phone that she wants you to come home … all of this is hard. The kind of hard that draws tears even though those memories are almost a decade gone by.

Those words are necessary, though. Necessary for the young private who reaches out and says, "Hey, I read your book. Can you give me any advice for staying in shape during my pregnancy?"

Necessary for the Gold Star mom who wrote that she felt like she got her daughter back when she read one of my books set in the years between the 1st Cavalry Division's deployments to Iraq. Necessary for the spouse who is struggling to understand her husband's Post-Traumatic Stress Disorder, so that she knows she's not alone.

Necessary to help an Army leader build the arguments for why women shouldn't be excluded from Ranger School, because they are not excluded from the combat we've been engaged in for the last two decades.

I write because literary fiction generally only included female soldiers as "the enemy" of spouses. These literary achievements didn't bother to include the lifelong friendships built among the women who serve at home, the women who serve at war, and the women who do both. It was cheaper to write about the divisions between us, rather than the friendships.

I write because the bulk of war fiction out there focuses on men's stories, and I wanted to see my sisters on the page as the stars of the show, instead of a side note. I wanted to see women and men serving side by side, fighting to protect each other, to bring each other home. I wanted to write about the bonds of deploying that are the same no matter who we are or where we're from.

I write because no one prepared me for how hard it was to come home, to become mom again. And I wanted the young mothers coming after me to know they were not alone when they were crying because their kids were crying again when they dropped them off at daycare. I wanted them to know they are not alone.

I write because Army life is funny and the dumb things that soldiers do is worth writing down and remembering. I write because I wanted to add another voice to the books on the shelves that maybe will help a future leader learn how to lead *all* of their soldiers a little better.

I write because I wanted my daughters to have something to show their grandchildren. In this digital age of transient ideas, a book is something tangible, that will still be readable in 50 or a hundred years.

I write alone, but words serve as a way of connecting others. Of connecting civilians to the military, of military moms to each other, of spouses to service members. Of telling the stories of "us," of "we."

That is why I write. Because our words will be here long after we are gone. And they will connect us to whoever comes after us.

And to remind us that we may write alone, but we are not alone.

Jessica Scott is a USA Today *best-selling author of more than 14 novels about soldiers returning from the war in Iraq. She enlisted in the U.S. Army as a private in 1995, and attained the rank of sergeant first class before commissioning in 2007. She is currently serving as an assistant professor at the U.S. Military Academy at West Point, N.Y. and holds a doctorate from Duke University, Durham, N.C. with interests centering on morality, moral judgments, group cohesion, and status. Follow her on Twitter: @JessicaScott09*

Remembering Private First Class Hutson

By Peter Van Buren

I write because Pfc. Brian Edward Hutson must remain silent.

Perhaps only ancient Sparta claimed to support its military more than the United States. From the "soldiers in uniform board first" ritual that happens only in American airports, to elections where a decision not to serve is forever held against a candidate, there are daily reminders that "the troops" are a presence in our society like few others.

The desire to claim a piece of that presence leads to elaborate lies, known as "stolen valor." People buy regulation uniforms and walk through society showing off medals, telling fake war stories, and accepting unearned thanks. They want the juice without having endured the squeeze. They are out there, and they are to be loathed.

Beside those who trade in stolen valor are those who claim virtue in the third person, by "supporting the troops." The bumper stickers, the writers who fetishize Sun Tzu, Homer, and Clausewitz, those one-time donations after some sad TV infomercial are shallow enough.

But zoom out. While some individuals fake service, society as a whole fakes support. We watch troops die because of long waits at veterans' hospitals. We pass 40,000 homeless vets on any given night, more than half of whom suffer from an untreated mental illness. We know some 460,000 vets from the Iraq and Afghan wars suffer Post-Traumatic Stress Disorder (PTSD); another 260,000 have Traumatic Brain Injuries (TBI). Statistics are hard to come by from America's other wars, but a working figure for PTSD of about 20 percent out of Iraq and Afghanistan suggests millions of Vietnam and Korea vets might also suffer. We read that military suicides increase among those who suffer brain injury and post traumatic stress disorder.

We are silent in the face of 20 veteran/soldier suicides a day.

All those of things are just numbers until you put a face on them. In my case, the face belonged to Brian Edward Hutson (name changed). I write about these things because of him.

I heard about Pfc. Brian Edward Hutson's death at breakfast and walked over to his trailer. As a U.S. State Department foreign service officer, I spent a year embedded with the Army in Iraq at several smaller Forward Operating Bases (FOB). Hutson had put the barrel of his rifle into his mouth, with the weapon set for a 3-round burst, and blew out the back of his skull. I saw the fan spray on the wall, already being washed off by the

Bangladeshi cleaning crew. The bleach solution they used was smearing more than cleaning, and the Bangladeshis had little stomach to wring out the mop heads all that often. The blood smelled coppery. Although I never smelled that before or since, I can summon it into my mind at any time I wish, and at some times I don't.

The ritual prescribed by regulation was the same, whether the death was by suicide or in combat. The chapel had rows of chairs set up, much as it would in Ohio or Georgia for a wedding, only at the front of the room was a wooden box with holes for the national and the unit flags, and a slot in which to stand the deceased's rifle. Hutson's human remains were likely already on their way home, on what the military calls an "Angel Flight." The box was made of plywood, stained and varnished like paneling, and reminded everyone of a high school wood shop project. The dead man's boots stood on either side of the rifle, with his helmet on top. The arrangement is called a "Battlefield Cross."

There was a program with the official Army photo of the deceased, posed in front of an American flag—you could see a few red pockmarks on the side of his face, a chicken pox scar on his forehead. All these photos showed a vacant stare, same as every high school graduation photo. The chaplain read the 23rd Psalm.

The required speeches were strained, because the senior officers who had to speak at these events rarely knew, given the many troops under them, the deceased. The dead man's job had something to do with radios, and most present didn't say much beyond that. The eulogy thus rang a bit hollow. You reminded yourself the words were not necessarily intended for you, however, and that the colonel may not have been the best man for the job. He was, however, a responsible man, trying hard to do something impossible. He probably felt bad for his lack of conviction, and that he was not a Pericles or Lincoln.

The last speaker was, by tradition, someone more personally acquainted with the deceased. In this ceremony, things were especially awkward. The dead man had taken his life after only a few months in the Army, and even less time at this FOB. Nobody had befriended him, and this being the third suicide on the FOB made the whole thing especially grim. The ceremony felt rushed, like an over-rehearsed school play, where the best performance had taken place the night before.

But sometimes things surprised you, maybe because of low expectations, maybe because every once in a while somebody stood up and said just what needed to be said. A young captain rose without notes. "I was his team leader, but I never really knew him. Brian was new here. He didn't have a nickname, and he didn't spend much time with us. He played Xbox a lot. We don't know why he committed suicide. We miss him anyway, because he was one of us. That's all I have to say."

The ceremony ended with the senior enlisted person calling the roll for the dead man's unit. Each member answered, "Here, Sergeant Major" after his name was called. That was until the name called was that of the deceased. "Brian Hutson?" Silence. "Brian E. Hutson?" Silence. "Private First Class Brian Edward Hutson?" Silence. Brian was not there and almost none of us had known him but yes, that day, at that place, we all missed him anyway.

We hear a lot about supporting the troops and thanking them for their service. Go ahead and do those things; they deserve it.

But don't traffic in empty words. We best remember Pfc. Brian Edward Hutson by taking care of the brothers and sisters of his that we created. If our nation insists on being so quick to send men and women into harm's way, then it best face its obligation to take care of them—beyond early boarding and discounts on wings'n beer. Food, shelter, health care, pre-/post-enlistment counseling—that's how you support the troops. One less fighter plane, or a few less tanks, would pay for much of what is needed.

For all the talk about how much we owe those who serve, no one ever demands we pay up.

Peter Van Buren is a retired U.S. State Department officer with more than 24 years of service. He is the author of We Meant Well: How I Helped Lose the Battle for the Hearts and Minds of the Iraqi People, *a memoir about failed reconstruction effects in Iraq. This essay is adapted from that book, and originally appeared in* The American Conservative. *Van Buren is also the author of* Hooper's War: A Novel of Moral Injury in WWII Japan.

On First Drafts and Embracing the Suck

By Teresa Fazio

I started with the part of my life I least wanted to write about. When I was U.S. Marine communications lieutenant stationed in Iraq, I had an affair that I hid from the world for most of a decade. In denying my experience, I wore a stifling mask through which I could only mumble that everything was fine. Pangs of guilt stabbed through my relief at returning from war.

But writing was soulcraft. I had always found solace in words. I was that kid scribbling in a diary at age 6, 16, 23. I wrote to make sense of what I'd witnessed and felt, to flush the river of anxious sludge undercutting my days. Words debrided my memories so scar tissue could properly form.

When I first started writing about Iraq, I thought, "oh, I'll just write a few vignettes about the war, maybe a book of short stories. I can't possibly write about this illicit-relationship thing." But it kept circling back. I couldn't *not* write about it.

Then I published the whole sordid tale in *The New York Times*. The day after the article ran was, at that point, the most liberated day of my life. The worst thing I'd ever done was on display, yet no mobs marched against me. Friends, family, colleagues, and strangers demonstrated shocking levels of compassion, of which I am only rarely capable towards myself. I finally felt like I had nothing to hide. And in letting go of shame, I made room for joy and gratitude.

The most surprising responses were from fellow Marines who said, "you're not alone; I have a story for you." I'd never suspected these folks of holding secrets beneath their uniforms. Just as, I suppose, they'd never suspected me. Paradoxically, strength lies in admitting vulnerability. Exposing secrets lessens their power.

After a few publications, I learned the hard way that my writing can hurt people, especially when my description of their behavior was unflattering. My clumsiness, however, stoked conversations that never would have happened otherwise.

I write to remind myself that it's OK to fail, whether by a misplaced comma, or by hitting bottom after a messed-up relationship. In telling myself my own story, I was able to reframe it as one of growth. In sharing my words, and accepting compassion from others, I learned that I did not have to be defined by my mistakes.

Despite positive responses to my shorter articles, I still worry about potential reactions to my book, both from people I'll never meet and from those I've known for decades. Sometimes the fear is paralyzing. But I know I need to release that fear and keep writing.

If you're anything like me, you will have spent years lying to yourself— "no, I'm OK, everything's fine." It is not fine, else you would not feel the compulsion to get it out of your head, your tapping fingers the crucial conduits from aching brain cell to blinking cursor. Write what is honest and true. It's OK if it sucks. It's OK if you burn it. Neither your mother nor your middle-school teachers will read your first draft. But what you must do, is to write the story that only you can write.

Teresa Fazio served as a U.S. Marine Corps communications officer from 2002 to 2006, deploying once to Iraq. Her writing has been published in The New York Times, The Washington Post, Rolling Stone, Foreign Policy, *and in several anthologies. Her awards include the Consequence Magazine Fiction Prize, the Sven Birkerts Non-fiction Prize, and a fellowship at Yaddo. Fazio holds a doctorate in materials science from Columbia University, New York City, a Master of Fine Arts in non-fiction from the Bennington Writing Seminars, and an undergraduate degree in physics from the Massachusetts Institute of Technology. Her memoir* Fidelis *will be published by Potomac Books in fall 2020. Follow her on Twitter: @DoctorFaz*

Writing Myself to Sleep

By Matt Condon

I was lost.

There I was, sitting in a small, dirty apartment, "sipping" cheap bourbon on a Friday night ... alone. The temperature outside had started to warm up, but the infamous Seattle rain had washed away any desire to go outside; discontent had driven away any need for social interaction.

That's the way it'd been for several weeks: no parties, no plans, no people. The only person keeping me company that night—most nights, really—was Evan Williams.

Sure I'd spent a few weeks "dating" a girl from the gym, but we knew it was going to end when she transitioned out. Yes, I had friends in the area, but they were all married and doing things married people do. Of course, I could go to the gym, but the laziness and warmth from the bourbon had already settled in.

It was just me, a bunch of movies I'd seen a dozen times, and my computer.

Like every other night that week, I couldn't sleep—turns out Evan Williams is not the Sandman—and, like every other night that week, my mind seemed to drift between thoughts. The hours dragged on, the thoughts continued.

Around two in the morning my phone buzzed—the closest thing to human interaction I'd experienced the whole night.

The girl I'd "dated" was in Europe, spending some time decompressing from her time in the Army before starting school in the fall:

Her: Croatia might be my favorite place in Europe.

Me: You say that about every place.

Her: Why are you awake? Isn't it like 3 a.m.?

Me: No. It's only 2.

Her: Oh—'cause that's different. Can't sleep?

Me: Nope.

Her: What's on your mind?

Me: Everything.

Her: So you're thinking about your Ex?

Me: ... maybe.

Her: You need to find a way to stop doing that. Forget about her.

Me: I'm drinking. What other ways are there to forget about her?

Her: Try writing about it.

Me: What?

Her: Try writing. You edited that awful recommendation letter I wrote, and you have a knack for it. So try writing about it. Didn't you say you used to write in high school?

Me: Yes.

Her: So give it a try. What's the worst that can happen, you won't be able to sleep?

(She had a point.)

(She always had a point.)

Me: What am I going to write about? I don't have anything to say, and I can't make my mind sit still.

Her: Just write what's on your mind and go from there. Maybe you'll find something positive and be able to sleep.

I was skeptical. I hadn't written anything for myself since I'd graduated high school. Even in college, I loathed every paper I'd been assigned. Every OPORD and CONOP felt like an exercise in sadism from my commander.

What could I possibly write that would help me sleep? How would jotting a few things down on paper shake the feeling of embarrassment that met me at every hour?

But, she had a point. What did I have to lose, a few more hours of sleep?

Me: OK. I'll try.

I pulled out an old notebook, looked through the chicken-scratched notes from a class I'd taken earlier that year, and ripped out the pages. The blank pages stared back at me, almost taunting me.

There's few things in this world more intimidating than a notebook full of blank pages. To this day, one of my biggest fears is leaving a notebook completely empty, leaving a story in my mind. That fear is second only to starting a new story.

The fear, irrational or not, started my pen moving.

The result was a few pages about why my divorce had hit me so hard; why, beyond the obvious betrayal of her affair, it'd been so hard to accept at first.

Fear.

Fear of change, fear of living alone, fear of being alone, fear of embarrassment, fear I wasn't worthy.

Surprisingly, my attitude changed. My fear had always been that by writing down and making tangible those thoughts, I was somehow admitting defeat, making those feelings worse and more ingrained.

It was quite the opposite.

By writing those feelings down, by putting those fears in black and white, they seemed nominal—almost laughable. It was as if by putting them on paper, I'd found a place where they couldn't hurt me.

I still didn't sleep that night, I was awake to watch the sun shine through my windows, but I was able to rest a little. I let relief overtake my anxiety. For once, I was awake because I wanted to be, not because I was unable to sleep.

In the succeeding weeks, I found catharsis in writing. Something about it put my mind at ease. I still held those fears, still felt their presence throughout the day but I didn't let them control my thoughts when it was just me, the TV, and a 6-pack.

Eventually, I started sending some of what I wrote to—another fear. Their feedback was overwhelming. They encouraged me to keep writing. If for no other reason, it was a healthy way of dealing with my emotions.

There was still one fear that wouldn't let go.

Most days I could get by. It wouldn't keep me awake or I could ignore it long enough to sleep. But every few weeks, it would pop back into my head.

Driving down the road I'd see a wreck, or watching a movie I'd see the protagonist atop a high rise, and suddenly the fear was ready to greet me. For the better part of two years, it was the one fear I couldn't force myself to deal with, couldn't make my hand write the words.

That changed when I took an on-line writing class about writing with emotional authenticity. The basic premise of the class was writing characters—real or otherwise—in a way that made them believable, was neither all bad and nor all good (think Deadpool or Wolverine).

Near the end of the 8-week course, the writing assignment forced me to look at those thoughts and events of which I was ashamed.

To that point, I'd managed to write around what I found the most shameful part of my divorce. Now, it seemed, I wouldn't be able to write around anything, I'd have face this one head on.

Here is what I wrote for that assignment:

I just finished writing a note to my then-wife, clicked the pen shut. I read it over one more time: "I hope you live forever." I nodded in satisfaction, looked around the office, folded the note and put it in my pocket.

The plan was set, the note was written and now there was only one thing left to do. As I drove home, I thought about our conversation the previous day. It had been three weeks since she told me what she'd done, three weeks of torment and torture. I'd begged her to stay, to give me another chance. But she told me no. She was in love with someone else. And so I told her I wanted to go to sleep and not wake up the next day.

Unfortunately, I woke up. Cloaked in the chains of sorrow, wanting only an escape. And only one escape would do the trick.

I passed each exit on the highway, firm in my commitment to rid myself of the pain forever. But then my mind started to panic. She would never believe I needed a shower after work. I'd never done that unless I went to the gym before I got home. My plan was quickly unraveling at the seams. I needed to execute my plan without conversation or confrontation. I needed her distracted so I could pull it off without any guilt. What was I going to do?

The answer was in the passenger seat of my truck. My gym bag was riding shotgun, like a best friend should.

I glanced at the clock, still time to make it to practice. There was still a chance I could make this work. The panic subsided and the fog of sorrow settled back in.

Warm-ups had already started by the time I walked through the door, but I wasn't upset about it. Wouldn't matter if they gave me shit for being late. I was already feeling low, already numb to anything they could throw at me.

It was a light practice, mostly drills and a few rounds of light grappling. My coach was getting ready for a fight, so he was rotating with everyone. I was mostly going through the motions, never really doing anything I wasn't supposed to, but not really putting any effort into it either. I think he noticed.

As we were grappling, he put me in an awkward choke. It wasn't tight, it didn't really choke me, but I was out of motivation and didn't care at all. I didn't move, didn't try to escape, I tapped.

"Was that even choking you?" he asked pulling out his mouth guard.

"Not really," I said, unable to summon up the urge to care or look at him.

"Then why the fuck did you tap?" he asked, fire in his eyes.

I had no response. I numbly looked down at the floor and somehow lower.

He went on, "Look at me. Failure is always an option. One-hundred-percent of the time it's always there and can always happen. But it's a choice. Choose to fail, or choose to succeed. You can't give up because you're stuck, can't tap because you can't deal with the situation you're in. It's a conscious choice to fail."

Suddenly, I felt everything. All the pain, all the sadness, all the sorrow, all the regrets, tears began forming, my throat ached with the swelling lump. Something clicked. The plan was forgotten.

I nodded, finished the round, grabbed my things and left. As I drove home the second time, I dug out the note I'd written a few hours earlier. I sat in the parking lot to our apartment, grabbed the lighter off my dash and burned the note in the cup holder.

And there it was: the fear I'd most wanted to avoid, the event for which I felt the most ashamed. I was ashamed that I'd almost let someone else's actions push me to the point of taking my own life.

A few days later, my instructor sent me her feedback and told me more stories like this need to be told, the hard conversations we're afraid to have with ourselves, let alone others, are the most important ones to have.

That's part of why I write, to contribute to the conversations that we're

WHY WE WRITE: CRAFT ESSAYS ON WRITING WAR

afraid to have, to talk about hard things. Through these conversations we can show the humanity rooted in the veteran community and, hopefully, bridge the gap between veterans and civilians. To show that, despite our differences, we're all just people.

We're doing ourselves a disservice by not having honest conversations that affect more than just the military community.

My reasons for writing are more selfish than that, however. Without writing at some point during the day, my mind wanders as I try to drift to sleep. I might contemplate how I'm going to develop a character in a story, or the best structure to present an argument in my next opinion piece. Tomorrow, I will write more. I drift off from there.

At the end of the day, I need to write to sleep.

Matt Condon is a former U.S. Army captain. He is currently a freelance writer and photographer for multiple publications. Follow him on Twitter: @goat_path

Writing as an Airman and as a Civilian

By Matthew Komatsu

It is 12 a.m. in the land of the midnight sun. Seventy-two hours until deployment. I should be at home with my wife, Jen, and 6-month-old son or unpacking the house we bought recently. Instead, I'm on my bike riding home from the University of Alaska, Anchorage. A rowdy group rides down another trail that merges with mine, cycling in a pack in front of me. They laugh, pull beers from messenger bags, see me and offer me one. The exchange is tour-worthy. An anonymous rider pulls out a cold Olympia and reaches toward me. His eyes remain on the trail ahead, as do mine. I extend a blind left hand, close the gap, find the front of the can. For a moment we are connected by cheap beer. Then he lets go and it is all mine. I toast the rowdies and ride ahead.

On January 13, my wife's water broke, just as I put the final touches on my application to the Master of Fine Arts program in creative writing at the University of Alaska, Anchorage. While I drove, frenzied, across town for a post office, she held out through rising contractions. Finnegan Shichiro Komatsu made his entry that night, and a month later a letter came in the mail. I was in, accepted into the creative non-fiction program.

The university program is low-residency: a correspondence course for all but two weeks every summer. During the residency, students from all over the globe—and from three genres (fiction, creative non-fiction and poetry) —converged on the Anchorage campus. For two weeks, it was 12 hours a day of writing: poetry, fiction, readings, lectures, manuscript workshops. Immersed in an unfamiliar world, windows to new material opened hourly.

Because the program required so little time on campus, I did not have to quit my job to pursue the degree. The course work for my first semester was on-line. When it was time for the residency, I took leave, shed my uniform, pulled on some civvies and rode my bike to class.

Among the better-known veteran writers of recent wars, Brian Turner, author of *Here, Bullet* and *My Life as a Foreign Country*, took his MFA credentials to the battlefield and returned with devastating poetry. Phil Klay got his degree not long after leaving the U.S. Marines and wrote an acclaimed collection of stories titled *Redeployment*. And Ron Capps, author of *Seriously Not All Right: Five Wars in Ten Years*, got a master's before serving with the U.S. Army and the State Department in various war-torn areas, including Afghanistan and Rwanda. He credits writing with saving his life.

Veterans who are writers are no different from civilian writers, in that we bring the same baggage to the keyboard. Emotional trauma, the minefield of cliché and self-doubt are common to all writers. However, what sets us apart is that we veterans arrive with a litany of cultural tags, some of which are self-enforced, others undeserved, all entirely unhelpful: the other 1 percent, uneducated high-school dropouts with no better options, mindless automatons.

I showed up for the residency, cautious after a semester of on-line classes. Nothing in my virtual interactions with classmates indicated a need to worry. But how much can you hope to learn about someone when your interface is limited to, say, trading on-line perspectives about Anne Lamott's essay on terrible first drafts? I arrived, sweating from my hurried bike ride, and looked for the boogeyman.

Instead, I found men and women genuinely interested in my writing, which occurs on the peripheries of war and military life. My classmates included pacifists, Occupy movement enthusiasts, stay-at-home fathers, touchy-feely poets, and backcountry risk-takers. But labels fell away when we workshopped one another's manuscripts.

We each submitted two manuscripts and for hours each day workshopped them, which was the core of the residency. Nobody got a pass. One of my manuscripts covered the Japanese tsunami of 2011— during which my grandmother died—and my subsequent deployment to Yokota Air Base in western Tokyo. An emotional facade crumbled during the workshop and I broke down. My classmates smiled and told me that the essay was good but that the structure needed work. My other manuscript, a retelling of my experience during an attack on Bastion Air Base in Afghanistan, was "confusing" and filled with "military jargon" that isolated the reader, they told me. During the workshop I was no longer an airman or a veteran. I was a writer, just like everyone else.

I asked a fellow Air Force Academy alumnus, Brandon Lingle, about his MFA experience. He joined Brian Turner's MFA program at Sierra Nevada College in Nevada, and later deployed to Afghanistan. During his first residency, Brandon's classmates wanted to know more about the veteran experience and understood that he was about to deploy, which, he said, "helped humanize the concept for those who had never been exposed to the military."

If there is debate over whether MFA programs produce good writers, none exists where connection is concerned. And that is precisely what I am after. Near the end of my first semester, a classmate asked the question in our on-line forum: "Why do you write?"

My response was two paragraphs. Both described what it was like to witness an airman receive a Silver Star, then drink with him and a man whose life he saved. The first paragraph described the ceremony, the heroics, everything you could absorb in a hurried read or on the Silver Star citation itself. The second paragraph characterized the struggles both men now face in negotiating simple day-to-day living.

You can get all of the former on your own, I wrote. I'm here to deliver the latter.

I balance an increasingly foamy beer while maneuvering my bike around and over frost-heaves in the pavement. Caught in the moment under the shadow of an evergreen canopy, I find a smile on my face. An unlikely beer. A shot off the page that hits the reader just right. While the former was serendipitous and the latter desired, both are inextricably tied to the risk I took when I sent in my MFA application. That decision positioned me right where I am. It will lead me ahead, converging and diverging with other paths as it may.

I finish the ride and park my bike next to garage boxes. I tiptoe into Finn's room, kiss his sleeping form, then find Jen in the bedroom, where she is unpacking. "Do I have a story for you," I say.

Matthew Komatsu is a writer and member of the Alaska Air National Guard. Follow him on Twitter: @matthew_komatsu

Finding "Ashley's War"

By Gayle Tzemach Lemmon

The path that led me to write about the military did not start with covering war from the front lines. Indeed, it began in an unlikely place: with a first set of interviews about women entrepreneurs in Afghanistan.

I landed in Afghanistan in 2005 while studying for an MBA, after years at ABC News. And I began writing about entrepreneurs: the challenges they faced, the opportunities they created, and the hope they manufactured.

And the deeper I got into the story of Afghanistan, the more time I spent writing about the challenges Afghan women faced in realms outside the economic. And the clearer it became that I would have to write about security if I were ever to understand—let alone communicate to an international audience—what the country's citizens faced on the ground.

And in the process of writing about Afghanistan for print and on-line outlets, and reporting my first book, I met an ever-larger number of those in uniform serving America. These were people I had never known or met in "everyday" life back in the United States. I, like the overwhelming majority of Americans, had little to no contact with the men and women serving in the nation's armed forces.

In Afghanistan, I met troops working to provide security in some of the most trying moments imaginable. They turned out to be people with whom I shared a great deal, even though we had arrived at the security conversation from different starting points. They were people who were doing their best to accomplish the mission they had been handed, people who were losing friends and brothers- and sisters-in-arms on the battlefield, people who wanted to serve to their utmost, people who found themselves changed by all of these things.

And I realized how little most of America knew about them. Less than 1 percent of this nation has fought 100 percent of its wars since 2001. Precious few people outside this narrow sliver have seen their lives changed by wars that have not yet ended. Yet for those who have deployed, and those who have spent time in the nations where America is at war, nothing is ever the same. The same goes for the families of those who serve—especially the families of those who are lost.

I ended up falling in love with Afghanistan, and the grace, grit, heart, and resilience of its people. And I ended up feeling the extreme privilege that comes with coming to have a front-row seat in the unfolding histories of this nation's service members.

It was the privilege of writing *Ashley's War* that offered me the latter. I first found out about the story from former U.S. Marine Claire Russo. She mentioned 1st Lt. Ashley White, and her service on this strangely named entity known as the Cultural Support Teams (CST). It turned out this was a benign name for a groundbreaking concept.

The story of *Ashley's War* started with a call to the White family. And it took over my life—in the best and most powerful sense of that phrase—nearly immediately. As soon as I met Lt. White's mother, in person, and saw the letters that had poured in to them, I wanted to meet the lieutenant's teammates. And the Rangers with whom she served.

It took me just a few months of reporting to understand one thing: This was an extraordinary team of women. They started as teammates, became friends, and ended their time at war as family. They were forever changed by the experience of serving at the tip of the spear at time when, officially, women remained banned from ground combat. And America had no idea they existed.

They had not set out to break historic ground, they set out only to serve to their utmost. Nevertheless, they had made history. I felt a responsibility, a burden, and a privilege to tell this story of friendship, of sacrifice, of service, of love for the first time to the nation in whose name they served. Whether that nation would pay attention, I did not know. But I knew in my gut that the story had the power to push past the idea of nameless, faceless people fighting nameless, faceless wars. And to connect readers to the women and men who set out each day—and, in this case, each night—to fulfill the missions America asks of them.

In the process of telling *Ashley's War* I had the opportunity to meet so many of the men who made the story possible. And to, in a way, embed myself in the lives of a number of special operations soldiers, most of whom had completed 10, 11, 12, sometimes even 13 or 14, deployments on their country's behalf.

I saw for myself their love for the work. And the tolls it exacted. I felt frustration and something approaching anger about how indifferent—and downright ignorant—most Americans were to what they asked of these men. I wanted to connect people to these ordinary individuals asked to do extraordinary things.

War is deeply personal, even if we don't talk about it that way. We must change that. Stories are the only tools we have, really, to break through the impersonal veneer of shapeless words we now employ to discuss combat. We must push America to engage with its conflicts, if we care about our country's future and the service members who go and fight our nation's battles. Showing these wars in the smallest details of their very human terms is one way—and the best way I know—of doing that.

Gayle Tzemach Lemmon is the author of The New York Times *bestsellers* Ashley's War: The Untold Story of a Team of Women Soldiers on the Special Ops Battlefield *and* The Dressmaker of Khair Khana, *about a young entrepreneur who supported her community under the Taliban. Lemmon's next book is forthcoming in spring 2020 from Penguin Press. The story is based in northern Syria and focuses on the women who spent four years leading the fight against ISIS and their push for the most far-reaching experiment in women's rights in the world's least-likely place. Lemmon is a partner and CMO at Shield AI and serves as an adjunct senior fellow at the Council on Foreign Relations in its Women and Foreign Policy Program. Follow her on Twitter:* @GayleLemmon

Some True Lies about Conflict Reporting

By Carmen Gentile

I've been asked more times than I can count why I write about conflict. And every time I'm asked, I give a different answer. Some of them are true, many are outright lies. But none come close to adequately explaining why.

The most popular reason given by many a conflict hack is considered the granddaddy of war journalism clichés: "It's important to bear witness."

This abhorrent contrivance aims at convincing the inquirer that not only is war reporting a noble calling, but its practitioners are impossibly brave, selfless martyrs who risk their lives to inform and educate the masses back home, who are living sheltered lives while they dodge bullets, sleep in the dirt, and poop in a hole.

This kind of self-adulation makes me sick, especially since I, too, trotted out this self-aggrandizing pabulum in my youth without an iota of shame. Mostly I did it to woo young women who listened intently to my casually tossed-off tales of supposed heroics, their mouths agape and hearts aflutter. Or so I liked to imagine. More often than not, they saw through my shtick and I went home alone.

That's not to say conflict journalism isn't important. It is, in my humble and completely objective assessment, some of the most essential storytelling ever committed to stone tablet, paper, and screen.

From *History of the Peloponnesian War* author Thucydides, to the American treasure of frontline journalism Ernie Pyle, all the way down to the lowliest of freelance hacks such as myself, conflict reporting helps us to understand the sometime-wicked ways of the human experience.

Without it, humanity's seeming ease with mutilating innocent masses in the quest for either money and power, or co-opted religious ideals masquerading their greed for money and power, would go unchecked and be even worse than already is.

However, even that isn't the real reason why I do it. Mine is one to which nary a conflict journalist will admit publicly, though I suspect is the motivation for many of them: It's a rush.

War can be a heart-pumping, heart-in-your-throat thrill ride. Perhaps this is why it seems to attract those with addiction-prone personalities. I would never presume to speak for others as to why they chose to cover war, but consider it an educated guess based on many years of anecdotal evidence gathered in the company of my tribe. Sex, drugs, booze, war— they're all ways in which to get high. Many of those spending time in war zones imbibe in these other indulgences to excess. I know I did until I finally had to call it quits. That's when I found a new addiction.

Now as I've grown older, my zeal for the wartime thrills has waned. Maybe it's maturity, but more likely it's the realizations that I already have more years behind me than ahead, and that I'd like to spend most of the time I have left with my young daughter.

But my passion for the work hasn't diminished. I still like to tell good stories, replete with human emotions that don't appear in stories told about conflict from a policy perspective by wonks in Washington.

For me, creating a compelling, true story—one of love of family and tribe and hate for your enemy—is its own addiction.

My desire to produce my best work under the most extreme conditions is me chasing another high. By comparison, those stories I report that are relegated to a handful of phone interviews and follow up e-mail, make me want to tear my eyes out from boredom.

Again, I readily admit, this is yet another terribly insensitive way in which to view the calamities of war. It's horrifying. I used to never admit it. Few of my colleagues do. But I can't deny it any longer, especially since my most ambitious writing project to date is a book about my personal experience covering war.

Back in the summer of 2010, the height of the Afghanistan surge, I was embedded in a foot patrol through a small village just a few miles from the Pakistani border.

While speaking to a group of young men squatting by the side of the road, I heard a loud *WHOOSH!* and turned around to see someone shouldering an RPG launcher. The ordnance screamed towards me, then collided with the side of my face, blinding my in the right eye and shattering all the bones in my cheek. By freak luck, the rocket didn't go off, but instead ricocheted off me to hit the platoon leader in the elbow before clattering to the ground.

I spent the better part of three years, writing, editing, and polishing a manuscript about my one-of-a-kind injury, recovery, and eventual return to conflict reporting. Writing about the most physically painful and emotionally miserable time of my life reopened old wounds, but I'll also shamefully admit gave me a perverse pleasure. I knew it would produce the most honest work of my career to date.

And once I found a publisher for my book, the type was set and the manuscript shipped to the printer, I immediately set about writing another book. This one chronicles behind-the-scenes tales from more reporting assignments in Afghanistan, as well as conflicts in Iraq, Haiti, and other countries I've covered.

It's gotten to the point that even when I'm not reporting from God-awful conflict, I'm revisiting those same battlefields to examine the cracks in my stories and my own understanding of its cost in human lives and suffering.

Bottom line: There is something probably seriously wrong with me. That's probably the closest answer to the truth about what I do—and why I do it—that I'll ever give.

Carmen Gentile is the author of Blindsided by the Taliban: A Journalist's Story of War, Trauma, Love, and Loss. *As a journalist, he has written for some of the world's leading publications, including* The New York Times, Time, Newsweek, USA Today, *and many others. He has also produced radio and on-line video reporting, and has published numerous photos with his work.*

Gentile began his international reporting career in the late 1990s, when he was based in Cairo, Egypt. In September 2010, Gentile was shot by a Rocket-Propelled Grenade while reporting on U.S. and Afghan forces in eastern Afghanistan. Following a lengthy recovery, he returned to Afghanistan, and resumed embed reporting for USA Today and others. Follow him on Twitter: @CarmenGentile

The Three Pillars of T.E. Lawrence

By Hal Wilson

> "[...] I long for the vanished gardens of Cordova.
> However, before the gardens must come fighting [...]"
> —Prince Faisel, as played by Alec Guinness,
> in the movie *Lawrence of Arabia* (1962)

In January 1911, a young man arrived in Aleppo, a city in what is now Syria. He had travelled via those two keystones to the ancient world: Athens and Constantinople. At the former, he had explored the Parthenon; at the latter, he had lived for a week aboard a broken-down boat, roaming the famous city as he awaited repairs.

This was no listless wanderer, however, loafing on the equivalent of a modern "gap year." He was a fresh graduate from Oxford University, with First Class Honours in History. His thesis title: *The Military Architecture of the Crusades*. He had arrived in Aleppo to further this knowledge of the Crusades, and to support architectural digs around Carchemish. His hunger detail was keen. Indeed, once in Aleppo, he found the city's sole-remaining chain-mail maker—and asked if he could learn the armorer's methods.

The young man was, in short, a budding genius. His name was Thomas Edward Lawrence.

As he busied himself with his digs and books and travels, he could never have guessed how he would one day return to the region as young staff officer in the British Army. He would go on to lead an Anglo-Arab army, and help smash Ottoman rule of Damascus forever.

Today, he is popularly known as "Lawrence of Arabia."

Thanks in no small part to actor Peter O'Toole, who starred in David Lean's 1962 epic movie, Lawrence has become a cultural touchstone of the 20th century: a man who united warring tribes, and who fought the endless desert as much as the Turks themselves. As an exemplar, Lawrence again came to prominence through the long, hard years of Iraq and Afghanistan, when author and U.S. soldier John Nagl borrowed Lawrence's aphorism on counterinsurgency for the title of his 2005 work, *Learning to Eat Soup with a Knife*.

Lawrence continues to inspire other soldier-writers.

By the time of his arrival at Aleppo, Lawrence had already demonstrated his skill with a pen. In 1911, he wrote to his parents of a novel entitled *The Seven Pillars of Wisdom*, "my monumental book on the Crusades." Lawrence would later re-use the title for his wartime memoirs. As the preface to the 1935 edition of the latter explains: "The title was originally applied by the author to a book of his about seven cities. He decided not to publish this early book because he considered it immature, but he transferred the title as a memento."

Sadly, this version of events is somewhat inaccurate: Lawrence actually burnt the manuscript to the original *Seven Pillars* at some point in 1914, before joining the Army. Whatever self-effacing thoughts Lawrence may have had of the manuscript, its destruction is surely a great loss. We know this given the eloquence of his pre-war letters home from the East. Consider his description of the Parthenon:

> [...] I, a stranger, was walking on the floor of the place I had most desired to see, the greatest temple of Athene, the palace of art, and that I was counting her columns, and finding them what I already knew. The building was familiar, not cold as in the drawings, but complex, irregular, alive with curve and subtlety, and perfectly preserved. Every line of the mouldings, every minutest refinement in the sculptures were evident in that light, and inevitable in their place. The Parthenon is the proto-cathedral of the Hellenes.

His youthful excitement practically bleeds from the page, with short, sharp clauses bouncing breathlessly across each line, as if he cannot write things down fast enough. Despite destroying his pre-war *Seven Pillars* manuscript, Lawrence went on to leverage precisely this sweeping, eager style for his wartime memoirs of the same name.

It is precisely because of that style—and its simple, powerful elegance— that today's defense and security writers should invest time on Lawrence's work. Whether writing fiction or factual reports, this approach offers a worthy guide for three key reasons:

Firstly, Lawrence's style allowed him to distill details to easily digested helpings. Consider, for example, Lawrence's dictum on counterinsurgency; that "war upon rebellion was messy and slow, like eating soup with a knife." Indeed, just a few pages after that remark, Lawrence went on to condense the complexities of desert war by explaining, "The invention of bully beef had profited us more than the invention of gunpowder [...] since in Arabia range was more than force, space greater than the power of armies." In this era of PowerPoint, in which details often are either too few or too many, Lawrence reminds us of the power of a pithy metaphor.

Lawrence's ability to firmly capture the imagination is the second key element of his style—and the reason his writing transcends the professional, military nature of his work. For instance, he describes Beirut almost as the poet John Betjeman describes the interwar industrial city of Slough: It was a

"Levantine screen through which cheap or shop-soiled foreign influences entered: it represented Syria as much as Soho the Home Counties."

Alternatively, consider his more reverent description of the Valley of Rumm. Here,

> [Its] crags were capped in nests of domes [...] they gave the finishing semblance of Byzantine architecture to this irresistible place: this processional way greater than imagination. The Arab armies would have been lost in the length and breadth of it, and within the walls a squadron of aeroplanes could have wheeled in formation. Our little caravan grew [...] ashamed to flaunt its smallness in the presence of the stupendous hills.

Take particular note of the conclusion to that paragraph. Lawrence has taken a place "greater than imagination"—and looped back to the human scale, a familiar reference point to help frame his readers' imaginations. Thus, whether describing the epic vastness of his desert treks—or even Beirut by reference to Soho—his writing more readily chimes with the reader's mental imagery, no matter how alien or distant the topic.

Lawrence drives this home with a third key aspect of his style: He bakes "character" throughout his material. Sometimes, this relates to his cast of soldiers and statesmen, so that even the slightest figures stand out in memory. For instance, the British sergeant "Stokes"—nicknamed for training Arabs with the Stokes mortar—"was driven by the Arab strangeness to become more himself, more insular. His shy correctness reminded my men in every movement he was unlike them, and English ... [which] elicited a turn of respect. To them, he was 'the sergeant' [...]"

Lawrence's final product almost reads more as a travelogue than a war story—indeed, his delivery is often distinctly conversational. One example out of many stands out vividly. One night on the trek to Aqaba, Lawrence is drawn into a lengthy discussion on the nature of the stars above with his Arab comrades. To which Auda, the chief, silences his fellows:

> "Lads, we know our districts, our camels, our women. The excess and the glory are to God. If the end of wisdom is to add star to star our foolishness is pleasing."

And then he spoke of money, and distracted their minds till they all buzzed at once. Afterwards he whispered to me that I must get him a worthy gift [...] when he won Aqaba.

The result is that Lawrence's reader is once again drawn in and placed on his shoulder, as if sharing in some private conversation. Today's defense writers would do well to consider the merits of this approachable, character-driven method.

After all, the marketplace for the time of today's audiences is fraught with competition like never before. Winning the attention of readers, who are otherwise besieged by high-quality video games, or Netflix offerings, or the demands of family—is its own type of insurgency. Like Lawrence, we must fight to entertain, as well as to educate.

To be sure, Lawrence is not a perfect writer. His exuberance can grow exhausting; his descriptions of his achievements are sometimes inflated. (He was, after all, a staff officer.) But his methods—whether the use of detail in winning hearts and minds, or imbuing character and approachability—offer a potential template for achieving the "value-add' needed in today's marketplace.

Ultimately, Lawrence deserves one's time for the simple pleasure of his craftsmanship. Wherever one finds them—as I variously have in a sleepy second-hand bookshop, deep in rural Norfolk; and the trendy shelves of a Vancouver hipster emporium—the crossed-gold scimitars of his *Seven Pillars* 1935 hard-back are the highest mark of quality.

Hal Wilson is a fiction writer specializing in the use of narrative to explore future conflict. His finalist entries have been published by The Atlantic Council's Art of the Future Project, the Modern War Institute at West Point, and War on the Rocks. *Wilson graduated with first-class honors in War Studies and History from King's College, London, and is pursuing a graduate degree on the Great War. is a member of the Military Writers Guild Follow him on Twitter at: HalWilson_*

Armour Against Atrocity:
Writing to Find One's Moral Compass

By Tom McDermott

"For we know enough, if we know we are the king's subjects;
if his cause be wrong, our obedience to the king
wipes the crime out of us."
—Bates, a soldier, to a disguised king in "Henry V," Act IV, Scene 1

Everyone over the age of 25 has their 9/11 story. Mine is about a forgotten moral compass, and the search for a new one through writing. When the attacks happened, I was a young officer cadet in the British Army, training at the Royal Military Academy. On the morning of Sept. 11, 2001 we were timetabled for a defense studies lecture entitled "The Causes of War."

Instead, we woke to a city, and a world, on fire. As good cadets, we dutifully trudged up for our lecture, more afeared of breaking the sacred schedule than of breaking world events. The experienced historian (noting the irony of his topic against the unfolding attacks in America) told us to go away and watch television. He said it would be instructive.

So we sat together as a young cohort in the academy mess hall, and we watched. In detachment and shock, we watched as first one, then the other tower collapsed. We knew that thousands would be dead.

If I'm honest, the first emotion I remember was a morbid excitement that followed. As America's closest ally we knew the British would be involved. We were about to commission.

We knew we would be part of it ... we just didn't know when.

Five-hundred-and-fifty-four days later, as a lieutenant in the oldest tank regiment in the world, I took part in the invasion of Iraq. While you can split hairs about counterfactuals and flawed intelligence, the decision to overthrow Saddam Hussein was not an action of last resort, and it triggered a chain reaction with tragic results. The big-picture outcome, however, isn't what I want to talk about. Instead, I want to narrow down to my own personal consideration of the *ethics* of the invasion at the time. In other words, did I, as a young combat officer serving a staunchly democratic country, consider the invasion of Iraq to be "right"? Were the Iraqis my enemies, and a threat to my way of life? Above all, was killing them OK? How much responsibility did I hold personally, if it all went wrong?

I look back with a sense of curiosity and shame as to how little I considered these questions. I don't recall any real process of moral reflection. The intelligence seemed so sound, and the prime minister so confident. Saddam Hussein was the villain of our era, and getting rid of him was the "right thing to do." I had seen the videos of the Iraqi chemical attacks on Halabja, and the images of dead children were seared into my mind. If I'm honest, however, all of this faded into the background compared to my own professional desire to go to war. I wanted to fight: to do the job I had aspired to do since I was a teenager. I thought little, if at all, about what would follow after we deposed Saddam. The importance of a "just" peace (*jus post bellum*), and our moral responsibility for the aftermath of war, didn't even register against my zeal for soldiering. The fight was all.

Even today, this lack of moral consideration surprises me. It wasn't as if I lacked the intellectual wit to consider it. I had grown up in a home full of traditional Christian values. I had studied English literature and then classics at a good British university. I had devoured the *Iliad* and the *Odyssey*, and had spent many hours debating fate, freewill, and the just cause of the Achaeans. I had read Thucydides, Plato, Aristotle. I could quote from war epics like Shakespeare's "Henry V." Nothing compared to the visceral excitement of a real, conventional war. When thinking of Iraq, I was all "St. Crispin's Day" speech. I believed I was a subject of my sovereign, one of the "happy few," the "band of brothers," and that those who did not deploy to Iraq would "think themselves accurs'd they were not here." Never did I consider that, like the foot soldier Bates, I should worry of my personal responsibility if it proved that the king was wrong. It seemed I had learned the theory of morality, but I failed to put it in practice. It wasn't so much that I lacked a moral compass—I had just forgotten it.

Seven years later, I was fighting the same war, but this time in Afghanistan. Our declared enemy remained "terror"—as undefined an opponent as you could ask for, and one that Sir Hew Strachan has since labeled as "profoundly astrategic." While the war was the same, however, the style of warfare had changed dramatically. In 2010, U.S. troop levels peaked at the height of the "Afghan Surge." At the same time, so did our collective ability to apply technologically enabled violence.

A vast array of sensors, listening devices, drones, and aircraft crisscrossed Afghanistan. It created unparalleled access—an all-seeing eye—into the lives of the Afghan people. Ultimately, it had one purpose: to create the lowest-risk and most-precise capture/kill machine in human history. For six months, I was part of a team that used this eye to remotely find, follow, and often kill insurgents. It was a surprisingly intimate process. We would watch suspected enemy commanders for hours, days, and weeks on end, never leaving the safety of a secure operations room. Once an individual of interest was located, the aim was to always know where they were ... we rotated assets, stayed focused, and never blinked. When we were sure—if the moment and rules of engagement were assessed to be correct—we would strike. It was designed to be clean, clinical. The target would know nothing before the explosion.

We were the quiet, surgical high-tech snipers of the modern age, figuratively as far away as possible from the model of overwhelming force delivered in the invasion of Iraq. Morally, it should have felt infinitely more proportionate; more discriminate.

It didn't. The clinical nature of the "machine" was somehow harder to morally square than the visceral experience of Iraq. It was ironic that the last time I had watched live death on television was on 9/11. Isolated from the actual violence being applied, I could feel myself becoming increasingly detached from the strikes. They became commonplace, a process to be followed, guided by targeting lists, flowcharts and rules of engagement. The life at the other end gradually lost some of its meaning. Worse, it was easy to get caught up in the thrill and challenge of the game. It was exciting, and entirely free of personal risk.

Older, a little wiser, and more experienced than in Iraq, I began to turn a critical eye to my own moral perception of my actions. I was by this time a committed professional soldier, and no pacifist. I firmly believed that killing in war was necessary and justified, but should never be free of moral cost. I realized that Bates was wrong. It was not enough just to know I was one of the King's subjects. I could not believe that obedience could wipe my moral responsibility for my own actions, somehow deferring them to the state.

I began to reconsider and rediscover my moral compass. I returned to theory, studying philosophy and the morality of political violence. I delved into the 2,000-year history of the traditions of *just war*, reading the works of moral philosophers such as Aristotle, Jeremy Bentham, Immanuel Kant, John Stuart Mill, and Michael Waltzer. Critically, I started to write down my experiences, stripped of secrets, to help me to understand my own cardinal points. I realized that, through study and writing, I could armor myself with a framework of theory that would allow me to square my own moral responsibilities in the context of conducting war.

In 2013 I returned to Afghanistan, this time as a squadron commander. I was determined that the soldiers in my care should not find themselves in the personal moral void that I had found myself in Iraq and Afghanistan. Yes, I wanted them to be able to kill. However, I also wanted them to be able to understand the ethical challenge of killing. I needed each of them to be able to square their own moral circle: to be able to look at themselves in the mirror 10 years down the line, and to be spiritually content with what they had done. So I taught them ethics, and I wrote it down for them.

As a unit, we held a tight line on the use of force. We killed, but we did so with caution and consideration. We guarded ourselves against the heady excitement of war. We avoided the slippery slope to barbarism. I like to think, as a group, we will look back on that time and be content with what we did.

In December 2014, not long after my departure from Helmand Province, the international mission in Afghanistan ceased. This placed a marker in the sand for the wars that were a direct result of the 9/11 attacks. The Obama Administration was clear that the so-called Global War on Terrorism (a war without geographical boundary and targeting an emotion) was over.

I had the dubious honor of being one of those who were both present at the declaration, and then part of the cessation. For 14 years, we had fought persistent, irregular, and broadly unpopular wars. Tens of thousands were dead. But there had not been another 9/11, and for a brief moment it seemed like the armies of the West might be gifted with a dividend of time for introspection. I returned to the United Kingdom to teach at the Joint Services Command and Staff College. On the back of a successful tour, my ethical concerns faded into a beautiful British summer.

Then, the Islamic State raged across Iraq and Syria, and all thoughts of a peace dividend disappeared in a field of black flags and beheadings. The next phase had begun of what was clearly now a generational struggle against extremism. Those of us teaching at the college, who represented the generation that had fought the first phase, realized the lessons-learned from 14 bloody years were rapidly being left behind. A next generation of soldiers and officers were themselves about to go through the ethical fires of irregular conflict. They would receive intoxicating power, and thus great responsibility, and we didn't want them to make the same mistakes. The solution, we thought, might lie in the written word.

A colleague and I began to write. There was no better place to do this than at the staff college. Also, not two buildings away, we found a real, live moral philosopher, a doctor of military ethics, who helped us distill our scattered thoughts into a simple and coherent model. We discussed theories and drafts with students and staff. The three of us dragged ethical theory down into the muck, using real-life scenarios to relate complex concepts such as deontology and consequentialism to the battlefield.

And you know what? It worked. Soldiers read it. Students at the college discussed it. Copies were passed around. Eventually the work was named "Armouring Against Atrocity," and published in the 2017 book, *Military*

Ethics and Leadership. It remains an enduring record of hard-earned lessons on morality in modern conflict. This record, no matter what, will now never be lost.

Through collaboration in prose and narrative, we were able to illuminate the darker corners of modern war. Professional writing helped me to reflect on my own experiences and to explore new ideas, but it allowed me to share my potential insights with others who were about to enter difficult times. I don't write for pleasure, or for fiction. I don't find writing easy; I agree with Ernest Hemingway, who reportedly said, "There is nothing to writing—all you do is sit down at a typewriter and bleed."

We need not bleed alone, however, particularly when technology enables professional interactions across generations and geographies. To paraphrase Shakespeare's King Henry: He (or she) who thinks and writes and bleeds with me this day, shall be my brother.

We need not be absolved by obedience, but by our own navigations.

Tom McDermott is an Australian Army officer who served 15 years in the British Army. He took part in the 2003 invasion of Iraq as a tank commander, and served three tours of Afghanistan. He was the creator of the Australian Army's professional network, The Cove, *and is a director of the Defence Entrepreneurs Forum Australia. A doctoral candidate at the Australian National University, he writes on strategy and ethics. Follow him on Twitter: @helmandproject*

Beating the Muse into Submission

By Robert B. Robeson

In 1967, at the age of 25, my first freelance article was submitted to Bee Nelson, the editor at *Straight*—a teen religious magazine. In 1965, I'd completed Officer Candidate School at Fort Benning, Ga. Three months later, I'd been activated as a second lieutenant with the California Army National Guard for six days during the 1965 Watts Riot in Los Angeles. In the summer of 1966, I was activated for the Hunter's Point Riot in San Francisco. As the son of a Protestant minister, I felt that these difficult and traumatic experiences could provide important lessons to teenagers. Bee Nelson agreed.

My compensation was $25, plus a few copies of that issue. Mrs. Nelson also showed this article to the editor of *The Lookout,* and he published it as a separate pamphlet. My next two articles, submitted to different editors, also sold their first time out. I was hooked. This freelance business didn't seem like it was going to be as hard as I'd originally thought.

With my fourth submission, however, when the rejection slips began descending like autumn leaves, it became clear that early acceptances don't always equal perpetual success.

Having completed two-and-a-half years of college in two different states, and zeroes being the only numerals in my bank account, I made a career decision. With the Vietnam conflict heating up, and being a military officer, I decided to apply for U.S. Army helicopter flight school. Upon graduation, I intended to volunteer as a medical evacuation pilot on active duty in Vietnam. If I survived that tour, I figured it would give me a lot more to write about. I was right.

In a year of combat flying, between 1969 and 1970, based in Da Nang with the 236th Medical Detachment (Helicopter Ambulance), I learned that risks are necessary if you're going to do anything of value in life. And that having a direct impact on other people's lives is one of the greatest gifts and blessings a pilot (or writer) can receive.

I flew 987 combat medevac missions and helped evacuate more than 2,500 patients from both sides of the action. Seven of my helicopters were shot up by enemy fire, and I was shot down twice. There are those who advise you to "write about what you know." But that "know" can often come at a high price.

I turned those Vietnam experiences into more than 900 freelance articles, short stories, and poems, published in 330 different magazines and newspapers in 130 countries and 60 anthologies. These stories have reached a readership of millions. They include the *Reader's Digest, Positive Living, Frontier Airline Magazine, Military, Vietnam Combat, Soldier of Fortune, Gung-Ho, Official Karate,* and *Newsday,* among others.

During 24 hours spanning Aug. 20-22, 1969 my flight crew had two helicopters shot up by enemy fire. Our medic, Spc. 5 John Seebeth III, had his larynx destroyed by small arms fire. The wound had swollen so fast that it was cutting off his airway. Two of our three radios were shot out. After we limped back to the battalion aid station at Landing Zone Baldy, I held John's legs while a tracheotomy was performed without anesthesia by Capt. George Waters, M.D. John survived. After 12 subsequent operations an army surgeon's skill gave him back a voice ... but not the one we were familiar with.

Even with a 100 percent VA disability, John later ran marathons and was elected student body president of his college in Ohio. He bicycled to the Arctic Circle, around Europe and from Seattle, Washington to Baja, California. He was my inspiration for publishing his personal story, and the story of that devastating mission, in five publications, which included both an English and Russian edition of *Soldier of Fortune.*

Many years later I discovered something else about the 150 wounded Americans we'd evacuated in 42 missions, 15 of which were without gunship support. One of the evacuees was a grenadier named Pfc. Rocky Bleier. He'd been in his rookie year with the Pittsburgh Steelers when he was drafted. We evacuated him and many of his unit comrades on three loads from Million Dollar Hill just east of Hiep Duc—about 30 miles southwest of Da Nang in the Que Son Valley. He was on our third and last load around 0200 hours on August 21st. Bleier would later win four Super Bowl rings with the Steelers from 1974-80 as a starting halfback. (These missions were also highlighted in the August 2008 *VFW magazine* article by Keith Nolan, titled "Hiep Duc 'Death Valley.'") I've recently published another article about this that has been reprinted five times.

On Sept. 13, 1969 I was shot down for the first time after we evacuated four American infantrymen from a landing zone encircled by enemy forces. Although our jet engine, both cyclic controls, and various oil lines had been shot up or shot away, our bird refused to immediately die.

The instant I greased our skids onto the bumpy ground at LZ Ross in a forced running landing, a few minutes later, our Lycoming jet engine's 1,100 horses all died *en masse*. The story of this mission has been published seven times, and won a ($1,000) national Amy Writing Award in 2005. (Two other of my Vietnam-related articles also won Amy awards, in 1998 and 2006.)

On the morning of Dec. 25, 1969 I was shot down for the second time, taking 19 hits in our aircraft during a supposed "cease-fire" period negotiated in Paris, France. Half-an-hour later, we climbed into a replacement helicopter and flew back to the same landing zone—and again experienced heavy fire. We successfully evacuated nine wounded South Vietnamese soldiers who'd been attacked in their isolated outpost on Barrier Island, about 20 miles south of Da Nang. This story has been published eight times in national magazines, and once in separate Nebraska and Iowa newspapers during Christmas 2008.

While evacuating seven wounded American infantrymen from an enemy minefield in early January 1970, I set our left skid on two mines (one of which was estimated to be a 250-pound, anti-tank mine). Miraculously, neither detonated. This escape from certain death for my crew—a story that an infantry lieutenant and his driver drove 40 miles in a jeep over insecure roads to relate to me over a week later—has been published six times. There were other similar situations in Vietnam, too numerous to mention here, that have also been written about and published.

A favorite adage among chopper jockeys in 'Nam, that I often recall, is "Helicopter pilots don't fly. They just beat the air into submission." I've applied this philosophy to my freelance writing career. Many people don't feel comfortable attempting what appears to be impossible. That's why there's so much room at the top in many professions and areas of life.

In my 27-and-a-half-year military career (of which 19 were in Army aviation), and my 51-year writing career, I discovered that each vocation is hard work and often risky. If I'd wanted an easy life, I could have taken up quantum physics, brain surgery, or attempted to open a McDonald's on the moon.

In combat, our aircraft and crews gave people hope. Your writing and how you do it can accomplish the same. It's essential, though, to log those hours and years, and to collect your share of rejection slips. (Tip: I don't ever give up on a piece of writing, even if an editor burns my manuscript and mails the ashes back to me.)

My 77-year journey on this spinning ball of clay has been one in which I've learned to make a variety of fears my companions and friends. They have helped to stretch my understanding of the literary life, love, and our unsurpassed liberties in America.

Face your individual fears of not being published, of feeling unworthy or of being rejected. Be turf-tough. Your experiences in life—like exquisite jewels or fine paintings—can inspire, bring joy and hope and provide insight to fellow travelers. Encourage your readers to be risk-takers, too. Challenge them to find their own special niches in life.

The bottom line is that publication is achieved by trying, and trying, and trying some more. Memorable writing does not come from just the head. It comes from the gut and heart. If what you write is important to you, there's a chance it will be interesting and of value to someone else. And if it "rocks and rolls" and is good enough to catch an editor's eye, there will always be a market for it somewhere.

It's like trying to hit the ground when the enemy shoots out your jet engine at 1,500 feet. You can't miss! And I should know. Just remember our old helicopter adage and just "beat that muse into submission."

Robert Robeson is a professional life member of the National Writers Association, Veterans of Foreign Wars, Dustoff Association, and the Distinguished Flying Cross Society. After retiring from the U.S. Army, having served and flown on three continents, he transitioned to being a newspaper managing editor and columnist. He has an undergraduate degree in English from the University of Maryland-College Park, and has completed extensive undergraduate and graduate work in journalism at the University of Nebraska-Lincoln. He lives in Lincoln, Nebraska with his wife, Phyllis, of 50 years.

Sharing Stories of Service Between Generations

By Chad Corrigan

Initially, my writing was strictly personal and secretive. I did not start writing in earnest until 2015, during my second deployment to Afghanistan. At some point, I realized that writing had become important to me—sort of like how I ran for over a decade in the U.S. Army before I realized I was a runner and started to take that seriously, too.

What I was doing was largely reflective journaling. Eventually, I noticed that my private notes had evolved into something bigger. I still had no intentions to publish, but felt that putting my wartime experience down on paper would be something that my family would appreciate down the road.

For much of my childhood, my mom was a single parent and Grandpa Frank was the closest thing I had to a father to me. The Francis Ferreira that I knew was a kind, loving, straight-talking retired barber who had served in World War II. Unfortunately, his war stories would die with him. I did not want the same thing to happen with me.

Grandpa Frank would never talk about the war, despite my asking. At best, he would tell me the wave tops: That he was in the infantry in Germany. The last time I asked him about the war, I was in middle school At this point, my grandparents were no longer snowbirds from Massachusetts, but had become full-time Floridians. I noticed he was reading a book on World War II. He volunteered very little information. He mentioned that he was cold in Germany. I learned not to ask.

While in elementary school, two of my most-prized possessions were a small black and white photo of Grandpa from during the war, and one of his identification "dog tags." The photo showed a handful of soldiers wearing steel pot helmets, in a snow-covered foxhole with cigarettes hanging out of their mouths. Grandpa Frank did not smoke! But there he was, in Germany, smoking in this wartime snapshot. It blew my 8-year-old mind. When I confronted him about it, he gently brushed it off, saying it was a different time back then. Everyone used to smoke back in those days.

Maybe once or twice he mentioned trench foot. He was always telling me to change my socks, and would worry if my feet got wet. When visiting during my 4th grade year, and he took me to Busch Gardens in Tampa. We got caught outside in a heavy, sudden spring shower, and my feet got soaked in my white and red Reebok high-tops. Those sneakers are how I can place the year in memory. They were the first "cool" pair of sneakers I ever had and an expensive gift from him. I remember him being very concerned that my feet and socks were wet. He made me take them off and he tried to wring them out. To me it all seemed a little kooky. I was not worried at all, but he was genuinely concerned. I gradually came to realize his emotional response was invisible scar tissue from the war.

Nearly four years later, Grandpa Frank passed away from a heart attack in his sleep. We never did talk about his service.

More than 20 years later, my mom and octogenarian grandmother brought out a small stack of Grandpa Frank's pictures from his time in uniform. We sat around the kitchen table looking at them. Because I had become a soldier myself, I was able to decode his uniform from his pictures. The patch told me he had served with 102nd Infantry "Ozark" Division. My grandmother had previously mentioned him shipping off to Fort Dix, N.J. from our hometown of Dighton, Mass. Armed with these few facts, some pictures, and a library, I was able to piece together some of his service. At that time, I was an officer stationed at Fort Leavenworth, Kan. and spent a lot of time in the library doing my homework and research. I located a dusty history book that contained some information about Grandpa Frank's division.

The 102nd Infantry "Ozark" Division was one of the last units to enter the fight in the European theater in World War II. They did not participate in the famed Normandy invasion, but instead were part of the final attacks into Germany. Following the German surrender, the unit transitioned to occupation duty. Grandpa's photos mirror the action depicted on the maps in history books. In early pictures, he wears a dirty field uniform during the advancing attacks. Later, on occupation duty, he looks more spit-and-polished. Sergeant's stripes are sewn onto his uniform, and a Combat Infantryman Badge is pinned on his chest.

Like Grandpa Frank, I do not talk about the war much with my family. While I enjoyed the research to find out a little more about his wartime experiences, I was also motivated to pass on more of my own story to my family, especially my sons. By writing, I can preserve it for when they are older, or for a time when I am more ready to share it with them. My goal is to fill in some of the blind spots of their own childhoods. Added together, I have been gone for more than four years of their lives. They deserve to know.

In the long term, I intend to share some of my writing with a broader audience than family and friends. After returning home from the Surge in Iraq, my squadron commander told us that we needed to "tell the Army story." Our story, about the war as we knew it, and what our soldiers did. The American people deserved to know.

Perhaps, by telling our stories, we can help other families learn about their loved ones' service. During my first deployment to Iraq in 2003, my aunt sent me the book *Duty: A Father, His Son, and the Man Who Won the War* by Bob Greene. In the book, Greene talks about his childhood growing up in Ohio. His dad was a World War II veteran. They were not close as adults. He remembered that as a kid his Dad would remark, "I saw the man who won the war today [...]" That man was Paul Tibbets, pilot of the Enola Gay—the B-20 Superfortress that dropped the first atomic bomb on Hiroshima, Japan—lived in the same town. Many years after his dad passed, the now-journalist son ended up befriended by Tibbets.

Through Tibbets and his fellow veterans, Greene came to understand his own father a little more, as well as his country, and the service that made them all.

Chad Corrigan is a U.S. Army aviation officer, and has served in the 101st Airborne Division, 1st Cavalry Division, and 3rd Armored Cavalry Regiment. He has a graduate degree in public policy and management from the University of Pittsburgh, an undergraduate degree from Stonehill College, Easton, Mass., and is a graduate of the U.S. Army's School of Advanced Military Studies. An AH-64 Apache pilot, he has deployed to Iraq, Afghanistan, and Syria.

Attention to Detail

By Steven L. Moore

Corporal Johnson had two fake front teeth. That was a detail about him. His two top-middle teeth had been installed by a dentist, recently, so they were a little more white than the others. Though you might not notice, unless you knew to look.

The story behind the detail was that one day, during training, Cpl. Johnson and his fire team were running across a road; they were going to storm a house where the pretend bad guys were hiding. As they ran across the road, Johnson tripped and fell, and the barrel of his rifle planted into the road like the pole of a pole vaulter, and the buttstock smashed into his face and knocked his teeth out.

So that was a detail about Cpl. Johnson: He had fake front teeth.

Soldiers have to know about details because sometimes knowing the details can prevent people from getting hurt. Guys were always stressing about paying attention to detail. But it was always rather unclear what *constituted* a detail. How unimportant something had to be to qualify. Because basically everything on the whole planet is details, or made of them. When a sergeant told his guys "pay attention to goddamn detail," what he was really saying was, "pay attention to goddamn *everything*," which was a lot to ask.

As a writer, too, I love details. But why believe in them so much? If details are, as the dictionary tells us, the parts that are *inconsequential* or *beside the point*, why are they so important to the story? Why do I sometimes, after reading something, have the instinct to say, "I loved the detail." If detail is the stuff I don't notice or pay attention to in real life, if it's really beside the point, why is it that detail is so important to making a story feel true?

And is merely a *feeling* of veracity? Or am I just picking out symbols and tricking myself? I want to be responsible for the ways I go about knowing the past, and knowing what matters in it.

As soldiers, we were supposed to pay attention to detail, to all the shit that *seemed* inconsequential, because maybe it really wasn't. A pile of rocks on the side of the road is no longer inconsequential, if the rocks conceal a homemade explosive. The meaningless detail, the pile of rocks, upon exploding, transitions into being consequential. The very notion of a detail is flexible and context-dependent.

Or for instance, if the gunner in the first vehicle of a convoy—let's say it's Cpl. Johnson, just for continuity—spots this pile of rocks on the side of the road. Let's say the point of the convoy had been to patrol this road, so the pile of rocks was (bear with me) literally *beside the point*. But now Cpl. Johnson spots it and the convoy halts, and the patrol leader calls up to the ordinance disposal people about this pile of rocks they're suspicious of, and the convoy waits for hours and hours and hours for the disposal people to show up, and in the meantime they form a security perimeter and clear away nearby civilians. The pile of rocks is no longer a detail of this patrol. It doesn't matter if anything is concealed there. It *was* a detail. Until they looked at it. Until they lingered.

It's like in a movie, when a camera lingers an extra breath on some seemingly random thing, so you know it's not a random thing. You know it carries weight, somehow affects the narrative. The moment I identify a detail, it immediately *becomes* consequential, no matter what, because I made someone look at it. Which is to say, it loses the quality that defined it in the first place.

And I think this is part of the fantasy I have: that any detail can be secretly full of meaning. If I just linger on the right one, if I pay enough attention, the detail will somehow pay me back.

Maybe it really is just a matter of choosing the *right* detail. Of curating and selecting. Choosing the detail that best distills everything around it. Like sometimes, the only thing I remember from a whole book will be one really good detail. In college, I was assigned to read Don DeLillo's *White Noise* in two different classes, in two different semesters, and I was a super-obedient student so I know I read it both times. Now, five years later, about the only thing I remember is the part where one of the children is muttering to herself in her sleep, and the word she's muttering is the brand name of a car: Celica. She's muttering "Toyota Celica."

And I think if I saw Don walking down the street, and for some reason I told him how almost the only thing I remember from his most famous book, which I read *twice*, is this child muttering a meaningless brand name in her unconscious, I think Don would be pretty satisfied with that; like, yeah, you pretty much got the gist. Because it was this *right* detail; it distills meaning. It was beside the point, but really it wasn't at all.

I know that taking any one detail in isolation is a mistake; it avoids the character and the larger story, but any one detail, isolated, still ought to retain something; the meaning shouldn't vacate so easily as that, and I want to know what we retain.

I'm skeptical about the notion that such Right Details really do surround us, or that I can know anything about the past through this act of locating and naming and arranging its ornaments. Or, at the very least, there must be an ethics to the ornamentation.

I used to think about details like they were the periphery of the story. Like details defined the boundaries. Details asserted the illusion of a perimeter. A story shows you an inconsequential thing, and it seems like this must be the edge of the narrative—if the thing was any *less* meaningful the writer would've left it out—but even the inconsequential thing is designed to make you consider the larger point. It directs you back inside the story. It's like a boundary—the detail turns you back around. When that happens in a story, it's beautiful. But I can never get the story of the past to work like that. I don't even know if it's right to try.

I prefer details to be both specific and absurd. The more specific and the more absurd, the more something strikes me as a good detail. For instance, one day our commander, Capt. Wilson, walked into the 1st Platoon tent. This was on an outpost in the Laghman Province of northeastern Afghanistan. Capt. Wilson looked really shaken up and he just stood in the doorway. He turned to our lieutenant, who had the cot closest to the door, and Wilson told the lieutenant: "So, I just came from a meeting with the Taliban ..." And he told the lieutenant about meeting these scary Taliban warlords and how it felt to talk to them.

Then a few minutes later, as Wilson was about to leave, a soldier called to him from halfway down the tent. The private said, "Hey sir!" And Wilson turned. The private said, "Did you hear, O.A.R. is gonna be playing in Iowa City the week we get back?" And Wilson's eyes perked up and he looked instantly normal, like the commander was just a guy from back home who probably went golfing sometimes. Wilson said, "No shit, I didn't hear that, when do tickets go on sale?" And the private said, "It doesn't say yet, sir." And the commander said, "Well keep me in the loop—those guys are fuckin' awesome." The private said, "Roger, sir." And the commander walked out of the room. The private caught me watching this exchange and he shrugged and said, "What can I say—that guy fuckin' loves O.A.R."

The anecdote has this specific rock band, and it's pretty absurd, so it sticks out to me. But I'm not sure if I've learned anything. The commander fuckin' loved O.A.R. Cpl. Johnson had fake front teeth. Everyone in the story was human.

Brenda Miller wrote in the craft book *Tell It Slant* that when relating true stories, "We resurrect the details" from our memory.

We *resurrect* them. Details exist on the level of savior.

Zadie Smith wrote that details, especially seemingly random details, serve to "confer the authenticity of the Real." I agree with Zadie here, that they have this effect, but it worries me that we need to do this; that we use details to assert or prove the real. It seems like it'd be easier if I just stapled my DD-214—the specific document issued at the time of separation from active-duty service—to the back of each piece of writing, and if a reader had any doubts about the authenticity of the Real, they could refer to it like an appendix and confirm I was there.

And I guess my question is, does that statement seem truer because I know the nomenclature for the paperwork is "DD-214"—does being more specific in that way make it truer? Or if I told you that DD stands for "Defense Department"? Does that detail make it truer? Does it confer authenticity? Or if I told you that one of the awards listed on my DD-214 is called the Combat Infantryman Badge, which was established by the War Department in 1945—back when it was still called the War Department— and how they established the badge because they had so much trouble convincing anybody to sign up for the infantry, because the job was so shitty and terrible, they had to incentivize the experience of violence, so they invented this badge, and it proved really successful, and now infantry guys care a lot about their CIBs and I'm really proud of that line on my DD-214.

Are we yet in the vicinity of truer?

Would it seem more real if I told you that for each CIB that gets awarded, before you can be officially certified as having been in combat, you have to write a short narrative about the violent moment and a battalion-level officer has to literally approve the narrative, so that your encounter with violence can be officially documented? Then you get a small badge to wear on your chest. Or if I told you that when you're first given the badge, there's a kind of ceremony, and the badge has two sharp prongs on the back side and the officer pushes the badge into your uniform, then he punches the badge as hard as he can so the prongs stab you into the muscle? Then everyone in the company who already has this award files past and punches it also, again and again and again, and the badge digs through your uniform and your T-shirt and your skin and it's like this kabob effect happens on the prongs, and guys get awfully proud of the bloody holes they've earned by doing God-knows-what.

And what I mean is, isn't it funny how an experience can be represented by two bloody holes in your chest, *and* represented by official documentation with an official narrative and a signature, *and* represented by one line on a DD-214, *and* represented by the stories you tell about it to the people who were there and the slightly different stories you tell to the people who weren't, so that the experience is thoroughly and redundantly represented, it has a big huge constellation of what it is and what I know about it, and what I mean is: I think sometimes I have stories where I am not at a loss for details, but I am still at a loss for meaning.

And how can that be.

Steven L. Moore grew up in southeast Iowa and served for seven years in the Iowa Army National Guard. In 2018, he was recognized with an award for non-fiction writing by the Association of Writers and Writing Programs (AWP), which resulted in the subsequent publication of his manuscript The Longer We Were There: A Memoir of a Part-Time Soldier *by University of Georgia Press. His essays have appeared or are forthcoming in* Kenyon Review On-line, Georgia Review, Ninth Letter, Pinball, BOAAT, Entropy, *among others. He received his Master of Fine Arts in non-fiction writing from Oregon State University. He lives with his wife in Corvallis, Ore. and works at a non-profit in that city. Follow him on Twitter: @StevenLeeMoore*

Recovering the Rhythm of War

By Bill McCloud

> "I believe [Bill McCloud] was writing better
> and higher-quality letters home than many of us."—David Willson,
> *The VVA Veteran's Books in Review II*, Oct. 28, 2017

My family still has 52 letters that I wrote home to my parents during my year in Vietnam. All written in ink, in big, sprawling handwriting. They arrived in envelopes addressed to that two-story house on Otoe Street in Ponca City, Okla. Each one traveled a distance of 8,817 miles from my unit's mail collection point to the little box on my family's front porch.

In the upper right-hand corner of the envelope, in place of a stamp, I wrote the word "FREE." There was no charge to mail a letter if you were lucky enough to be fighting in a non-declared-war while on duty in a temporarily named nation.

For all other Americans who were not that fortunate it cost them $0.05 to mail a similar letter: Too bad for them.

We'll get back to those letters shortly.

In the spring of 1967, I dropped out of my first year of college to join the U.S. Army, knowing full well I would probably be sent to Vietnam. After basic training at Fort Polk, La.; advanced training at Fort Gordon, Ga.; and vaguely noting tears sliding down my father's cheeks, I was off to South Vietnam.

I served at the height of the war, but in a relatively safe Chinook helicopter company, which provided combat support. When I speak to groups of Vietnam veterans, I always take care to lower my voice and sort of run the words together when I mention that 50 of my 52 weeks in-country were spent on the airbase near Vung Tau, a major Rest and Recuperation (R&R) center.

After completing my three years of military service, I returned to college and began chasing down a degree in education, specializing in history. In less than a decade, I had a master's degree and was teaching social studies at a junior-high school in Oklahoma.

I later learned that the fact that I was a Vietnam War veteran had played a positive role in me being offered the job. Otherwise, my military experience during wartime had no obvious effect on my day-to-day life. Even as a history teacher, I talked very little about Vietnam in class; we were always hard-pressed to have enough time to get beyond World War II.

Then, in 1987, the principal of the school told me that some students had approached him to ask if they could study about the war in Vietnam in history class. A number of popular Vietnam War-themed films at the time had apparently sparked a great deal of interest in the subject. I was encouraged to address it in class.

I was fully aware that teaching about the war using only my personal experience would be an inadequate pedagogical approach. As a veteran, I also had my own questions about the period. To open my lens as an educator more widely, I wrote to almost 200 people, and asked their opinions on the most important things that I should be teaching my students about the Vietnam War. All were people who had been involved in the war in some way: enlisted soldiers; politicians; prisoners of war (POW); military officers; nurses; veterans of the anti-war movement; refugees; writers; and parents of soldiers who died in the war.

Among the 132 people who responded with answers were: George H. W. Bush; Jimmy Carter; Geraldine Ferraro; Allen Ginsburg; Barry Goldwater; Timothy Leary; G. Gordon Liddy; "Country Joe" McDonald, Robert S. McNamara; Tim O'Brien; Oliver Stone; and William C. Westmoreland.

I compiled the responses into a book titled *What Should We Tell Our Children About Vietnam?* Published by the University of Oklahoma Press, it was a finalist for the Oklahoma Book Award and remains in print, three editions and 29 years later. It gained some national attention, and was praised for providing a variety of viewpoints without seeming to push any specific one.

For decades, I used my book as part of my curriculum. The voices it contained certainly helped to flesh out—added its own heart and soul—to the basic history books that were continuing to be written. Throughout this time, I intentionally avoided talking about my own experiences in-country. It eventually became clear to me, however, that the farther time moved me from the war, the more interested I became in telling my role in it.

After all, I could almost consider myself an "everyman" among Vietnam War veterans. I served at the height of the war, served a full 12 months, and spent my time in combat support. Around 75 percent of American soldiers served in some area of support, as did I. Only a small fraction experienced the sort of fighting that excited viewers when they watched movies such as *Platoon, Hamburger Hill,* or *We Were Soldiers.* My experience was much more in line with what was shown in *Good Morning, Vietnam.*

Nonetheless, I had some stories to tell about certain events, interesting characters, displays of bravery, and even a few stories of human loss. I felt that my stories would have greater significance when placed in an accurate chronology and not just randomly told. The final boost of motivation came when I learned that teachers Laurie Walczac and Chuck Taft were using my first book in their classes at the University School of Milwaukee, Wis. Talking to them allowed me to feed off of their energy.

That's where the war letters I wrote home come back into the picture.

When we first return from war, many of us choose either to not talk about it at all (for a variety of reasons), or to talk about it strictly by describing our own personal experiences. We make no attempt, early on, to fit ourselves into the big picture.

I was ready to fit myself, the everyman, into the puzzle.

I placed my 52 letters, in order, on the floor of the living room, and began going through them taking notes, copying complete lines, and developing ideas of how to turn the information in each one into a poem. That's right. Somehow, I had come to the idea that the best way for me to tell all my stories from my letters was to turn them into poems.

I felt the technique would be within my capabilities, and that it also might be the best way to make my stories accessible to the most people. If I could tell each story on a single page, I figured, no one could be overwhelmed by the number of words in the book.

If I had relied solely on memory, it would not have been possible for me to create a book about my experiences from 50 years ago. Reading the letters anew, however, I was transported back in time and place: the incidents, big or routine, the details, the personalities, the emotions.

I worked for more than a year, and organized the resulting 106 poems into chronological order. Six "chapters" were:

- Here's How It Started! (which describes me dropping out of college to volunteer for the Army)
- In the Army, But Before Vietnam
- Vietnam (this makes up the bulk of the poems, about 70 percent)
- In the Army, But After Vietnam
- Out of the Army
- Today

I found an interested publisher, William and Lara Bernhardt's Balkan Press, and we began to put the book together. I had chosen the title, *The Smell of the Light: Vietnam, 1968-1969*, picked from a couple of lines in one of the poems.

David Willson, long-time poetry reviewer for *Veteran*, the magazine of the Vietnam Veterans of America, read the poems in manuscript and declared that they "rank right at the top of the heap" of Vietnam War poems. The poet laureate of the state of Oklahoma, Jeanetta Calhoun Mish, stated that the collection is "necessary reading."

In December 2017, *The Smell of the Light: Vietnam, 1968-1969*, was No. 1 on the "Oklahoma Best-Sellers" list, according to the state's largest newspaper, *The Daily Oklahoman*. You might say, however, that writing that book had started decades earlier, letter by letter.

Bill McCloud served in the U.S. Army between September 1967 and September 1970. Between March 1968 and March 1969, he deployed to Vietnam as a flight operations coordinator for the 147th Assault Support Helicopter Company, Vung Tau Air Base. Now an adjunct professor of American History at Rogers State University, Claremore, Okla., McCloud is the author of the 1989 non-fiction book What Should We Tell Our Children About Vietnam?, *and the 2017 poetry collection* The Smell of the Light: Vietnam, 1968-1969. *In 2018, McCloud was inducted into the Northern Oklahoma College (Tonkawa) Distinguished Alumni Hall of Fame.*

Making Sense of What Went Wrong

By Jeremy H. Warneke

For me, writing has always been a coping technique, as well as a way to make sense of the world. I won't deny that there is a bit of egoism or historical impulse involved. George Orwell defined the latter as the "desire to see things as they are, to find out true facts and store them up for the use of posterity."

Posterity is nice, but writing is about here and now. Many would take issue with calling writing "therapy," but one shouldn't deny the therapeutic applications. "For years," a 2002 cover story for the *Monitor on Psychology* noted, "practitioners have used logs, questionnaires, journals and other writing forms to help people heal from stresses and traumas [...] research suggests expressive writing may also offer physical benefits to people battling terminal or life-threatening diseases."

My unit's tour in Iraq had been extended for only three months. Our deployment, outside of a few incidents, had been a cakewalk. Yes, we were Military Police company, stationed at the now-notorious Abu Ghraib prison, but we'd arrived only two days before the prisoner abuses there were exposed on *60 Minutes*. There was no way we could have participated in or had knowledge of the torture, rapes, and other abuses that had previously happened there.

Still, one of us was suddenly dead.

In January 2016, I published in *Task & Purpose* my first piece of writing related to my experience as a soldier in Iraq. Called "The Tragic Truth Of Accidental Deaths In Combat Zones," it received a good deal of praise from former members of my unit. You could say that I wrote it in part for them. But the real reason I wrote about the a fellow soldier's death and others—and I said so at the time—was for my daughter, who was born in late 2015.

I wrote that first essay for more than just posterity, however. I wrote it for political purpose—or, as George Orwell would say, I had a "desire to push the world in a certain direction, to alter other peoples' idea of the kind of society that they should strive after." In other words, I was attempting to persuade. But there is one more thing I was doing or attempting to do: Deal with my own personal trauma.

In July 2016, I published a *Wikipedia* page about Landis Garrison, the first and only member of my unit to die while wearing the uniform. Eventually, a relative of Garrison's rebuked me for the act. I responded:

Keep in mind that writing has been a form of therapy for me. Writing about Landis and others has helped me process and learn from my own experience in ways I have never imagined. Did I create the *Wikipedia* page as a sort of memorial to Landis? Yes. I was unfortunately sleeping when the accident occurred. His death, the near-death of my friend Garriga and others have weighed on me over the years. My writing about them has been a sort of release. At the same time, I think about the senselessness of the events, how they could have been avoided, which has also spurred my writing. The fact that I've educated people on what really happened to Landis was unintentional. What was intentional was stressing the fact that too many of our uniformed service men and women have been lost due to accidents and other preventable causes. One-fifth of those who died in Iraq or Afghanistan died of non-combat-related causes. This, I know, does not ease your suffering. I cannot imagine what it is like to lose a child in any manner. I can only apologize and wish you and your family the best. For what it's worth, I again apologize.

As I wrote in *Task & Purpose*:

We were in our living quarters, when Garrison, just playing around, inadvertently shot himself. [A fellow soldier later reported] that he had this 'oh crap' look on his face, as if Garrison realized what he had done all too late. There was evidently a round in the chamber of the pistol he had pulled out from behind a friend's back.

First aid was administered, and a group of men rushed Garrison out on one of those green- or brown-colored Army blankets. It took an hour, but eventually, we were told of Garrison's passing. He had been my age at the time: 23.

What didn't make the cut was the description of me waking up, thinking we were being mortared before I realized what had happened. It had been in mid- to late-afternoon when Garrison shot himself. Some were quick to label the news a "suicide"—that our company's one-year-and-counting deployment, which had just been involuntarily extended, had been too much for him.

Even as late as 2016, some people thought Garrison had intentionally committed suicide, but nothing could be further from the truth. He was a happy-go-lucky guy. As the *Chicago Tribune* noted, three days after his passing, "he was unwaveringly optimistic, the kind of guy who could look at the Iraqi sand and imagine a beach."

While I had unintentionally wounded a Gold Star family with my writing, I also recognize the necessity of dealing with traumatic events, as an individual and as a society. Garrison and other young soldiers died or were seriously injured for no apparent reason. Garrison died at 23. At the age of 19, my buddy Garriga had received burns on at least 45 percent of his body. My writing, published and unpublished, were attempts to make sense of these incidents.

I got lucky in Iraq. I got very lucky. I got lucky here at home as well: Beginning in 2009, I started attending free writing workshops for veterans. Eventually, the stories I read in these workshops and elsewhere forced me to confront my own experiences. I also revisited the stories I had read in college or high school, and didn't necessarily appreciate at the time.

I had never before read much Hemingway, for example, but a single paragraph helped me articulate fear. Hemingway was not a military veteran, but he did experience combat. In a story titled "Chapter VII," with his protagonist's pleading of "oh jesus christ get me out of here [...] Please please dear jesus," Hemingway wrote about an emotion and an experience to which I could now relate.

When I read essays by other writers, such as Jamaica Kincaid's "Those Words That Echo ... Echo ... Echo Through Life," I say to myself, *Yeah, I can relate to that, too.* Writers don't know *why* we write exactly, we just *do*.

Some don't like the idea of writing as therapy. Some don't like potentially boiling veterans down to a stereotype, one of being emotionally or mentally broken. To me, however, writing will always be driven by a psychological motivation. Even if it is only, as Orwell had put it, that "same instinct that makes a baby squall for attention."

Jeremy H. Warneke is a U.S. Army veteran whose publication credits include NYC Veterans Alliance, Daily Kos, *and* Scintilla. *In 2017, he was a* War Horse Writing Seminar *fellow, and a second-place in poetry for the Col. Darron L. Wright Memorial Writing Award, administered by the literary journal* Line of Advance. *In 2015, he received an honorable mention for photography in* Proud to Be: Writing by American Warriors, Vol. 4. *He currently teaches a Voices From War-sponsored writing workshop in the Bronx, New York City.*

The Perils of Spilling Your Guts

By David Chrisinger

Back when I was teaching a writing seminar for student veterans at the University of Wisconsin-Stevens Point, I would wake up an hour or two before my wife and kids did each morning and brew a pot of coffee before heading down to my dimly lit basement office. The house I lived in then had been built in 1871, when insulating a basement was unheard of. In the wintertime, it was especially cold down there, but I liked it that way. I tried to let my work warm me until the coffee was done. Before I could begin, I would sit down at my oak desk, a castoff I found in the university's surplus store, and open my laptop.

On one particularly cold morning in February several years back, I opened the draft essay Mike Goranson had sent me the week before, and read it without typing or trying to fix anything. I did that with most essays I edited. It's hard for me to find the right fix if I lose the forest for the trees. By the time I finished reading, my coffee was usually ready. I liked it when I could drink that first cup in the kitchen, while I processed what I had just read. It was quiet, and a bit warmer, there. Once I finished that first cup, and after I poured a second, I was ready to head back down to my office.

I've helped lots of military veterans tell their stories. Most make the same mistakes any novice writer does in a first draft. Above all else, they don't seem sure of their essay's purpose. Their first drafts are for them, not for me or anyone else.

I didn't know much about Mike when I first started working with him on his essay. All I knew was that he was captain of the Chicago chapter of Team Red, White & Blue (aka "Team RWB") and that he was finally ready—after more than a decade—to tell his story. Before my first cup of coffee that morning I'd already learned quite a bit more about Mike. He'd written about his "Alive Day"—the day he almost died in Iraq—and the difficulties he faced when he got home.

It was November 29, 2004—my birthday, coincidentally—and Mike was a U.S. Marine deployed to Ramadi. The rest of his unit was conducting a door-to-door patrol, while he and another Marine guarded a T-intersection outside. An insurgent popped out from behind a building and fired off a burst from his AK-47. One of the rounds ricocheted off Mike's truck and struck him in the ankle, just above the top of his boot. The round burst through the back of his leg, and Mike began bleeding uncontrollably.

Before he bled out, he was able to radio in that he needed to be evacuated. Not long after, another truck came to Mike's rescue. He doesn't remember much from the rest of that day, except the Corpsman helping him into the truck, and hearing mortars landing near the field hospital as the anesthesia kicked in before the first of many surgeries. After the field surgeons in Iraq were able to stop his bleeding, Mike was flown to the American military hospital in Germany for more surgery. From there, he was sent to Walter Reed in Washington, D.C. The doctors there told him he was probably going to lose the foot. But like Lt. John J. Dunbar in *Dances with Wolves*, Mike was determined to keep it, no matter what it took.

He sustained permanent tibial nerve damage. But with his foot still attached and healed enough to be transported, Mike went home to Illinois. He was given a hero's welcome, complete with a call from the mayor.

All was going relatively well until he flew to San Diego to welcome back the rest of his unit from their deployment. It was then that a buddy told Mike that the other Marine he'd been with the day he'd been hit had told everyone in the unit that Mike had given up on the fight after he was shot. That he had quit.

When I came back to my desk after finishing my first cup of coffee, I wasn't sure if I could read Mike's essay again. It seemed he still had lots of processing to do. His language and tone were defensive, and I had the overwhelming sense that he was searching more for absolution than for understanding. He wanted me to believe him—that he hadn't quit, that no one knows how they're going to react when they get shot, and that he had done the best he could. My stomach ached in anxiety over what I could possibly say to help him with his story.

The first time I met Mike was at a Panera Bread store in downtown Chicago sometime after that February morning. I arrived at the restaurant before Mike did, hoping that if I got there first, maybe it'd signal to him that I took the meeting seriously, and that I wasn't just some guy dropping in to doll out life and writing advice like prescription meds at the VA.

I had seen pictures of Mike on Facebook, so I knew what he looked like: dark, short hair; baby face unmarred by a razor; kind eyes; and a sheepish grin. When he arrived, I was surprised by how tall he was. I'm 6-foot-4 and played defensive line in college, but Mike towered over me.

We shook hands, and I introduced myself. I could tell by the way he was looking at me—sizing me up, really—and by the way he was standing at a diagonal to me, that he was apprehensive. He knew I had read his story, but I hadn't yet given him feedback. I wanted to talk with him about my first reactions, rather than send them in an e-mail. It was like a first date. I couldn't help but wonder what he was thinking, and he seemed to be aching to know what I was thinking.

We turned to face the menu board and Mike blurted out, "So, where'd you serve?"

I hate that question. I get it all the time. "I'm actually not a veteran," I said. "I work with them, help them tell their stories."

I could tell he was disappointed. He nodded his head and looked away, as if to say, *Great, this fuckin' guy*. He didn't say another word, except to order his lunch, until we sat down to eat.

As Mike took the first big bite of his sandwich, I cut straight to the chase: "Take me back to that day," I told him.

"Nobody really knows how they're going to react when they get hit," he said, swallowing his first bite. After he got hit, he told me, he dropped his machine gun in the dirt and scrambled for cover. He made a point to say that, even though he didn't have his big gun, he still had his sidearm. He said he would have died if he hadn't dropped the big gun. He was leaning, elbows on the table that separated us. He didn't look away as he talked or hang his head. I could feel how badly he wanted me to believe him.

He told me his heart dropped when he heard what some of the other guys had said about thinking he'd quit. "And worst of all," he continued, "the guy who said that shit died in a motorcycle crash a couple of days later, so I never even got a chance to confront him about what he said."

Only then did I understand where all the defensiveness was coming from. Mike was still hurting, more than 10 years later. He didn't want his fellow Marines—anyone, really—to think he was a quitter. He was a good Marine. He had served honorably. He knew that, but it still hurt to think there were people who felt differently.

The problem with Mike's first draft was that it was a confession. I don't mean that he did something wrong and felt the need to be forgiven. It's more complicated than that. He knew he had done the best he could. He told his story not to get me to better understand him, but rather to get me to take his side, and to believe that he was the person he thought he was. Instead of ripping open his shirt, and showing me his proverbial scars, he simply spilled his guts, like a drunk vomiting in the gutter after a long night of binge drinking. The experience may have been cathartic for Mike, but it did nothing to help me connect with him.

In all honesty, Mike's essay made me feel bad for him, even pity him. That's not what Mike was looking for. He was in a good place when we met. He wanted to tell his story so that others could know who he was, what he had been through, and why he does what he does now.

I had so many questions for Mike. I barely ate my own food. Mike, to his credit, answered truthfully, like a friend confiding in another. As he talked, I jotted down his answers in a small notebook. The more he talked, the more he seemed to decompress. His shoulders, which had been pulled up to his ears most of the time we were together, began to relax. He laughed and smiled more. It no longer seemed to matter to him that I was not also a veteran.

When we were finished, I ripped out the sheet of paper and gave it to him. "This is your story," I told him. "No one else's. Not your friend's. Not anyone's. Just yours. Tell the reader what *you* went through and how *you* felt. Don't try to put words in others' mouths or defend yourself against what they *might* say. Don't make excuses or try to defend yourself. Confide in the reader, and they will connect with you on a level you can't even believe."

After Team RWB published Mike's revised essay on their blog, I shared a link to it on Facebook. A good friend of mine—who's also a civilian— sent me a message to tell me how much she connected with Mike's story. "I've never been in combat or anything," she wrote, "but I know exactly what it feels like to think I've let someone down."

My friend connected with Mike's story because it wasn't really about war. It was about simply being human, about feeling like a failure, about doing the best you can anyway.

David Chrisinger is the director of the Harris Writing Program at the University of Chicago, and the author of Public Policy Writing That Matters. *In addition to his work in public policy communication, he leads week-long writing seminars for post-9/11 military veterans and their families for* The War Horse News, *the only non-profit newsroom that focuses specifically on military affairs and issues affecting veterans. In 2016, Chrisinger edited a collection of essays,* See Me for Who I Am, *written by student veterans in a first-of-its-kind writing seminar he taught at the University of Wisconsin-Stevens Point from 2015-2017. He is currently writing a book about famed war correspondent Ernie Pyle for Penguin Press, due out in 2021.*

Building Bridges
& Platforms

Why I Launch "The Grenade"

By James M. Thompson

The weekly newsletter for the Service Club of Indianapolis is called *The Grenade*. The club is composed of military veterans from all previous and current combat operations. It was founded in 1920 by World War I veterans who wished to continue the camaraderie found in military service. Grudgingly, they later allowed veterans of World War II. Since that time, the rules have changed to admit any military veteran. The paper consists of four 8 1/2-by-11-inch pages, mainly reporting on the weekly meetings. Page 3 is always devoted to a short story pertaining to military life. It is the hardest page to fill.

As editor, I prefer to use stories from a given member's military experiences. Most have not experienced actual combat, but all have some humorous or interesting tale to tell. You would think it an easy job to get veterans to write about their tours of duty, but it takes some effort.

Besides the normal hesitancy in speaking about combat, members from World War II or Korea are not, as a rule, computer literate. They can't dash off 800 words in any computer format, let alone e-mail the result. To them, a computer is a strange instrument of science-fiction known only to their grandchildren. On top of that, most of them are not gifted writers. I've found a more productive technique is often to interview them, and put their stories on paper for their approval before publishing.

Younger, more computer-savvy veterans are capable of writing their own stories—sometimes delivering too many words. In these cases, I pare them down and seek approval if necessary. Many of the members have learned to trust my editing skills.

Personal stories are, by far, the most interesting to my readers. Readership also consists of several widows of members who delight in reading the adventures of other military men. After all, military wives are as much a part of a veteran's career as the veteran himself.

When members' stories are not forthcoming, I either provide one of my own stories, write a story on some military subject, or seek war stories from other sources. There are several on-line sources where veterans have told their stories. The Internet has saved my editorial bacon several times.

Books are another source. A good summary of a book with a military subject can prompt a member to read the entire volume. One member provided me with an excellent book titled *Military Anecdotes*. The author is Geoffrey Regan, and he's included 454 anecdotes, ranging from a few lines to some more than 1,000 words.

A great fount of information on any subject is Wikipedia. That source provides basic facts, which I weave into a Page 3 story. I use it for weapons information quite often. Such content can help trigger the memories of other members. One article I wrote on the Browning Automatic Rifle (BAR), for example, prompted a member to tell me about his own experiences with the weapon.

My experiences from 23 years in the U.S. Air Force have also provided several Page 3 fillers. I had no combat experience, but my tours with the 62nd Troop Carrier Wing's "Hurricane Hunters," and as an advisor to the Republic of Vietnam Air Force's (RVNAF) 3rd Air Division at Bien Hoa Air Base, have provided many tales.

An interesting story about *The Grenade* itself involves getting extra copies of the paper to the weekly meeting. Usually, the editor brings copies to the meeting for any member who may have missed theirs. On one occasion, the editor would not be able to attend the next meeting, so he dropped the extra copies off at the president's home. The president was not home at the time, so the editor called and left a message on his phone as follows, "I left the extra *Grenades* on your porch." As luck would have it, he dialed the wrong number. As the answering machine had a generic message, he was not alerted to the fact he'd made a mistake.

When the owner of the phone returned home and checked his messages, he contacted the FBI immediately. They found no actual grenades, but agents arrived at the editor's door the next day. The editor had to show then copies of the paper before they would believe his story.

I've had this job off and on for over three years, and I never tire of it. The response of the members to a good issue is enough fuel to keep me going for several weeks. The deadline is short, less than 24 hours after the meeting. It has to be this short because quite a few members still receive the issue by snail-mail. More and more members are using the e-mail edition, but only time will eliminate the postal version. One advantage of e-mail is that it's in color, while the snail-mail version is limited to black-and-white to reduce printing costs.

I'll keep editing as long as I can, or until a younger member has the desire to take over. It's a labor of love for me, and a duty to my fellow veterans.

James M. Thompson is a graduate of Purdue University, West Lafayette, Ind. with a degree in aeronautical engineering. He spent 23 years in the U.S. Air Force, and retired as a lieutenant colonel. He is an author of five books. He is a past president of the Service Club of Indianapolis, and he now edits the organization's weekly newsletter. Jim is the recipient of two Sagamore of the Wabash awards, one each from former state governors Mitch Daniels and Mike Pence.

Podcasts: Writing to be Heard

By Mick Cook

The popularity of podcasts—exemplified by the success of the 2014 investigative journalism program *Serial*—has made it an attractive alternative to listening to music, audiobooks, or radio. The on-demand nature of podcasts means that an audience can choose to listen to content without the restriction of a programming schedule. The consumer demand for "programming control" mirrors trends in other media, such as film and television. Unlike other media formats, however, podcasts are relatively cheap to produce. Many have flocked to this medium to, quite literally, make their voices heard.

Many independent (or "indie") producers are not professional journalists or broadcasters. Instead, each of us undergoes a unique journey in the development of our craft. This is particularly true for those who either come from a military background, or seek to influence a military audience. Audiences that center around military topics often set high bars for qualities of content and presentation, as well as regular, timely production.

Getting the right mix can require a bit of luck, and a lot of learning.

I want to explore how these processes are similar to writing, and how applying a deliberate analytical process to producing independent podcasts requires competency in writing. I currently produce two independent podcasts that relate to war, politics, and military theory. I have also previously produced an "official" podcast on behalf of a military organization.

My first podcast was *The Dead Prussian* podcast. The podcast tips its titular hat to Carl von Clausewitz, a 19th century Prussian military theorist. Launched in January 2016, our episode count is now more than 80. The podcast features engaging interviews and "dad-joke" style humor to promote discussions amongst national security professionals, academics, and policymakers. The show has exceeded the initial success metrics established upon launch, but not in a way that I anticipated. In fact, the regular audience—the one that tunes in fortnightly for its dose of lame jokes about obscure war-based topics—is not the audience I'd originally targeted.

My aim, I had thought, was to encourage engagement with military theory and history among junior military officers. I wanted to make the material accessible. I had dabbled in writing and media production, including covering sports events as a photographer. I needed to "show, not tell." I understood that merely telling officers to read a book would not get results. I could lead a lieutenant to a library, but I couldn't make them read.

What goes for books also goes for blogs and professional reading lists. I took a page from my own habits, and realized that much of my own intellectual engagement was taking place via podcasts and audiobooks. Such formats allow audience members to multitask, and to consume information more easily while on the move.

Selecting the right format for the job was the first step in successfully reaching an audience, but it wasn't the last. I also encountered challenges in episode structure and content development.

The first episode I that planned, wrote, and recorded was never released. I am lucky enough to have a spouse who is an expert in media studies. She is the co-producer of the podcast, and not only taught me some technical skills, but also lent her voice to the intro and credits of the show. Having a co-producer or proofreader has been essential to content development. It's also surprisingly helpful when that individual doesn't have experience or a keen interest in the subject matter. Nothing is assumed.

In the initial stages, my co-producer was able to provide some frank advice about the project. The first, unaired episode was ... boring. I started over, and began to experiment with a variety of templates for future episodes. Of these, one has been the mainstay of the show. Most others have never been used.

What ultimately proved successful was an interview format. This was unexpected. So was the audience with whom the show began to resonate. Where I'd originally aimed at junior officers—those just starting their careers—the podcast proved popular amongst mid- to senior-level military officers, academics, and policymakers in the national security sector.

Every soldier knows that after every "ready, aim, fire," you either correct your aim or change your target. I did both. By reviewing and revising my content structure, I was able to make slight changes that didn't alienate the regular listeners and appealed to members of the original intended audience. The implementation of these changes was valuable, not just in achieving results in audience impact, but also providing me on-the-job training.

A broadcast veteran with whom I was co-producing a different project at the time offered additional advice. I had been using each episode plan only as a rough guide, without understanding the impact each plan had on an episode. Every detail counted: the way each question was written, whether it had a cue for a joke or follow up question, and even the way in which a guest was introduced. Each could influence the tone and pace of the episode and the impact on the listener.

I changed two significant aspects of how I wrote episode plans. First, I wrote an introduction before the standard greetings that preceded each interview. I call this the topic "hook." An audience generally decides in the first two sentences or 10 seconds whether or not they will read a complete article or continuing viewing a video. In early episodes, I had been offering the audience no knowledge of what a given episode was going to be about. I was failing to hook them on the topic.

Second, despite featuring a similar number of questions per interview, the initial episodes varied considerably in length. I revised how I structured my questions. I had always tailored the questions to each guest, but I hadn't always ensured each question was easy to answer. I needed my questions to be open-ended to give guests freedom to expand upon the topic.

Now, to ensure my guests are prepared, I provide them with a "run sheet" that includes five questions about their topic, as well as a sixth question that all guests are asked to answer.

I ensure the core of each of the first five questions is an open question on a specific aspect of the topic, but also include a note for each question that allows me to ask a closed question on the topic as a follow-up, or to provide a joke related to the guest's answer. This "open-closed-joke" format allows me to better monitor and control the tempo of an interview. As a result, I now produce episodes in which answer lengths fall within a defined range, based on listener preference survey data.

The sixth and last question has become a hallmark of the show, and many listeners have commented that they eagerly anticipate each guest's answer to this recurring prompt: "Complete the sentence 'War is …'"

By making changes to target audience, format, content, and program length, *The Dead Prussian* program increased both audience size and engagement—all within the first seven months of the production's life.

If there is still a gap between the initial target audience and those who now tune in to the podcast each fortnight, I don't see this as a failure. I see it as a lesson in understanding what you want to communicate, how you want to communicate it, and to whom you want to communicate. This lesson applies whether you are writing a blog, producing a podcast, or delivering a set of orders in the field.

Mick Cook is an Australian writer and digital content producer. He currently works at the University of New South Wales' Defence Research Institute. Cook writes and produces digital content on war, warfare, and professional development of military professionals. He is passionate about strategic communications and enabling discourse on public issues. Cook is a non-resident fellow at the Modern War Institute at West Point and a sessional academic in the School of Arts and Communication at the University of Canberra. Cook spent 18 years as regular officer in the Australian Defence Force before transferring to reserve service. Cook's research focuses on strategic narratives and information warfare. He is a member of the Military Writers Guild.

"Semper Write": One Aviator's Opinion

By Carl Forsling

Marine aviators have lots of opinions. All you have to do is ask—and, really, not even then.

While it's one thing to express yourself bantering with your friends, however, it's quite another to write them down for posterity or public comment. My first published opinion essay may not have changed the world—it was an article for the *Marine Corps Gazette* about how to streamline night-vision training for my fellow aviators—but it did change me. It got a lot of "right ons" from peers, as if I'd said things they'd been thinking for a long time.

That was probably the most satisfying part—feeling like the *de facto* spokesman for the ready room on that issue. I was helping to shape and articulate others' opinions.

My next big piece was about changing the U.S. Marine Corps' policies surrounding safety while on liberty. Then I wrote about changing tactics for assault support aircraft, and buying specialized targeting equipment.

My writing was still something of an *ad hoc* affair. When I got an idea or an issue bugged me, I wrote an article about it.

Gradually, I widened my scope from writing about tactics to writing about operations, then about strategy. Along the way, I even wrote for some non-military publications. Eventually, I was offered the chance to regularly contribute articles for the website *Task & Purpose*.

For a would-be thought-leader, the biggest bang is from professional journals of the armed services, such U.S. Navy's *Proceedings* and the *Marine Corps Gazette*. The U.S. Air Force has *Air and Space Power Journal*. The U.S. Army has *Military Review*, and others.

While depressingly few junior personnel read those journals, they have a fairly strong audience among senior leaders, or at least their staffs. Well-researched, -reasoned, and -written articles occasionally do shape the dialogue at the service level and sometimes higher. I've told many Marine Corps company-grade officers that writing in the *Marine Corps Gazette* is like putting a note in a suggestion box. Believe it or not, however, after one of my articles was published, I once got a call from the Commandant of the Marine Corps. We had a friendly discussion about the topic, and I think we both got something from the discussion.

If your goal is to write on military strategy or history, or to review books, look at on-line publications and forums, such as *Strategy Bridge, War on the Rocks*, and *Small Wars Journal*. These are venues for serious analysis, and have audiences that range from casual military buffs, to think-tank fellows, to serving military officers.

Outside of those spaces, the world of military writing gets very complicated very quickly. There's the military news, culture, and editorial space, exemplified by sites such as *Task & Purpose* and *We Are the Mighty*. Then, there are places like *BreachBangClear* or *SOFREP*, which aggregate general military news, but also cover topics such as individual tactics and gear. There are military-spouse writing spaces, too.

Bottom line: The Internet is a chaotic, challenging, and ever-changing environment. Just keep one hand on the cyclic, and one hand on the collective. Maintain situational awareness at all times. Most of all, remember: Small course-corrections can lead to big results.

Carl Forsling is a senior columnist at Task & Purpose, *and a business development manager working in military aerospace. Previously, he flew helicopters for the Baltimore Police Department. He is also a retired U.S. Marine officer who served 20 years piloting the V-22 Osprey and CH-46 Sea Knight. He is a graduate of Boston University and the University of Pennsylvania. He has a son and daughter, and lives in Arlington, Texas. He is a member of the Military Writers Guild.*

The Power of Op-Eds:
How to Inform & Influence

By John Spencer

In 2015, I had the opportunity to take a class on "Op-Ed" writing. The instructor was a former reporter and writer for the *The New York Times*. I wasn't even sure what Op-Ed stood for (a legacy term from newspaper journalism, it means "opposite the editorial page," rather than "opinion editorial" as I initially thought), but I attended nonetheless. The one-hour class covered how to write a short, newsy opinion essay; how to pitch an editor a topic; and what types of topics editors want to see.

Each of us, we learned, had a perspective that editors and people in general want to read about: first-hand experience. And that's something that military service delivers by the truckload.

The oft-cited statistic is that only 1 percent of the U.S. population serves in the military. Many debates or discussions about war and other military topics fail to incorporate the experienced view of the practitioner.

As I was then just a U.S. Army major, I had never considered myself an expert in anything. I have since discovered that good, meaningful writing can and should come from more than strategists, historians, general officers, or academics. Writing Op-Ed essays, stories of real-world, first-hand experiences—complete with reasoned arguments and calls-to-action—can make a real impact.

Beyond that, there were no secrets to writing revealed in the Op-Ed class. The same essay format I had learned in high school—an introduction paragraph with a thesis, supporting paragraphs with topic sentences, and a conclusion paragraph—was still the starting point.

There were, however, a few small tricks or techniques that applied to news-and-opinion markets, including writing for newspapers, magazines, and websites. Such writing, for example, has to be current. Topical. Newsworthy. Journalists call this factor a "news peg"—something on which to hang reader interest. Quality writing also counts. Good articles—and, by this, I mean the ones that editors are most likely to purchase and publish—start with a "hook." Something to grab a reader's attention.

Finally, each pitch and essay should answer two questions: "Why people should read this now," and "Why should they listen to you?"

One of the first essays I pitched ran counter to what then seemed a consensus opinion from U.S. Army leaders: that women soldiers couldn't handle the job of being in the infantry. I applied my experiences as a career infantry soldier and former Ranger Instructor (RI), observing that many popular arguments against women serving in the infantry were founded on opinions more than facts.

I sent the essay to *War on the Rocks*, an on-line, subscription-based news and analysis website.

It was rejected, but not without feedback.

The editor said the idea of my article was super, but that the central point wasn't clear. I had also failed to provide a strong case that my opinion was based on credible experiences. Most importantly, the editor said that if I was willing to do a major rewrite, he would reconsider the submission.

I learned a lot from this episode. That writing is important, but so is editing. If you don't feel confident in either skill set or both, look for help from others. From that point on, I have always had someone else (usually multiple people) look at everything I write before submitting it somewhere. I also gained the encouragement that I could make a strong argument founded on first-hand experience.

Later, after I'd collected a few by-lines, I decided to expand beyond first-hand experience to address a topic on which had I both observed and studied: the impact of technology on small-unit cohesion. I had done research on small-unit cohesion theories while in school. Reflecting on my deployment experiences, I began to wonder if soldiers' ability to connect with family and friends at home via social media and e-mail, might have had negative effects on forming shared bonds with their fellow soldiers.

I took my personal observations, and combined them with academic research on the effects of social media on relationships and society. I wrote an opinion essay, shared it with friends for feedback, and submitted it to *The New York Times*. To my major surprise, it was accepted.

The amount of positive feedback was overwhelming. I received e-mails from across the world, from soldiers in combat—ironically, using social media to contact me—from senior military officials, and others who told me they had observed the effects of phones, e-mail, and social media on unit cohesion, or who also had the same concerns.

Later, I wrote an essay inspired by my 2008 deployment, a time when it seemed all I had done was emplace concrete walls. I never thought that job was particularly noteworthy, but after I argued in conversations with friends about how effective the walls were at reducing violence in Iraq, I realized that most people—including myself—had no idea just how much concrete we had used putting up those walls, much less why they were effective.

Research + first-hand experience + news peg + hook (+ editing) = !!!!

The article went viral. It was read more than 100,000 times on the blog maintained by the Modern War Institute at West Point. It was republished by *Yahoo! News*, *National Geographic Education*, *Vice*, and other outlets.

Needless to say, I was convinced of the power of the Op-Ed.

We each have multiple roles. Each identity is a vital part of who we are, and a set of experiences rich with story and meaning. For most of my adult life, I have considered myself a soldier, a Ranger, and a leader. When I had children, I became a father. Now, I am also a writer.

My only regret is that I discovered writing at the end of my Army career. Writing has made me a better thinker. It has helped me to communicate with clarity. I can only imagine how much better of a soldier, leader, and person I would have been if I had discovered the process of writing earlier in my life.

John Spencer is the current chair of Urban Warfare Studies at the Modern War Institute at West Point, N.Y. A former Ranger Instructor, he has held the ranks of private to sergeant first class, and lieutenant to major while serving in Ranger, Airborne, light, and mechanized infantry units during his 25 years as an infantry soldier. His writing has appeared in The New York Times, The Wall Street Journal, The Washington Post, USA Today, *the* Los Angeles Times, Military Review, Foreign Policy *magazine, and many other publications. Follow him on Twitter:* @SpencerGuard

Creating Better Alternatives:
The Story of "Divergent Options"

By Phillip A. Walter

One word motivated me to begin writing: "Destroy."

It was September 10, 2014, the day before the anniversary of the 9/11 attacks, and U.S. President Barack Obama was outlining his strategy to counter the threat posed by the Islamic State of Iraq and the Levant (ISIL). While addressing the nation, Obama said, "Our objective is clear: We will degrade, and ultimately destroy, ISIL through a comprehensive and sustained counter-terrorism strategy."

I was stunned. I was speechless. I felt like Marlon Brando as Col. Kurtz in *Apocalypse Now*, describing his reaction to horrors he had seen on the battlefield: "I cried, I wept like some grandmother. I wanted to tear my teeth out; I didn't know what I wanted to do!" Surely, the president and his staff understood that "destroying" an ideology, without inflicting the kind of physical destruction the United States and our allies did to our enemies during World War II, was impossible. At most, based upon U.S. political will and world opinion, all the United States could do was undertake efforts to manage threats of this kind. They knew that, right? Didn't they?

Partly to give my ideas a voice, and partly to exorcise various demons associated with other experiences, including deployments, I purchased a domain name, established a Twitter account, and three days later wrote and self-published my first article: "World War II, Foreign Policy, and the Global Effort to Manage Threats." As time went on, I met other writers. Together, we continue to think, write, tweet, occasionally podcast, and try to change the world for the better, one sentence at a time.

After two years of writing, I felt there was something missing from the on-line national security landscape. As I surveyed this virtual terrain, I saw conservative and liberal websites advocating their respective lines of thought; I saw middle-of-the-road websites suggesting minor adjustments to current national security activities; I saw elite websites that new voices likely could not enter; and I saw research websites that published amazing products that I assessed would not be read due to length.

Based upon this assessment, I came up with my idea for *Divergent Options*—a website that publishes articles providing national security options, without advocacy, and assessments of national security situations, in a short (1,000 words or less) and easy-to-read format that fits into busy lifestyles. I wanted *Divergent Options* to be a place that focused on its writers' ideas, rather than their pedigrees.

At home, pacing around the house in my robot pajamas, I wondered if my idea had merit. I sought out a second opinion from Steve Leonard, the creative force behind the Doctrine Man!! web comic. Leonard supported my idea wholeheartedly, and asked if he could partner with me on the project. Together, we brought on Bob Hein, a retired career surface warfare officer in the U.S. Navy, who previously commanded USS Gettysburg (CG-64) and USS Nitze (DDG-94). The three of us have been moving forward smartly, ever since

Editorially, we have kept our shot-group tight. We will never be [Insert Amazing National Security Website Here], and that is OK. Conversely, [Insert Amazing National Security Website Here] will never be us, and that is OK as well. These days I sleep well knowing that I can write for myself, write for other websites, and help people broadcast their own ideas through *Divergent Options*.

Phillip A. Walter has served in the military, the intelligence community, and the interagency. All of his written works and podcasts, which do not contain information of an official nature, can be found at: www.philwalter1058.com

My First War Novel

By Rachel Kambury

Before I was old enough to vote in an election, rent an apartment, get a tattoo, buy cigarettes, or walk out of a liquor store with a bottle of bourbon, I wrote a war novel. Go big or go home.

My interest in World War II history had all the makings of a phase. Given the opportunity to do an investigative research project in the 6th grade, 11-year-old Rachel decided to tackle the Holocaust. Susceptible to imprinting on things like so many a duckling, I latched on to the subject assuming the interest would fade in time, doomed to join previous obsessions like the Titanic, ancient Egypt, and dinosaurs in the figurative jar of childhood curiosities. No such luck.

Four years later, sitting in bed one cold February evening, I opened a notebook and started writing a World War II novel. In hindsight, beginning the work felt as natural as anything. But after nine months of writing, I had a first draft of a story that was more a messy amalgam of varied interests and half-known facts about the war than a real novel. Were they fighting in Albania? Italy? North Africa? How did they end up in Germany?

It was an unmitigated clusterfuck, and as such, *Gravel* became my first exercise in cover-to-cover rewriting. I had spent the previous nine months telling people about my novel—had relished the expressions of shock and interest and bewilderment, to the extent that *Gravel* was no longer my little writing project, but an expectation in the minds of others. And the more their expectations grew, the more I felt compelled to meet them.

Knowing a second draft *had* to happen made discarding all but a few lines from the 350-page, handwritten manuscript easy. The question on my mind at that point wasn't "how do I rewrite my first war novel," but "how do I get this *right?*"

The answer came during my junior year of high school. By then, I'd watched HBO's *Band of Brothers* approximately 8 billion times. (My connection to and feelings about that miniseries is its own essay.) Like the subject of the war, itself, I imprinted on Easy Company hard. I breathed the series day in and day out—it was a resource as much as it was a comfort. The second draft of *Gravel*, meanwhile, ostensibly became my single extra-curricular activity, a thing that was costing me sleep, friendships, and, unbeknownst to me, my mental health. Still, I decided to follow the old adage "write what you know" to the letter.

Felix joined the 101st Airborne Division. So it goes.

Here's the thing about writing a war novel when you're 15, 16, 17 years old: You know you have no idea what you're doing, but you do it anyway. There is a delightful, unbridled chaos to being that age—an unselfconsciousness that lends itself to creativity, productivity, and self-destruction. Even awkward, retiring types with poor fashion sense, bad acne, and an idiosyncratic taste in music lose all inhibition when it comes to doing the thing we love most.

There was also the fact that, growing up in a small town, I had yet to be confronted with the wider literary world. I had no concept of markets or comp titles or target audiences. I started writing a war novel because I had an idea I couldn't shake. But, even after it became clear *Gravel* was becoming a bigger project than I originally intended, there was never any intention of finding an agent for it, or getting it published by a big house in far-off New York City.

Gravel was going to be the imperfect, incredible achievement it was always meant to be. That I knew.

I became a new person going through the process of writing *Gravel*. Here was the culmination not only of a decade of practicing writing, but proof that my 11-year-old vow to do what Kurt Vonnegut did and write novels wasn't just wishful thinking—I'd actually followed through. The proof was taking shape as I moved through the last year of high school on a billowing wind of determination, much to the bafflement of the people closest to me.

Other things were happening, however, under the surface of all that creation. A Hydra of severe mental health issues, which had lain dormant for years, had begun to raise its heads. This was also the period when I first encountered the particular kind of sexism that dogs me to this day, when I first encountered comments like: "You write about *war*? But you're a *girl!*"; "Maybe you should write under a male pseudonym, that way people will take you seriously"; and "But it's such an ugly subject, why would you want to write about that?"

Friendships fizzled out over the course of the two-and-a-half years it took to write (and re-write, edit, and eventually self-publish) *Gravel*. I share the blame for that. I made writing the priority, the thing that outweighed everything except homework; it kept me at home on the weekends and at coffee shops four hours after school every day, writing myself to the point of exhaustion, the kind that sleep can't undo, day after day after day.

I wrote myself sick, to tears, to nightmares.

Then, there was a pustule of a man who called himself a "publisher" and almost got me to give up writing when I was 16. Jimmie and I met at one of my go-to coffee shops, and got to talking about what I was working on. He asked to read my manuscript, which by that point was a year-and-a-half from completion. In a state of naive, starry-eyed excitement, I e-mailed him the first few chapters. Two days later, on a dusky evening in September, I received a phone call while staying at my stepmother's house.

"There's nothing here that's gonna grab people," he said. "I know I said we'd be interested in helping you with this, but I just don't see it going anywhere. I know this book matters a lot to you, but it's just not good enough."

Today, when I re-read portions of *Gravel*, I realize there was a lot about his "critique" that held water. *Gravel* was a soft book. Many of the characters are painfully one-dimensional. It is not particularly well-written or -paced, and it's historically inaccurate in ways that strain credulity. Bending facts is one thing in realistic historical fiction, but *breaking* them is another. Were I to re-write *Gravel*, I'd do it from scratch. Again.

I can be rational about his words now. But at 16? Writing my first real novel? I wallowed hard for weeks after that phone call. Questioned my ability to write, my commitment to this story, whether or not there was any point in seeing this project through to the end. Was *Gravel* worth anything to anyone besides me, or was I kidding myself and them?

Then, in the full flush of youthful stubbornness, I went back to work. A burgeoning mental health crisis, my social life, and sexism could wait.

(For what it's worth, I had to click back through nine years of e-mails, 22,000 of them, just to find the name of the guy who almost made me stop writing nine years ago. Damnation, thy name is Gmail.)

Earlier this year, I had dinner with my high-school health teacher in New York City. "What was the reaction at the faculty meeting the day *Gravel* came out?" I asked her.

She laughed, the bright sound drowning out the roars of the hard-drinking Staten Islanders at the next table. "Some of us didn't even know you'd been working on it, so all of a sudden we have this student who drops a war novel on us and we were just shocked. Shocked!"

At the Senior Most Likely "awards" ceremony in May 2009, I was voted "[Girl] Most Likely a *New York Times* Bestseller." There was triumph in that, but more so in learning that the only other writing category—Senior Most Likely to Write a Novel—had been nixed because of me. I felt indomitable. *Gravel* was the greatest accomplishment of my life up to that point. It made even the most dry-eyed members of my immediate family cry, a monumental achievement in and of itself.

Since 2009, the book has sold about 100 copies, which is about 96 copies more than I ever could have anticipated, and a thousand less than I'd hoped for. But I'd done it—I'd written a novel. Between April and June 2009, not a day went by someone didn't refer to me as "The girl who wrote a war novel." Looking ahead toward college, toward the next book, toward a career—I saw nothing but potential.

Naturally, that's when it all fell apart.

The aforementioned mental health crisis bubble finally burst not long after I moved to New York City in August 2009. I am glad it waited until after I made pilgrimages to Normandy, Eindhoven, Dachau, and Bastogne. But the writer I had become through the wild and spectacular process of writing *Gravel* was gone within a year of its publication—lost to severe depression and Post-Traumatic Stress Disorder (PTSD). All that fire of momentum, snuffed out.

In the years since, it has become clear that writing *Gravel* effectively did away with my resistance to a battery of mental health issues. If my mind was a tin can, writing *Gravel*—more specifically, writing about war—was the rusty, jagged-edged can-opener, slowly serrating through the psychological defenses I'd spent years building up and fortifying.

The fallout was nearly catastrophic. But as counterintuitive as it sounds, writing about war, despite being the thing that almost did me in, had also become the lens through which I could best make sense of my own traumatic experience. What happened to me as a child transpired far from any battlefield, but there was still meaning to be found in my study of them.

In writing war stories, I learned that for almost every person who finds healing and understanding in the peaceful and the quiet, there is someone like me, who doesn't.

In many ways, it feels like *Gravel* never happened. Reading it now is like reading a book written by somebody else. But there are moments of remembrance, when I can recall where I was and how I felt writing this or that chapter. There is, for example, the D-Day landings scene, which made a veteran and survivor of the Bataan Death March tell my best friend's dad, "She gets it." A scene I wrote a few months after Jimmie told me to give up on the whole thing.

There are moments like one recent December, when I found myself spiraling in doubt, questioning whether it was worth it for me to continue trying to write when I had, besides *Gravel*, nothing to show for my efforts. It was then I turned to an *Ashland (Ore.) Daily Tidings* article from 2009, in which a starry-eyed 17-year-old Rachel is quoted saying: "About halfway through writing *Gravel* I started thinking of myself as a writer ... I'm definitely going to pursue being a novelist."

In September 2010, following an unprecedented 17 months of total creative inertia, I began writing my second World War II novel. By February 2016, I'd started a fourth draft, effectively shelving the 500,000 words I had written over the past 6 years. Once again, I started over from scratch, asking myself not if I can do this all over again, but how do I get it right *this* time?

While my writing resumé is still relatively short, I am satisfied that the first thing on it will always be my first war novel. Whatever shame or embarrassment I might feel toward that sparse page, let alone the amount of time it's taken me to write my second war novel, is always supplanted by the pride I have in the work I did when I was a dauntless teenager caught in the grip of something bigger than herself.

So, yes. For now, and for a little while longer still, *Gravel* stands alone. I can live with that.

Rachel Kambury was born and raised in Oregon. She self-published her first World War II novel, Gravel, *in 2009—two months before she graduated high school. In 2013, she earned an undergraduate degree in literature from Eugene Lang College of Liberal Arts, New York City, and has studied war history at the American University of Paris. Her work has appeared in* The Wrath-Bearing Tree, Consequence Magazine, The Quivering Pen, Columbia Journal, *and the United States World War I Centennial Commission blog. She lives and works in New York City, and can often be found in the war/military history section of the nearest bookstore. Follow her on Twitter: @rkambury*

A Passage of Lines:
Starting a Literary Journal

By Christoper Lyke

When I'm writing and editing, I try to tell the small stories. Those are the true ones: like the look of fear in the Afghan woman's eyes as she huddles her children behind a boulder during a gunfight. It's not the bang-bang stuff that's good. That all comes across like *Tarzan* movies. You need it for flash, but it's not the truth. That mother's eyes are the truth. Her black and red and green robes, the gold stitching on her son's cap, the way they melt into the space where the boulder touches the terrace near the river is the truth. The ghostly puffs of smoke that rise around them from the rockets' spent energy are the truth. They are so white against the green by the river.

I watch that family like they're on television, while I'm slung in my seat. Brass and links rattle from the turret down to the floor. All of that is true. The story is in there.

It's important for all of us to try and sing a little bit, whether it springs forth like an arcane chant or even a death wail. I like to think of it as casting a spell. It takes months, but getting the words just right—getting the rhythm down with comma and period and breath—is a powerful thing. Tell the ghosts and the djinn when to move out and find another home. It's the old magic. It's an exorcism. And if it's art, it is that, too.

We balance this singing with the rest of our lives. Every day, I get up and go to work. I teach at a high school in Chicago—I talk about books the kids don't read and fix grammar they'll promptly forget. I talk with other school personnel with a smile. I try not to get angry. Sometimes, I want to scream.

That's not exactly helpful. So, I go to work and stay in my classroom. I talk to exactly three people beside the students. This way, I don't get into trouble. Sometimes my mask gets caught on a piece of clothing and a little bit of the light shines through. I say fuck too often or drink too much or tell a coworker, "I've already got a wife, stop complaining at me." It comes out way hotter than they're used to, though. To civilians, it seems extreme.

I was an adult when I joined up, so I can understand their confusion at this "military thing." I remember what it was like to see the military as faceless and thoughtless. I grew up with memories and movies of the Vietnam War clouding everyone's opinions. (I went to see *Platoon* when it came out. We were in an idyllic Cleveland suburb. I was 15. My grandpa, who had fought the Nazis at Remagen, took me. All he said when it was over was, "Bullshit. It ain't like that, Grandson.")

I leave at the bell. That's frowned upon, but someone has to take my kids to soccer and dance. If I don't, they'll be late and then their only lives will be sitting inside of a condo with no backyard in Bucktown, Chicago. I wait till they're done and drive them home. We do homework while I make dinner. We eat and then the wife gets home. She eats and sits on the couch. I make us drinks and the kids go to bed. We go to bed with half-done drinks left by the couch. I get up at 4:45 in the morning and start it all again. It goes on like this. No one is immune.

Every year, some of the students enlist after graduation. The school administration says a word of congratulations, but at heart they look down upon this. In ratings for each school, the city doesn't give credit for graduating new soldiers or sailors. Enlistment is looked on as a student somehow not having a sound plan for after graduation.

Most people believe what they've seen on TV. They look at the military as a "less than." It's a mystery to them—a life "on the gun" seems horrifying. If they know that I'm a veteran, they usually stumble around in their speech. They apologize and smile and give a few "I'm sure you know what I mean"-type sentences after it spills out. I don't say anything. I didn't join up till I was 30. I had already established a working civilian life. I know how odd it might seem, that the soccer dad who is trying not to curse and trying desperately to not wear the same clothes every day, who is also teaching English like he gives a damn, was a grunt sergeant in Afghanistan.

The good part of being a veteran is that our hots burn hotter and our cools are hyperborean compared to "civilians." It's like when someone without kids talks about their pets as though they were actual, human children. I don't think they can't understand, it's just that they haven't ever had the fear furnace turned that far up. Their gauges for what is real are calibrated differently.

They haven't, for example, seen rocket fights between villagers fighting to recover a stolen 12-year-old, taken as a child bride by a 30-year-old fighter from the village down the way. As it happened, that one went on for a while—a lot of the wedding party didn't make it. And they didn't see the sad prostitutes in Africa, who serviced both our Ethiopian allies and our Al Qaeda enemies in the same night, and who spent the interludes in-between serving beers, smoking hookahs, looking out with half-lidded eyes. Stories like that usually don't register with anyone stateside, unless you're talking to a cop in a bar.

My versions of human cruelty and human potential go way beyond a brief conversation. So, I carry on. I don't say much. Sometimes the mask slips off and some of the fire shows through. Maybe I scream, maybe not.

So, I dream instead. And I write. I do so for that open sky at 8,000 feet. The dreams of the boredom and the beauty. The all-of-a-sudden fights with men from the past, armed with jug bombs and Russian weapons. I dream of finding my voice.

It once dawned on me that I may not be alone in this half-life, so I started an on-line literary journal with a veteran friend. We called it *Line of Advance*. I get to put other people's work out there in the ether, and put some of my own out there as well. And we do our best. We all help each other. We all celebrate one another's victories.

Some days, I don't even think of the war—then, suddenly, there it is again and it feels like yesterday instead of years ago. I read some Ambrose Bierce recently. He said the same thing about the American Civil War. It stuck with him until he disappeared down Mexico way. I'm pretty sure the old Mediterranean boys would echo the same thing. It's a part of us now. We're in the club.

I think that's why we keep working. That's the trick. If we can keep the river rushing, and put our canoes in and start paddling, we should be good to go, singing our stories along the way.

Christopher Lyke is a writer and teacher living in Chicago. He served in Afghanistan and Africa as an enlisted infantryman with the U.S. Army. He edits and publishes Line of Advance, *an on-line literary journal for veterans. He can usually be found running with his dog in Logan Square or watching the Buckeyes at Vaughn's Pub. Chris has been published in such venues as* BlazeVOX *and Military Experience & the Arts' literary journal* As You Were, *and won the short-story award in* Proud to Be: Writing by American Warriors, Vol. 4.

Novel or Memoir?
It's the Stories that Matter

By Wayne E. Johnson

After chow one evening in 1971, a few of us short-timers were sitting around the G-1 barracks in Seoul, Korea, chuckling about some laughable situations that had happened in the office during our tours. One of the guys said, "Somebody should write a book about all this." Another guy replied, "Nobody would believe it."

Over the years, I became that "somebody," penning short stories based on events that happened during my two-year Vietnam-era military career, with a focus on my year at 8th Army Headquarters.

I eventually had enough short stories, published and unpublished, to fill a book—maybe a novel. To create a readable fiction, however, I needed a backbone, something to tie the stories together—a protagonist. A character with a developmental arc, so that my stories wouldn't just be an episodic collection of events.

If you have a protagonist hero, you also need an antagonist—someone or something that keeps the hero from achieving success. In my book, that villain is the U.S. Army, embodied by a nasty character I based on a real sergeant major. I added a love-story subplot, and another about a G.I. and his Korean wife. I wrote it in first-person, to give it immediacy and the feel of a memoir. My novel, *The Militarized Zone: What Did You Do in the Army, Grandpa?,* was published at the end of 2016 to positive reviews from *Publishers Weekly* and the Vietnam Veterans of America, among others.

Author Harold "Hal" Walker and I later created a 2-hour program encouraging our fellow veterans to share stories of military experience by recording them in some way. Our program was conducted in partnership with the Aurora (Ill.) Public Library, and underwritten by a grant tied to the release of 10-part Ken Burns documentary on the Vietnam War.

We focused our presentation on self-publishing, either in print or as an e-book. Hal is a retired U.S. Marine lieutenant colonel, and was a helicopter pilot in Vietnam. He kept an excellent, detailed journal about his time in the service, and he's turned his Vietnam experience into a work of non-fiction, a memoir. To help double-check his accuracy with the details, he contacted fellows who served with him.

While it's good to try to get facts such as unit information correct, a memoir is your story, your view of the events. You're not writing a history textbook. If you can't remember a detail or a date, say so. Someone who experienced the same things right alongside you would have his or her own view of the events, and their view could be quite different from yours. Who's right or wrong? Both are describing what took place the way they saw it.

I chose to write my book as a novel rather than a memoir. While the content is based on actual events, fiction gave me more freedom to elaborate, and to add some humor. Examples of such an approach include *M*A*S*H* and *Catch-22*, and the movie *Good Morning, Vietnam.*

These days, with the advent of Publish-on-Demand (POD) technologies and services, it's easier than ever to publish your work as an e-book, or even a trade paperback. Write your text in Microsoft Word, then upload it to CreateSpace or similar provider. They offer plenty of help for authors. If you want something more permanent, POD providers can output your work as a printed book as well. The format is up to you.

What's most important is getting your story told. A few years ago, I attended a memorial service for a World War II veteran from my group, the Fox Valley Veterans Breakfast Club (FVVBC). He was a Pearl Harbor survivor. When his son took his turn at the podium, he said the best and most important thing his dad did for the family was to record the events of his military life. He'd rarely mentioned anything about his service while he was alive, but left a notebook and pictures behind.

To help others to share their stories, the breakfast group began selecting a Veteran of the Month. The selected individual is interviewed by a reporter from *The Voice*, a regional northeastern Illinois newspaper, and awarded a certificate and an encased flag that has flown in our nation's capitol.

The FVVBC has twice sponsored The Moving Vietnam Veterans Wall in our area. A woman who regularly attends our FVVBC meetings lost her brother in Vietnam. For the last 20 years or so, she'd been trying to find someone who could tell her details of her brother's service in Vietnam. The day this woman visited the wall, she came upon a man with tears in his eyes, who was lightly touching her brother's name on the wall. She asked if he knew her brother. He told her they were best friends from basic training, and was with him the day he died. They hugged and cried, and have been in contact with each other ever since.

There are people out there waiting for your story. Share it.

Wayne E. Johnson is a Vietnam-era veteran. He was drafted in 1969 and spent two years in the Army. He's been an actor, musician, forklift driver, advertising manager and creative director for Sourcebooks, Inc., among other occupations. Currently, he's a self-employed book designer and writes a humor column for The Voice, *a northeastern Illinois newspaper. He lives with his wife, Pat, two cats and a yard full of chipmunks in Aurora, Ill.*

My Grandfather's Thumb

By Michael Lund

As early as I can remember in my childhood, I was troubled that half of the thumb on my grandfather's hand was missing. Carl was a master craftsman. On his son's (my father's) 10th birthday, for instance, he made a drop down oak desk with the name, "Louis," and the date, "1929," inlaid in walnut. A microscope wouldn't show a space at any seam. How could the man who so carefully built this exquisite piece of furniture slice off half of his thumb with his own table saw?

In the year when he would have been 138 years old, I am composing an answer to that question. Why I write that story reveals a desire to recover a part of my grandfather's identity, and to present to others a reason to value national service.

Here is the family line:
- Carl Lund (b. 1890)— Sadie Wyrick (b 189?)
- Louis Lund (b. 1919) — Marian Macy (b. 1910)
- Michael Lund (b. 1945) — Anne Casteen (b. 1945)

On regular visits in my childhood, I watched Grandpa unconsciously sweeping his fingers over that still-functional stump as he relaxed in his easy chair. Rhythmically, steadily, continuously he rubbed the half-thumb because, my boyish imagination concluded, it still itched or ached years after he lost it. While I was curious about that unconscious action, as well as the accident itself, I could never ask this taciturn, stoic man—or his very private son, my father—how it had happened. One didn't bring up that kind of question in our restrained, if not repressed, Midwestern family.

Recently, I have come to conclude that Grandpa's fingers were not so much touching what remained of his thumb as passing over the place were the rest of it had been, outlining a full digit as if its substance and function might somehow be recovered through the process. As I enter what I generously term my "mid-seventies," I similarly want to hold onto or recover mental and physical abilities that are inevitably fading. So I'm going to use a theory of imaginative restoration to fill in a missing part of my grandfather's personal history: his 12 months in the Swedish Army. To do so, I must highlight features of my own two years of military service that I had obscured for years, even from myself.

My grandfather Carl's mother died when he was 6 (after bearing six children), and he was raised by his older sisters into his teenage years. According to family legend, hard times in his native Sweden meant that, at the age of 13, he had to go to work with his father in the coal mines near Bjuv. Around 1900, he and brothers Nils and Oscar emigrated to the United States, where they became skilled carpenters, painters, and wallpaper hangers near Salinas, Kan. Before he left his native country, however, Carl had to serve one year of active duty in the military.

According to my father, Carl resented this mandatory service. He thought of it as "a waste of his time." I also suspect he didn't support the country's military buildup in a time of relative piece and security. Looking at a picture of him in uniform, however, I can possibly see pride in his expression. Still, as a U.S. citizen 20 years later, he was pleased that his son Louis could grow up in a free country—one that, following the 1918 Treaty of Versailles, had no conscription. The woman my grandfather married, a Missouri school teacher, had a beloved older brother who'd been gassed in World War I and was an invalid. The two parents each insisted, for different reasons, that their one son use his brains not his hands to serve the nation, in a civilian rather than a military capacity.

When World War II came, Louis' poor eyesight initially kept him from being drafted. By 1943, however, he knew he would be called. He used his university credentials as a scientist to secure a research position for the U.S. Navy. He never left this country, and, after the war, returned to his Ph.D. studies, in 1949 becoming a physics professor at a Missouri university. Although a talented athlete throughout his college years—baseball pitcher, tennis player, boxer—he took care as a professional man to protect his hands. It was not vanity or a sense of social superiority that led him to wash them regularly and to keep the nails carefully trimmed; it was a sign that he had fulfilled his parents' dreams of a second-generation child rising above the working classes.

The following generation, my brother and I, also went to college and on to graduate school, using student deferments to separate ourselves from the 18-year-olds who were filling the draft quotas needed to pursue the war in Vietnam. I never heard my father speak against America's efforts in Southeast Asia (my grandfather had died in 1963); but it was an unspoken family conviction that my hands, like his, were to be preserved, as my mind moved me into the ranks of the professional class. In 1968, however, I received my "greetings" from Uncle Sam as a graduate student in an English department. Suddenly, I had to anticipate holding a gun rather than a pen for a period of two years or more. For decades, I did not connect my (intact) trigger finger to my grandfather's maimed thumb. Later, however, I came to believe the U.S. Army excised two years out of my professional life as neatly as the table saw had removed half of my grandfather Carl's thumb.

I have had a full professional life after the Army, partly because the military assigned me to a role for which I was well qualified: information specialist/correspondent. Soldiers holding Military Occupational Specialties

71-Quebec (print journalist) and 71-Romeo (broadcast journalist) had a much higher rate of survival in Vietnam than did those that were assigned 11-Bravo (infantry).

In 1971, I returned to my doctoral program, picking up a pen once more to resume what I thought of as my destiny—to read, teach, and write about literature. I pounded out finished papers, including my dissertation, on an Underwood upright manual typewriter. All eight fingers and two whole thumbs produced letters—and spaces—on paper to qualify me for the same life my father had enjoyed, that of a college professor. There was a gap in my adult history, however, that has been only recently filled in. As I write out my military life in the forms of personal essays, as well as two collections of short stories, and a five-volume series of novels, the reasons for doing so have become evident to me: I am reflecting on my past, to see its shape more clearly, year by year. I also hope that the life I have built and documented in words might offer a guide in some way to others.

From its earliest chapters, my chronicle has included my grandfather. His figure—the boy thrown into manhood at the age of 13—certainly inspired my father to work hard and to succeed. That sense of responsibility was passed on to me in the next generation. The missing half of a thumb never belonged in such a trajectory. And now what was not there becomes for me what is perhaps most important.

I believe that Carl did not resent the obstacles he faced in life; they were all things he could overcome with physical, mental, and emotional strength. The lack of formal education, the early loss of parents, the challenge of learning a new language in a new country—he could handle these so long as he was free to act on the basis of his own beliefs and abilities. Even with one deformed hand, Carl built cabinets, furniture, houses, barns—beautiful, sound structures for a growing America. What he resented was what one loses in the military: the freedom to build what you desire with the resources you earn. You have some choices in the military, true; but they are largely determined by others, by a sometimes impersonal system. Especially if you feel you know more than those who limit your choices—as I suspect my grandfather did—resentment is inevitable.

I knew this resentment at Fort Bragg, N.C.; Fort Campbell, Ky.; and at Long Binh, Vietnam. I had been taken from a promising career as a teacher and a scholar to work within an environment governed (and that's the right word) by others. By the time I arrived there, the reasons for the Vietnam War had become confused and its goals vague. My resentment subsequently erased the places I'd served, and my military experiences, from my public biography and personal history.

However, in recent years, as I've re-composed a history that includes those phases of my life, I have found that the very loss of liberty has given me a greater understanding of its value. My grandfather and four of his siblings, after all, were drawn across the Atlantic to gain this freedom. And he wanted it for his son and grandsons. With my pen—well, now, of course, with a computer and powerful software—I have run my mental fingers over and over the phases of my life I had previously skipped in memory. And I have discovered the centrality of individual freedom to this nation, recognizing more fully the sacrifice of others who gave up their liberties, not with resentment but with a profound desire to preserve freedom for others.

Several years ago I founded a program, Home and Abroad, that encourages military, veterans, and family members to write about their experiences in this country and overseas. I promise participants printed copies of their finished products to give to family and friends. At the same time, I offer my professional skills as an instructor of writing. These interactions have given me ideas about service that I failed to recognize when I was in the Army. In listening to others' stories, helping them shape their thoughts, and seeing their pasts take material form on paper, I can only shake their hands in gratitude for what they have taught me—no matter how many digits we each have or how well they function.

When my grandfather was in a hospital bed and dying, he returned to his native Swedish. My father, who had never learned much of his father's language, grieved at his beside that no one could understand his last words. It is, on the one hand, outrageous of me now to propose what he might have been saying. It is also a genuine effort of respect for my ancestor, however, whose story guided me in ways neither one of us might have recognized at the time. If he made one slip in an otherwise exemplary life—and lost half of his thumb because of it—I, who have made many errors, hope in a sense to restore his carpenter's and his soldier's hand with my authorial pen. In addition to the tools of his trade—the hammers, chisels, saws—I see that he also grasped the liberty that he felt mandatory service had taken from him for one year, and that this land provided for the rest of his accomplished life. With my free hand I offer thanks to all those who sacrificed to give him, his son, and his grandson that freedom.

Michael Lund is a native of Rolla, Mo., who lives and writes in Virginia. He is author of At Home and Away, *a Route 66 novel series that chronicles an American family during times of peace and war from 1915 to 2015; and two short-story collections:* How Not to Tell a War Story *and* Eating with Veterans. *A professor emeritus of English at Longwood University, Farmville, Va. he teaches part-time and conducts writing workshops with Home and Abroad, a free writing-instruction program for veterans, active-duty military, and families hosted by the university's Department of English and Modern Languages. He is a past finalist in the Col. Darron L. Wright Memorial Writing Award competition conducted annually by the literary journal* Line of Advance.

Veterans' Voices: Our Shared Story

By J.A. Moad II

As a kid growing up in an Illinois steel town, I was surrounded by men who'd served in the military—family and friends who'd fought in World War II, Korea, and Vietnam. Their stories of adventure inspired boys like me to serve, as well—to leave our Midwestern hometowns in the Rust Belt for a chance to see the world, get an education, or challenge ourselves with something different and exciting. If nothing else, it gave us an opportunity to escape the singular narrative of graduating high school, and going to work in the factories that lined the Mississippi River. While I no longer live in the area, I carry the stories of those people with me, and like so many children of veterans, my life has been shaped by their experiences, both good and bad.

After two decades in the U.S. Air Force, I found myself drawn back to the Midwest. I settled in a small Minnesota town, just south of where the Mississippi River snakes into a dividing line between Minneapolis and St. Paul, before it continues south on a 2,000-mile journey to the Gulf of Mexico. It glides past the struggling industrial towns along the river towns that once churned out the raw materials to build our weapons of war, just as the surrounding communities produced the young men and women to fill the ranks of today's armed forces. I've driven through these communities again and again on trips to see my parents: towns like La Crosse, Wis.; Davenport, Iowa; Quincy, Ill.; and Cape Girardeau, Mo. Towns where so many of the veterans from our current wars live, work, and do their best to bear the burdens of their experiences.

For years, I've considered how to tell a story about my father, a veteran of the Vietnam War. I've been hesitant, concerned it might come across as a cliché or as an embarrassment for him, and uncertain if I could render it with the justice it deserves. But, after performing in New York in my play, "Outside Paducah: The Wars at Home," I realize it needs to be heard. Of course, I should have known this. After all, my play is part of a broader initiative of mine that began at the Minnesota Humanities Center in 2014, and resulted in then-Gov. Mark Dayton declaring October as "Veterans' Voices Month." It's a project grounded in the power of stories to help us shape our understandings of war and what it means to serve.

The proclamation recognized that "Minnesota is home to more than 400,000 veterans" and that we should honor them by "sharing and studying veterans' experiences through stories, essays, poetry and art from the men and women who have served [...]." At its core is an acknowledgement that such stories provide a narrative that needs to become part of the public consciousness. Stories help us recognize that the trauma of war is always with us, down through generations. Their story is our story, after all, just as my father's story is a part of mine—a story I'm finally honored to share.

I don't remember my exact age when it first happened, but I must have been 8 or 9, because the talk was all about the war in Vietnam that was coming to an abrupt and disappointing end. All I know for certain is that I was at an age when a boy still looks up to his father as someone to emulate, his young eyes studying a man who seems so strong and certain, a kid longing to be like the old drill sergeant—a beer in hand and a cigarette dangling from his lip—as his stories capture everyone's attention.

What I remember most is the power of his presence. The way people were drawn to him, a group of men standing around in the back yard and my older brothers' friends tucked into lawn chairs, their faces turned to him as he spoke, told jokes or pontificated (his word not mine) on what it meant to be a soldier and a man. He was broad-shouldered and stocky, with a thick mustache and booming voice that always pulled you in and made you believe. He had a soft confidence, balanced by a hard strength that could inspire fear with a sharp look. More than anything, however, he had this disarming sincerity—an ability to push aside any doubt that what you were hearing was the unfiltered truth.

It must have been a Saturday afternoon, because he'd just finished cleaning the fish from the morning's catch. His fillet knife rested on the thick wooden cutting board covered with blood and scales. It was a warm day, late in spring and the humidity from the Mississippi River clung to our T-shirts. When the conversation turned to the war, my younger brother and I grabbed our baseball gloves and slipped deeper into the back yard, just out of range of the hard words sure to come. This was his stage, the old drill sergeant and natural storyteller, playing the part of military strategist who could have won the war if only he'd been in charge.

No one ever questioned him, even though his conclusions weren't always rational, and a story would occasionally lose its main thread inside a bottle of Jack Daniels. He was the neighborhood authority on the subject throughout my teenage years. As a boy, that authority is what builds the foundation of the truths on which you build your sense of self. It would inspire my two older brothers to enlist in the U.S. Army. It would inspire me to attend the U.S. Air Force Academy to become an officer and a pilot, instead of (as he put it) "some grunt in the jungle being told what to do by idiots." I listened to my father, just like those men who admired and respected what he'd done, piecing together his words into a narrative that would become part of my own. But there was never enough for me. I listened on the perimeter, clinging to every detail, and hoping to discover everything he knew. In my imagination, I constructed my own war where I killed the Viet Cong in the jungles of my mind.

He must have been on edge that day. The daily barrage of news was depicting the Viet Cong's advance on Saigon, our military bases getting overrun, and the boats of refugees crowding the South China Sea like a bathtub full of children's toys. I recall a clear sense of bitterness at the foregone conclusion—and my father's frustrations—about the decisions culminating in our defeat. "A lost war that wasn't a declared war and therefore not a real war," as so many of his buddies liked to say. In time, many of those who hadn't served would lose interest in such a war, and they would tire of his stories. But it was real, a devastatingly real loss to the men who sacrificed their youths in Southeast Asia, and there wasn't anything my father or the greatest military in the world could do about it.

I recall the conversation clearly, not in the way it actually happened, but as a composite of the narratives he would cling to in the decades to come— flawed narratives that I would suck up as definitive until I would disprove them with my own education and experience. He's not talking about the war exactly, but he's talking around it, about how we should have been more assertive back in the early '60s when he was in-country, and they were making headway. He never talks specifics about what he did on the ground, because he knows his audience isn't interested in the hard truths. He avoids the reality of what it was like to be a 19-year-old struggling to make sense of it all. Instead, he speaks to what we didn't do, how we let the communists win, failed to hold our ground with that god-damn, take-a-hill-leave-a-hill strategy, and all because the idiots in charge didn't have the guts to make a hard choice. And I can see the cold, hollow look in his eyes when he says, "we lacked the guts to bomb more, failed to use everything in the arsenal, and were too weak use tactical nukes in the name of freedom."

For years, I've pictured what comes next, something I never saw, but have reconstructed as if watching from a distance like a scene in a movie. An old Chevy glides down our street, and as it passes our house, the engine coughs into an explosive backfire. The sound reverberates into the backyard like a shock wave, and I see heads twisting toward the noise, everyone except my father, who has thrown himself onto the ground screaming, "incoming." And suddenly every face is looking down on him, his hands covering his head in a fetal position as they wonder how to help and if they should. There's nothing wrong with him, after all, and then, in a slow, defiant maneuver he stands and brushes himself off. He doesn't look at anyone, his eyes locked on the cutting board, as he contemplates how to proceed. And then he picks up the knife and buries it into the wood with a deep, guttural "fuck" before he walks into the house alone.

There were more moments like this in the years that followed, but this is the first one I recall with such vivid detail. And when I say recall, what I really mean, is *felt*, and what I felt was the embarrassment and the shame of a man who couldn't acknowledge his own fragility—a man terrified of painting himself as weak. The message was clear to me, and as a kid, I believed my own sense of strength was grounded on his. So I took it all in, feeling the unspoken pain and the rage he couldn't hide. And, like so many boys, I packed it all up inside me, a kind of base-level rage that we learn to hold onto and conceal like a sheathed knife ready to wield. I was being pulled into a cycle of which I wasn't aware, an unsuspecting ally in the perpetuation of war trauma reverberating down through generations. Like so many men who fought in Vietnam, he spun in a cycle of frustration at the powerlessness to affect the outcome of the war, and of their inability to combat the trauma they brought back with them. Post-Traumatic Stress Disorder (PTSD), after all, wasn't considered a medical condition until 1980. Even more so than today, it was a diagnosis fraught with complications and the stigma of being weak instead of strong. It wasn't until my father was into has late sixties before he quietly confided in me that he "might have some of that PTSD stuff."

Over the last decade, I've come to recognize that his stories were a way to deflect attention from the emotional struggles inside him. They gave him an outlet to vent his frustrations, and to turn a spotlight on the much more damning embarrassment of losing the war. He became an expert at unraveling the strands of rational thinking into a jumble of bitterness and anger directed at hippies, the news media, and college students—anyone who shed light on the harsh reality of the war, or believed it couldn't be won. It was as if he were guiding us deep into the heart of our failures as a nation. Any other perspective made us not only weak and ignorant, but complicit, as well. And in a sense, he was right. We were complicit— complicit in dismissing the trauma of those men who served in Southeast Asia. The war itself was a wound in the nation that festered in the silence, and we wanted to pretend it would heal on its own. In doing so, we turned away from those who served. We denied the emotional struggle of all veterans, just as my father denied his own, and by not recognizing the burden that he and so many veterans have carried in silence, we failed to acknowledge their suffering.

When I first started thinking about Veterans' Voices, I realized that despite the overwhelming support for veterans today, civilians are more distanced than ever from those who fight on our nations behalf. The All-Volunteer Force has created a gulf between those who have served and who haven't. Over the last few years, I've watched two simple narratives emerge in Hollywood and on TV, that of the victim and the hero. These narratives limit our abilities to engage in a productive dialogue on how to understand the cost of war on a personal level. I also realized that many of the children of veterans shared similar experiences to mine. I pictured hundreds of thousands of kids across the nation, struggling to understand a father or mother who'd been forever altered by their experiences in combat. Kids who are confused and ashamed with a quiet rage building within, many of them who had or will endure childhoods underscored by anger and violence, broken families and suicides, as well as drug and alcohol abuse.

The sad truth is that we've talked *around* the harsh realities of war for far too long, limited our perceptions to a few simple narratives and avoided the difficult work of recognizing the emotional struggles of veterans and their families. We've looked away and hesitated, unsure how to help, telling ourselves that the military or a broken Department of Veterans Affairs will do the job for us. But the simple fact is that those organizations are failing, and we are complicit in that failure. It's time to accept hard truths and to push past the clichéd "thank you for your service," and find new ways to move forward.

As we navigate another year of this seemingly forever war, it's time to work toward a more-complete narrative—one grounded on the stories of the veterans themselves. I picture Veterans' Voices as the foundation on which we create an environment where vets feel safe to stand up and discover the power of their own stories. I envision connecting with communities up and down the Mississippi River, reaching out to Veterans of Foreign Wars and American Legion posts, and partnering with local colleges, universities, and civilian organizations to organize 3- or 4-day events with panels, workshops and performances facilitated by professors and veterans who've honed their own craft of writing on the topic of war. Most importantly, though, I imagine it as a celebration of understanding and acceptance, where we recognize the power of their voices to create a new narrative—a shared story—as a reminder that we must acknowledge what they have to teach us. Because their story is our story.

J.A. Moad II is former U.S. Air Force pilot with more than 100 combat sorties in the C-130. He served as a professor of English at the U.S. Air Force Academy, and continues to serve as a fiction editor and blogger for the journal War, Literature, & the Arts (WLA). *His short stories, poetry, and essays have appeared in a variety of journals and anthologies, and include the 2014* Consequence Magazine *Fiction Award. In addition to writing, he has performed on stage at the Library of Congress and The Guthrie Theater as part of The Telling Project. He performed a play he wrote, "Outside Paducah: The Wars at Home" in November 2016 in Minneapolis. He currently resides in Northfield, Minn., and is busy editing a novel about an American military in a not-too-distant future.*

Writing to Build Social Capital

By Will Meddings

In December 2016, the British Army launched a new Centre for Army Leadership. The centre was to be located in Robertson House at the Royal Military Academy Sandhurst in Camberly, England, the site of all initial officer training in the British Army.

Given the centre's mission to improve the practice of leadership throughout the British Army, the location is appropriate. Robertson House is named after Sir William Robertson (1860-1933), the only soldier to have enlisted in the British Army as a private and later rise to the rank of field marshal.

As it exists today, the centre:

- Produces action-research papers on relevant leadership topics.
- Acts as guardian of the British Army's Leadership Doctrine.
- Acts as a focus and library for the British Army's academic leadership papers.
- Provides leadership presentations and speakers to military and civilian audiences.
- Organizes Army leadership conferences and events.

On launch day, however, there was little about its design, mission and operating model that was defined. In retrospect, I think it's sufficient to say that simultaneously designing, testing, and launching a project is not the best idea. Nevertheless, that's where we were. The formal direction for the establishment—our marching orders, as it were—was written on a mere four sides of paper.

Perhaps it was appropriate for a "Centre for Leadership" that we had been issued a broad intent with the details left to the execution team. Field Marshal William Slim (1891-1970) once famously commented that the rules in his headquarters were "No details, no paper, no regrets"—leave the details to the doers, don't write what can't be verbally briefed, don't regret what doesn't work out. Apt words indeed.

During our early discussions, the three initial team members sat in our bare office drinking coffee from our Centre for Army Leadership-branded mugs (one of our first purchases). We spent hours discussing and analyzing how we would go about improving the practice of leadership in the Army.

We disappeared down rabbit holes and flew away on flights of fantasy, yet tried not to lose sight of the ultimate end. Whatever we did had to improve the practical application of leadership. It was easy, therefore, to focus on what we already knew: Off-site courses. In other words, taking officers and soldiers and sending them away from units for a month, pouring leadership into them, and spitting them out as better leaders. One might call this a "human-capital" view of investing in leaders.

Our efforts continued. We met with our counterparts in the U.S. Army, and spoke with academic researchers. We quickly realized that such a human-capital approach misses something key. Developing leaders and leadership is about building *social* capital.

An organization that cares about leadership must create a culture where leader development is a central pillar of what it does. Sending people on leader-development courses has an effect—it creates an inescapable baseline of human capital leader development. But the real development of leaders happens through a social process that takes place inside organizations day-in, day-out. It happens when senior leaders mentor and support junior leaders, encourage peers to mentor and support each other, and create an environment where thinking about being a better leader is valued and encouraged.

Leaders train and mentor new leaders.

We based our nascent culture of learning on Connectivist pedagogy. This theory of learning is based on creating a connected community of professional mastery in which peers, apprentices, and experienced professionals share knowledge. For the community to prosper and develop, it has to work on four principles:

- **Autonomy:** People must have ownership of their development.
- **Openness:** The body of knowledge must be easily accessible and revisable.
- **Diversity:** Arguments and views, especially of those outside the community's normal experience base, must be present and encouraged.
- **Interactivity:** A feeling of a "live" environment of mutual professional exchange, in which ideas can be tested and changed, must be created.

As the team travelled around the British Army, lecturing on and discussing leadership with others, we encountered soldiers and officers who would have loved to have readily available leadership and job advice. I also came across soldiers and officers who were more than ready to offer that advice. We began to consider the question of why more British Army leaders were not in the practice of sharing ideas and insights in writing.

I discovered a list—a list of what one might call "Why We *Don't* Write."

First, the British Armed Forces have a strictly enforced policy on commenting on defense issues without clearance, backed up by career sanctions for those who break the rules. The rules themselves are rather loose, and generally allow the sharing of leadership thinking and advice.

Still, serving soldiers seem concerned they risk career damage.

Second, potential authors are afraid that, by raising their heads above the parapet, they might become the butt of their peers' jokes. (In a macho military culture, no one likes a "swot"—what American soldiers might call a "spring-butt" or know-it-all.) Likewise, there is a general feel that the average soldier is in no better position than anyone else to offer advice.

Finally, the few British Army outlets that do exist to facilitate the writing and sharing of ideas set a high bar for publication. Infrequency of publication (many professional publications appear only once a year, or quarterly), editorial style and formatting standards, and required word-counts are all potential obstacles to soliciting participation from officers and NCOs. All assuming, of course, that one successfully solicits the necessary permission from one's commanding officer.

In short, we have made writing for publication an intimidating process.

Leaders help remove obstacles for their peers and subordinates. We needed to create some intermediate, accessible steps for budding authors. First, we decided to publish 1,000-word *Leadership Insights*, creating the opportunities for junior leaders to discuss their thoughts on leadership. These were (and still are) good-quality, official, open-source articles hosted on our website. Authors didn't need to be "leadership experts" and we actively supported those wanting to submit work. All are welcome: The centre features submissions from lieutenants and majors, colour sergeants and corporals.

What these articles didn't offer was the ability to comment. To create opportunity for discourse or debate, I also launched *The Army Leader*, a leadership blog and entry-level outlet for writing. This blog is unofficial, but helps demonstrate that soldiers and officers of any rank can write on leadership, and be appreciated for what they are doing. Leaders, after all, recognize and reward the successes of others.

In my own practice as a soldier-writer, I have tried to pursue the centre's objectives. The end is important—the sharing of knowledge. But the process itself has value. Writing helps me collect and analyze my thoughts. It develops my own "human capital." But most importantly, it creates social capital; it creates a culture of peer support, of leaders supporting their subordinates, that values thinking and exchanging ideas.

Will Meddings is an infantry officer in the Royal Anglican Regiment of the British Army. As well as deploying on operational tours of Iraq and Afghanistan, he has served as an instructor at the Royal Military Academy Sandhurst, and the Infantry Training Centre, Catterick. In 2016, he was one of the founding members of the British Army's Centre for Army Leadership, before going on to head the centre in 2017.

Confessions of a Reformed PME Critic

By Kelly Dunne

"Even junior positions of command require outstanding intellectual qualities for outstanding achievement."—Carl von Clausewitz

Early in my career in the Australian Army, I attended a military parade where medals were presented to some fellow soldiers, in recognition of their commitments to service. I recall thinking, as I listened to the biographies being read out of people who had been serving longer than I had been alive, that "there's no way I will be in the Army that long.'"

Recently, however, another thought occurred to me: There will soon be people joining the Army who were not even born when I was first fumbling my way through initial training. From this, three conclusions sprang forth:

1. I am seriously getting old!

2. Somewhere along the way, without necessarily making a conscious decision, the Army had become for me not just a job, but a professional career path.

3. This journey had demanded greater personal investment to ensure I remained effective and relevant, and could contribute meaningfully to the Australian Defence Force.

For most of my career, my personal approach to Professional Military Education (PME) was not very well-balanced. I skewed toward the subjects in which I was interested, or at which I believed I was good. I felt like a bit of a fraud—many might call it "imposter syndrome"—always fearful that I would be exposed for not knowing enough about topics like strategy, operational art, and military history.

As an Army instructor, I lived in fear of being allocated the military history lesson to deliver. I felt that all it would take was a single question from a trainee history buff to steer the topic off my carefully memorized lesson, and to unravel my professional reputation.

In short, I lived and worked in something of a self-limiting bubble, attempting to convince myself that professional writing and reading weren't essential parts of being a good leader and proficient military officer.

In 2017, however, I executed a decisive 180-degree maneuver. A close friend had started a professional development blog for service members. A number of peers were involved with other emerging defense forums. Perhaps most importantly, key Army leaders were driving the conversation about the importance of reform in professional military education.

On this shifting cultural terrain, I was assigned to a team tasked with enhancing the intellectual edge of the Australian Army.

I was thrust into a world where reading Clausewitz and Sun Tzu, meeting with prominent historians and university professors, and designing content for a PME website was part of the job description.

Initially, many conversations with academics went over my head. I relied on taking copious notes during meetings, later consulting my good friend Mr. Google to translate what I'd heard. I soon learned, for example, that casual conversation references to "Lawry" and "Hew" referred to the works of Lawrence Freedman and Hew Strachan, experts in strategy and military history in the world. My new job had unlocked a whole new world—I was out of my PME comfort zone, and I loved it.

One of my favorite lines from *The Enlightened Soldier* by Charles Edward White stresses why military professionals must read and write:

> For [Gerhard Johann David von] Scharnhorst, the profession of arms was not just a craft or technique (which is primarily mechanical) or an art (which requires unique talent or ability). It was instead an extraordinarily complex intellectual skill requiring comprehensive study and training.

Why do we write? We write because we must. If we are serious about the profession of arms, and about doing what is necessary to defeat the enemy in war, then we must be committed to the pursuit of lifelong learning. We may not love every moment of it, there may be times where it is tedious or uninteresting, and it will certainly be challenging. Still, we read and write the same way we learn to fight—and we always fight to win.

Kelly Dunne has served more than 17 years in the Royal Australian Army Medical Corps. She has served as commander of the 8th Close Health Company and adjutant of the Royal Military College–Duntroon, and has operational service in the Middle East and South Pacific. She has a Master of Emergency and Disaster Management, a Master of Military and Defence Studies, and is an associate fellow of the Australasian College of Health Services Management. She is currently the military assistant Head Military Strategic Commitments. Follow her on Twitter: @KellyDunne54

Writing as a Catalyst for Change

By Gary M. Klein

My writing journey began in graduate school, before I commissioned as an officer in the U.S. Army. At that time, I wrote to meet academic requirements, but I started to realize the personal benefits of writing.

As a graduate student in chemistry, I started to understand that reading and writing were critical to higher learning. Students had to learn more material than they could access through formal classes. Students had to dedicate time to self-development.

I believe the same challenge exists in the military. The Army develops its leaders through Professional Military Education in the institutional domain, and training and leader development in the operational domain, but soldiers must seize the initiative. Leaders must seek out opportunities for self-development as well.

Graduate school included a similar spectrum of development, from a focus on classes (institutional domain) in the early semesters, to a later focus on research, which is comparable to training (operational domain) and guided self-development. My research required me to read material pertinent to my project, and to write a thesis. This contributed to my first academic publication in *ChemMedChem*. I learned how researching and writing contextualize and synthesize information. I also learned the value of a peer-reviewed publication process; how sharing information enables group learning. I conditioned my mind to think in terms of questions.; a skill that continues to benefit me today as a military officer.

After my initial article in 2008, I did not publish again until 2011, following graduation from the U.S. Army's Cavalry Leader's Course (CLC). One instructor encouraged me to write, and I discovered a topic that interested me: reconnaissance and security orders. Throughout class, students discussed different ways to develop and write orders. We began most discussions with doctrine, which some perceived as prescriptive. We quickly discovered, however, we could use doctrine descriptively to convey new ideas.

One example involved how leaders could develop reconnaissance tasks and purposes using Named Areas of Interest (NAI) and Commander's Critical Information Requirements (CCIR) in place of doctrinal tasks and purposes. This technique is not explicitly described in doctrine, but it supports the primary function of reconnaissance: to improve the commander's understanding, visualization, and decision-making.

Following graduation, I ended up working with one of my instructors to draft an article for *Armor Magazine*. I wanted to share our insights with our branch community—fellow leaders and soldiers. Ranger School had promoted a similar idea: Graduates were encouraged to use what they learned to lead and accomplish their mission, but also to share their expertise with their fellow soldiers back at their respective units. Writing is a multiplier.

Another example: Writing a *Strategy Bridge* article enabled me to share ideas gleaned from a temporary duty (TDY) experience at the 2015 Captains Solarium. This event was designed as a forum for junior officers to provide feedback to senior leaders, but also served as a broadening and learning opportunity. While the solarium included only 100 participants, through my writing, I was able to share that experience with a larger audience.

Writing creates opportunities to coach, teach, and mentor others through co-authorship as well. When I was a Headquarters and Headquarters Troop commander, for example, I co-authored articles with my medical officer. Working in partnership creates a catalyst for bringing together new insights, expertise, and experiences. The challenge is to develop a process that integrates the thoughts of both authors, to ensure a consistent narrative.

One way to approach a co-authored project is to brainstorm collectively a thesis and supporting points or subtopics. Then, assign authors to each of these parts. Designate a lead editor, who will be responsible for integrating the pieces and ensuring a consistent narrative. To facilitate continued discussion and build consensus, the lead editor should share assembled drafts frequently. Co-authoring articles is an outstanding way to broaden learning, build relationships, and mentor aspiring authors.

Writing is an exceptional way for soldiers and leaders to advance their own professional development. It forces them to synthesize ideas, ask questions, and think about topics more broadly or deeply while enabling them to contribute to the profession. Working alone or with co-authors, military writers can help others create the conditions for success. Writing is a catalyst for positive change.

Gary M. Klein is an officer in the U.S. Army. His military assignments include tank platoon leader; troop commander; Observer-Coach, Trainer (OC/T); Maneuver Captain's Career Course instructor; and squadron operations officer. His civilian education includes a graduate degree from the University of Illinois–Chicago and an undergraduate degree from the University of Michigan, Ann Arbor. His work has been published in Armor Magazine *and* The Strategy Bridge. *He is a member of the Military Writers Guild. He currently lives at Fort Bliss, Texas with his wife Andrea and their boys.*

The Quill that Bridges the Divide

By Dale R. Wilson Sr.

As a veteran of the U.S. Navy, I have a great deal of respect for those who serve our military, and those who lead them. Over the years, I've become fascinated with the subject of military leadership. I've immersed myself in the study of great military leaders and strategists throughout history, such as Napoleon Bonaparte, Carl von Clausewitz, Dwight D. Eisenhower, George S. Patton Jr., William "Bull" Halsey Jr., Chester W. Nimitz Sr., Douglas MacArthur, and H. Norman Schwarzkopf. Jr., among others. I began a collection of books to study the fundamentals of military leadership.

One such book, *The Challenge of Command: Reading for Military Excellence* by Roger H. Nye, emphasizes the attainment of military excellence through reading. Written to help men and women prepare for positions of higher responsibility in the armed forces, it discusses various facets of military leadership, then offers a reading list for each one.

From my own research and reading, I have come to the conclusion that there's a correlation between military leadership and corporate leadership. The line drawn between those who lead military organizations and those who manage civilian enterprises shouldn't exist. There is common ground among those who lead people into battle, and those who lead companies and teams of people competing for market share. Leadership of people is universal.

I decided to create a WordPress blog to write about my views. In December 2011, I launched *Command Performance Leadership* to discuss military and corporate leadership competencies, as well as principled values, virtues, and wisdom that can guide military and business professionals to victory. The intent of my writing is to apply experience and knowledge from military leadership to corporate contexts.

As a companion to the blog, to bring people into interactive discussions about organizational leadership, I started a LinkedIn group, Command Performance–Military and Corporate Leadership.

Across these platforms, I sought to create content that was educational and inspiring, and to spark dialogue across military and civilian domains. I've been fortunate to engage service members from around the world, as well as corporate leaders. Notable authors and fellow bloggers have also joined the conversation. I am proud to have earned a place among this community of international writers who advocate, collaborate, and promote military writing in all its forms.

The fine men and women of the U.S. military live by and are committed to core values, such as loyalty, duty, respect, selfless service, honor, integrity, and personal courage. Such principles can help both individuals and organizations gain confidence, earn respect, and foster loyal cooperation among followers, peers, and superiors.

I'm committed to writing with the quill that bridges the divide that may exist between the civilian and military communities. Through my writing, I attempt to contribute to the dialogue in an effort to educate, clarify, and inspire. Ultimately, I hope that my writing will find its way into the eyes of those who may have doubts, or are not completely aware of the enormous talents and qualities that our military men and women possess.

It is why I write.

Dale R. Wilson Sr. served in the U.S. Navy from 1986 to 1994. He is a business manager in the private sector. He hosts the Command Performance Leadership *blog, which discusses the synergies between military and corporate leadership competencies, and ties experience and knowledge from military leadership to its application in a corporate environment. He is a member of the Military Writers Guild. Follow him on Twitter: @5StarLeadership*

Operationalizing "The Field Grade Leader"

By Josh Powers

I write for the leader serving their first tour on staff—likely, a new major preparing to become a battalion operations officer (S3) or executive officer (XO). When I held such an assignment, I did my best to "coach" lieutenants and captains in the shop. I treasured opportunities to interact with and learn from these young leaders. When I departed the unit, I wanted to find a way to continue to engage in professional dialogue.

I started to write, about topics such as management and organizational systems. Soon, I began to explore comparisons between business and military practices. I distributed content on social media, and eventually created a platform for my work on a webpage called *The Field Grade Leader*.

Subscribers to this forum may not actually need me, but I certainly need them. I rely on this audience to hold me accountable, and to motivate me to engage and expand my own thinking and writing.

I try to write every day. Most mornings, I am awake at a time that feels unnatural yet efficient, an old habit from years of early mornings. With a cup of hot coffee in hand, I reflect on the previous day's notes. I might read a few business or military articles. I capture some fragments in a separate section of my notebook, with pages reserved for reflection, thoughts, and lessons-learned. Then, I consider these elements in the light of this question: Which of these thoughts could benefit someone else?

Many junior leaders perceive the Army as "zero defect," where mistakes are unacceptable or seen as weakness. I once shared these fears. Now, I write to demonstrate to others that not having all of the answers is OK.

Writing is an opportunity for me to give back to my profession, while improving myself as a leader. My writing stems from personal shortcomings and professional failures, and growing from those experiences. I hope that my writing contributes to a broader discussion, and that it results in successes for other professionals in the force.

Josh Powers is an infantry officer in the U.S. Army and founder of The Field Grade Leader, *a blog focused on organizational leadership in the military. He holds an undergraduate degree in history from the Virginia Military Institute, Lexington, Va. and a graduate degree in military arts and science through the U.S. Army's School of Advanced Military Studies. Powers is currently assigned to the U.S. Army Pacific Headquarters in Hawaii, where he serves as an operational planner. He is a member of the Military Writers Guild.*

Writing to Think: Writing Intentionally for Professional Development

By Ryan Hilger

It felt like a solid punch to the gut. After a series of major issues onboard, the squadron commander made the difficult decision to relieve USS GREAT STATE's commanding officer a mere four months from a scheduled deployment to the European theater of operations. I had been onboard as the chief engineer for just over two months.

More than a year-and-a-half before I set foot on the submarine, I had begun preparing for the role of department head. I would be directly responsible for six junior officers and more than 100 sailors in five divisions, a nuclear reactor and its associated propulsion plant, and nearly all of the hull, mechanical, and electrical systems onboard a billion-dollar warship. I would also be trusted to lead a watch team of more than 20 sailors each day at sea, with the safety of the entire crew in our hands, to execute the national tasking at hand.

Early on, I vowed to be the best department head and submarine officer that I could be. My preparations centered on my small group of mentors, and my love of reading and writing.

The short ride out on the tug to report aboard USS GREAT STATE was a chaotic mixture of emotions. In the few weeks since my orders had arrived, I had learned more about the world into which I would be stepping. It was going to be a crucible—a "defining moment in my career," as one of my mentors would later tell me.

When they had heard my pending assignment, friends and colleagues winced and wished me luck. The scuttlebutt was that GREAT STATE was struggling. The boat had passed its inspections thus far during the year, but doing so with a passing grade had required a herculean effort on the part of the crew—and some outside assistance. The material condition of the boat was poor. Morale was the lowest on the waterfront, as evidenced by the frequency at which sailors were leaving GREAT STATE. The previous engineer had been detached for medical reasons for a few months; I would be relieving the squadron engineer. Plans called for the ship to deploy to the European theater of operations in six months.

A senior commander at the submarine squadron specifically requested that I meet with him to discuss the challenges that I would soon face. Only a few colleagues related positive stories to me, and then, only about my engineering department master chief. At least, I thought, it sounded like I had a solid right-hand man to help run the engineering department.

I once read an article that would fundamentally change the way I approached reading and writing for professional development. In the article, titled "The Relevance of History to the Military Profession: An American Marine's View," retired U.S. Marine Lt. Gen. Paul K. Van Riper related how reading shaped his growth as a commander at all levels. The article spurred me to action. I spent time reflecting on my strengths and weaknesses, and devised a succinct plan to help me shore up my deficiencies, enhance my strengths, and further challenge my mind. I continually whittled down the list, added new material, and assessed how these books were going to help develop me.

While on shore tour prior to being assigned to USS GREAT STATE, a key mentor had also encouraged to write professionally—not for publication, but to hone my thinking. The value of mentors can't often be tied to a singular event, but is cumulative over the years of the relationship. Often, they do not provide direct answers to problems, but prompt young leaders to think critically by asking the right questions.

Our conversations would occur every few weeks, each lasting about an hour. Those conversations forced me to think critically about my objectives as a future department head: What does success look like? What standards do I want to uphold? How would I describe my role as a department head? How would I assess and improve my future department? My mentor forced me to write my answers—spoken answers would not do—and to refine my thinking through multiple revisions. It took months of thinking, writing, discussing, and revising to finally arrive at concise statements.

I ended up with a page-and-a-half centered around four themes, each with a half-dozen or so precisely crafted supporting points. It was not a trivial exercise. It forced me to think critically about each questions. I couldn't just wave them off with shallow answers. Writing to think was an invaluable contribution to my development.

Figuratively gasping for breath—we'd been working 100-hour weeks aboard GREAT STATE when our commander had been relieved—I reached back out to my network of mentors.

Our conversations were not usually long, but my mentors delivered good questions and advice. They saw through the fog of issues, and helped me focus and refocus my actions. They not only helped me weather the tumult now engulfing GREAT STATE, but also to emerge as a stronger leader, ready to lead GREAT STATE out of the doldrums. Above all else, they helped me continue to objectively and daily assess whether or not we were meeting the required standards.

After the first few days as the engineer on an unfamiliar class of submarine in an unfamiliar homeport, I realized that most of what I had done to prepare myself had not directly prepared me, at all, to lead in such a challenging environment. I took solace in a well-worn passage from President Dwight Eisenhower to the National Defense Executive Reserve Committee in 1957:

> Plans are worthless, but planning is everything. There is a very great distinction because when you are planning for an emergency you must start with this one thing: the very definition of "emergency" is that it is unexpected, therefore it is not going to happen the way you are planning. So, the first thing you do is to take all the plans off the top shelf and throw them out the window and start once more. But if you haven't been planning you can't start to work, intelligently at least. That is the reason it is so important to plan, to keep yourselves steeped in the character of the problem that you may one day be called upon to solve—or to help to solve.

I kept reading whenever I could find a spare moment, but my writing tapered off. I struggled to even find time to sleep. Slowly, however, our efforts began paying off, and I was able to spare moments to reflect. I realized that all my preparatory thinking and writing—Eisenhower's "planning"—had developed in me the ability to more rapidly process information, and to holistically assess the problems I faced.

Less than seven months after my coming aboard, USS GREAT STATE and I somehow made it onto deployment.

Not long afterwards, I pulled the document out that I had spent months writing and revising. I read it carefully, then read it again. I pulled out a pen and scribbled brief statements in the margins, annotating how I thought I measured up against each of them. Then, I wrote some more, brainstorming what I wanted to do to improve on my identified weak areas. I would repeat this process every few months, talking with my mentors at about the same intervals. Most importantly, toward the end of my GREAT STATE tour, I began to use the same techniques to help further develop my junior officers professionally, just as my mentor had done with me.

Ryan Hilger is an engineering duty officer and former submarine officer in the U.S. Navy. He has a broad education, completing his undergraduate work in political science and history at the University of Kansas; and mechanical engineering, anti-submarine warfare, and regional security studies at the U.S. Naval Postgraduate School, Monterey, Calif. His articles have appeared in United States Naval Institute Proceedings, The Submarine Review, InterAgency Journal (IAJ), *the Center for International Maritime Security (CIMSEC), and* War on the Rocks. *He and his wife, Heather, and two children, Charlotte and Henry, live where the Navy sends them.*

The Arts of War
& Writing

Dreaming of Ishtar
In the Land of Two Rivers

By Jonathan Baxter

I knew I would come back to her, eventually.

The Etihad Airways flight delivered me into Baghdad International Airport, and I was back home. When I left Iraq on my last military deployment there in 2009, I had the feeling it was only temporary, and I would eventually wind my way back to the Land of Two Rivers.

It was weird this time, entering the country three years later as a civilian. I managed to get through customs and collect my bags without too much incident. A private security team was waiting to drive me from the airport to the U.S. embassy, where I would start my new job as a member of the embassy's static security element.

We pulled out of the airport, and I blinked as we drove past what had been the U.S. "Victory" and "Slayer" base complexes during the American occupation. Three years earlier, the land outside the airport had been a sprawling metropolis of Containerized Housing Unit (CHU) trailers. Street after street of the white boxes had run amid a labyrinth of concrete T-wall barriers and earth-filled Hesco fences. The American bases had run up to and around the former pleasure palaces of the Baath party members, whose opulent mansions had overlooked beautiful man-made lakes.

"They drained the lakes, too," I observed, as we made our way out of the airport's perimeter. The concrete barriers remained, but everything else was a wasteland. Acres of weeds stretched up to the base of "Commo Hill." The tiny promontory, now empty, had once bristled with the antennae from the surrounding bases. Funny how much a place could change in only three short years.

There had also been many changes in my life since my last trip to Iraq. I had done two trips to Afghanistan with the military, and then separated in 2011 to seek my fortune in the "real world." That hadn't really panned out as I expected. I quickly found out that being a former non-commissioned officer with the 75th Ranger Regiment hadn't made me a shoe-in for premium jobs as I imagined it would. It did, however, open doors in the private security contracting community. Here I was, back in the world I had briefly left behind.

Going in, I didn't know much about security contracting. I had seen the news footage of the tattooed, steroided guys with M4s and cargo pants, and

I fancied I was embarking on some grand adventure with some elite, paramilitary outfit. I was rapidly shown the error of my thinking.

The equipment I was issued was old and mismatched. My coworkers were mixed bags of experience and skill sets. Some were seasoned combat vets; others were ex-cops with no military backgrounds. Our supervisors, Department of State Regional Security Officers (RSO), were comparable to second lieutenants in the military ... but less competent and without the military experience.

The job was about as high-speed as everything else. We did essentially nothing, 8- to 12-hour shifts at a time. Occasionally, our RSO superiors would decide they needed some positive bullet points for their end-of-tour evaluations, so they would concoct circus-style drills for us to perform.

The days dripped by like water drops from cave stalactites. In our ready room, we surfed the Internet for hours. We lifted weights. Car bombs detonated in the city outside our walls. I read *Heart of Darkness* and found some resonance in the story of an expat making an interior journey in a savage, absurd world. We conducted silly drills for the benefit of the RSOs. The civil war raged in neighboring Syria. We got "spun-up" to break up an embassy bar fight between two women. I re-read *Heart of Darkness*.

I have never done time in prison, but I imagine it to be a similar experience. Spending months at a time behind heavily fortified walls with no view of the outside world, and no purposeful tasks to focus the mind. While in the military, I had spent months at overseas Forward Operating Bases, but there we'd interrupted the monotony by rolling out on missions almost every night. Here, there were no such diversions from the daily routine of chow, duty shift, chow, gym, chow, sleep.

The other difference between this job and the military was that I was no longer special. I certainly didn't feel elite anymore, as I walked around in the contractor "duty uniform" of beige flight suit and drop-leg holster. I looked like a tactical Egon Spengler from the movie *Ghostbusters*. More importantly, I wasn't part of something bigger than myself. The brotherhood that was the cornerstone of my military service was not there. I was very much alone this time, exiled from family and friends in the states, trying to sustain a long-distance relationship with my girlfriend, and working a mindless job that gave me too much time to think.

Somewhere in there, I started writing again. I had dabbled in writing since my third deployment. Reading and writing poetry were certainly not pastimes I had advertised among my fellow Rangers ... for obvious reasons. Yet, I have always felt poetry to be the most immediate of the literary forms. It was a vehicle in which I could articulate some of the more nuanced emotions I had been experiencing overseas. I had memorialized a friend in "Death of a Ranger." I had written about the timelessness of Iraq in "Back to Babylon," and a conversation with Death in "The Jester Skull."

Now, on this new job, with nothing but time and memories on my hands, the words started flowing again. I wrote the first of several meditations on Ishtar, the Mesopotamian goddess of love and war. Unlike the Greek and Roman gods, who represented only one of those attributes, she embodied both. Love and war. Sex and violence. She was the apotheosis as well as the eroticization of combat, and in my mind, she became everything I missed about being in the military: The night raids. The helicopters. The electric rings that would glow around the rotor blades. The way fields and villages looked under night-vision. The smells of cooking oil and roasted lamb. The sound of metal gates being eased open slowly. The rhythmic barking of stray dogs while the assault squad quietly emplaced the breaching charge. The calm before the storm.

I wrote to make some meaning of the time I was losing. I would never get back the hours of my life I wasted on that stupid contract. The hours I spent sitting in a ready room or driving aimlessly around the embassy compound. The long-distance arguments with my girlfriend via Skype. The year-and-a-half of my life I spent on that gig, until I got picked up for a better contract. I wrote to avoid it all being a complete waste.

I wrote about the car bombs going off in the city outside. I wrote about the few glimpses of the city I could get beyond our concrete walls. I wrote about the Ferris wheel outside our compound, and how it looked at night. I wrote about the sculpted archway of scimitars I could see from the roof of one of the embassy apartments. I wrote about the way the city lights reflected off the Tigris River, and the way the plumes of flame ascended from a distant oil refinery at night. I wrote about my insomnia, and the difficulty of sleeping during the day after a night shift. I wrote about boredom. I wrote about loneliness. I wrote to give my life a meaning that it did not have at the time.

Eventually, I left that contract and Iraq. I watched in the news as ISIS launched their blitzkrieg attack and overran whole parts of the country. I thought about the years America had spent in that country and the blood, sweat and tears that had been poured into those deserts. I thought about the years I spent in that country. I thought about the wasteland of weeds by Baghdad International Airport. In my mind, I saw the faded graffiti on the T-wall barriers, the fading emblems of the 101st Airborne Division, the 82nd Airborne Division, the 10th Mountain Division—the Americans who had come, done their time, and gone home, many in flag-draped boxes.

Violence still continues in the Land of Two Rivers, as it has for millennia. The occupiers come and go: Sumerians, Babylonians, Persians, Greeks, Arabs, Mongols, Ottomans, British, Americans ... The land endures, the Tigris and Euphrates still flow to the sea, Ishtar still bides over the land where they once worshipped her. There are those of us who keep the faith still.

JONATHAN BAXTER

Our policymakers struggle to find solutions that would validate the time we spent there. For me, I wrote to try to find a meaning from my time there. If I couldn't find a meaning, I'd make one. I hope this generation of veterans will continue coming forward with artwork from their experiences. I think that's the closest we'll come to find meaning or sense or beauty from that land.

Jonathan Baxter spent six years in the U.S. Army with the entirety of his service with the 75th Ranger Regiment. His first volume of poetry, The Ghosts of Babylon *is a reflection on his experiences in Iraq and Afghanistan. His poetry was also anthologized in* In Love... & War: The Anthology of Poet Warriors. *He continues to deploy to the Middle East as a private security contractor, and writes under a pseudonym. His website can be found at www.mercenarypoet.com*

"It" Shoots: Zen and Writing

By Eric Chandler

A week before the winter solstice, I pulled my skis out of the back of my truck. I walked through the gap in the fence to the trailhead. I stripped off the rest of the day like layers of clothing. I put the skis down on the snow, stepped into the bindings, and started to cross-country ski.

I take it for granted. I've been skiing since I was 2. The rhythms and movements of skiing feel like home. Unlike running, cross-country skiing is a sport with zero impact. Kind of like compressing and releasing a spring. No pounding of the pavement with each stride. You move by gliding. I sense the trees pass by. I adapt to the terrain as it tips up or down. Turns left or right. Sometimes, I get into a meditative state (interrupted by my wheezing, but even that, at least, is rhythmic). I don't think about anything. When I come out of that mode, I sometimes have no idea where I am. I forget which trail system I'm on. Even what month it is. I get mildly disoriented. Maybe I just admitted I have early onset dementia.

The disorientation is a marker. Not an Alzheimer's symptom, but a sign that I've been in a desired frame of mind: "I'm skiing" is transformed into "I *am* skiing." There's no separation between me and the snow and my poles and my boots and my skis. It's a cornball thing to say, but it's everything, all at once, at the same time.

In high school, I attended a clinic for people who wanted to try biathlon. That's the Olympic sport that combines cross-country skiing with rifle marksmanship. I was a good skier. I was a good shot. I thought if I put them together, I could be somebody. An Olympian there named Lyle Nelson told me I had potential. So, I spent my life savings on a biathlon rifle. Now, I had to become one with a rifle, in addition to my skis, boots, and poles.

In biathlon, you ski into the rifle range and try to calm yourself as your heart hammers in your rib cage. You take the rifle off your back, load a magazine with five rounds and settle in to fire at one of the five black circles 50 meters away from your shooting position. When you hit the target, there's immediate feedback: When the bullet hits the target, it flips a hinged white metal cover over the black target. There's a reassuring clank as the black turns to white and you chamber the next round.

In marksmanship, you're supposed to slowly squeeze the trigger so you're surprised by the rifle shot. For me, when I was shooting well, the shot was very surprising. I heard the clank of a successful shot halfway through working the bolt for the next shot. Sometimes. OK, it was rare. But it was the feeling I wanted every time I was on the shooting range in a biathlon. It was the same feeling as forgetting where I was while skiing.

By the time I went to pilot training for Uncle Sam, I had already spent years trying to grow nerve endings into inanimate objects like skis and rifles. It was time to become one with airplanes. Eventually, I went to F-16 school. I flew the Viper for the next 23 years. You bound yourself to the ejection seat with a lap belt and shoulder harness. You plugged your G-suit into the airplane to keep blood in your brain. You plugged your comm cord into the airplane so you could speak and listen. You plugged your oxygen hose into the airplane so it could help you breathe. You plugged an umbilical into the airplane so your helmet-mounted sight fed you information no matter where you looked. In his memoir *Fighter Pilot*, Robin Olds wrote something that rings true after you spend so much time connected to one piece of machinery:

> Man merges with machine; he doesn't simply use it. You don't climb into an aircraft and sit down. You strap the machine to your butt, become one with it. Hydraulic fluid is your blood; titanium, steel, and aluminum, your bones; electrical currents, your nerves; the instruments, an extension of your senses; fuel, the food; engine, the power; the control surfaces, the muscle. You are the heart, yours is the will, yours the reasoning power. You are something more than earthbound man. You are augmented and expanded by the miracle of the machine. You are tied to it physically and you are part of it emotionally.

"Yours is the will," indeed. The machine made anything possible. Flying was easy. It was using the machine for combat that was hard. Knowing all the tactics. Knowing all your weapons. Applying the knowledge in practice. Running a tactic properly with a formation of four airplanes, eight airplanes, even as a mission commander of 80 airplanes (not just F-16s) took a lifetime of training. I can only hope I was at least average.

I repeatedly think of one day in Afghanistan. My two-ship formation was supporting ground troops on a Close Air Support (CAS) mission, as we did on every sortie on that deployment. My wingman and I were yo-yo to the tanker, which meant we took turns going alone to get air-refueled so the troops on the ground had at least one of us overhead at all times. I returned to the radio frequency after getting gas. I flew back over the river valley where my wingman was in the final stages of setting up a strafing run with his 20mm cannon. I wanted to get into position to support him, but the weather and the terrain made it difficult. We were under a cloud deck that had ragged bottoms and was barely high enough to safely start our attack.

There were banks of clouds, some open weather when you could see green orchards below, and then more gray fingers reaching down, obscuring the view of the mountaintops, of my wingman, of the target. When he started his strafe pass, I was so concerned about running into a hill or going back into the clouds by accident that I didn't see his attack.

The reason I remember this specific moment is because I felt like a spirit. My only concern was for my wingman and the ground troops. To quickly understand the scenario by listening to the radio and using my avionics. To fly the airplane into position to support and run a follow-on attack, if necessary. To not fly into a mountaintop beside the river valley. I was the rain. I was all the voices on the radio. I was my eyes, searching for the enemy position. I didn't feel tired. I felt nothing. I felt completely unaware of myself while trying to be aware of everything else. There was no "I." Up to this point in my life, the skiing, the shooting, and even the plain-old flying were just gateway drugs. This was up a notch.

I just finished watching episodes of the *Vietnam War* television documentary series by Ken Burns. Karl Marlantes, author of *Matterhorn*, spoke about his experiences. He said something that resonated with me:

> Combat is like that. You're scared. You're terrified. You're miserable. But then the fighting starts. And suddenly everything is at stake: Your life, your friends' lives. It's almost transcendence. Because you're no longer a person. You lose that sense. You're just the platoon.

Afghanistan was my last combat deployment, in the last year of my military career. On my very last sortie there, my last venture into combat, I took a young wingman from the unit replacing us out on his very first combat sortie. I sit here four years after that flight and I have mixed feelings. I want to write about my experiences in war, but at the same time, I want to move on. Korean War fighter pilot James Salter pretty accurately describes this sentiment in his memoir *Gods of Tin*:

> When I returned to domestic life I kept something to myself, a deep attachment—deeper than anything I had known–to all that had happened. I had come very close to achieving the self that is based on the risking of everything, going where others would not go, giving what they would not give. Later I felt I had not done enough, had been too reliant, too unskilled. I had not done what I set out to do and might have done. I felt contempt for myself, not at first but as time passed, and I ceased talking about those days, as if I had never known them. But it had been a great voyage, the voyage, probably, of my life.

ERIC CHANDLER

I write for many of the reasons we all do. I write to figure things out. I write to create a record of what has happened to me. I do this with most of my outdoor-related writing. It acts as a long, drawn-out diary entry about my family. (I'll need it so I can read it later when I'm old and drooling into a gin and tonic at the cabin, unable to remember my own name.) I write to bear witness. To try to share my awe. To try to influence opinions. This isn't the whole list.

The horsepower for this list comes from feeling of being temporarily immortal. I write because, when I do, I don't notice the passage of time. I often sit back in my chair after typing and realize I haven't moved for an hour. I make old-man sounds as I rise to my feet and run to the bathroom because, it turns out, I really have to pee. What I am and what I'm trying to write are all the same. Even editing a completed draft has that effect on me. I probably shouldn't admit that last part.

It's the same feeling I had on the ski trail a few weeks ago. And when I heard the bullet hit the target. And when I flew the F-16. Lately, I'm chasing the ultimate high: Getting "the feeling" from writing about having that same feeling while flying in combat. It's like a double espresso: Transcendence while trying to explain transcendence. For me, writing is a compulsion that happens to have a long list of useful side effects.

When I was in high school and first getting into biathlon, I managed to find *Zen in the Art of Archery* by German philosopher Eugen Herrigel. From 1924 to 1929, he studied Kyudo, the Japanese martial art of archery under Awa Kenzô. Herrigel had a hard time. Herrigel wrote:

One day I asked the Master, "How can the shot be loosed if 'I' do not do it?"

"'It' shoots," he replied ...

"And who or what is this 'It'?"

"Once you have understood that you will have no further need of me. And if I tried to give you a clue at the cost of your own experience, I would be the worst of teachers and deserve to be sacked! So let's stop talking about it and go on practicing."

For years, I had a close-up photograph of an eye looking into the rear sight of a biathlon rifle. I taped it inside the door of my locker. At the bottom, I wrote the words: *"It" shoots*. A handful of times in my life, I briefly grasped what "it" was. Skiing. Shooting. Flying. Fighting.

And now, writing.

Let's stop talking about it and go on practicing.

174

Eric Chandler is a former U.S. Air Force fighter pilot, outdoor sports writer, and author of military-themed poetry, non-fiction, and fiction. Chandler is a three-time winner in the Col. Darron L. Wright Memorial Writing Award competition administered annually by the literary journal Line of Advance. *Among other works, he authored the 2017 poetry collection* Hugging This Rock: Poems of Earth & Sky, Love & War. *In 2018, in Northeastern Minnesota, Chandler directed a "Bridging the Gap" writing workshop to help address the civil-military divide. He is a member of Lake Superior Writers and the Military Writers Guild. He is a husband, father, and commercial airline pilot who cross-country skis as fast as he can in Duluth, Minn. Follow him on Twitter: @ShmoF16*

I Left the CIA and Wrote a Satire of the War on Terror

By Alex Finley

Imagine if *Zero Dark Thirty* were funny.

There is a scene in *Zero Dark Thirty*—the 2012 film directed by Kathryn Bigelow and written by Mark Boal—where Maya, the intrepid CIA officer intent on hunting down Osama bin Laden, goes to her boss's door every day and writes a number in marker on his window. The number represents how many days it has been since she asked for a response to her operational plan to get the terrorist leader. She is intense, eager to move on with her plan, and angry that any response from Washington is taking so long.

What we don't see is what people at CIA Headquarters were doing while Maya was wringing her hands and making her boss crazy.

Sure, there were 7th-floor gatherings and inter-agency principles and deputies meetings and situation room huddles. And my guess is that the response cable they finally cobbled together required at least 32 people to coordinate, and of those 32 people, at least six were standing in line at Starbucks to get a latte before attending an Amish quilt exhibit down in the atrium, and at least two others were on flex-time or were at an off-site doing team-building activities.

I was once a CIA officer working on counterterrorism-related issues. For years, I helped process electronic paper in a global game—with life or death consequences—that was being played out to an official narrative on the world stage. But, sitting in my cubicle, the scene behind the magic curtain was so much absurdity: The Wizard at the end of the cable-strewn brick road was actually a dysfunctional old bureaucrat.

One day, just after something blew up in Yemen (it is a sign of the times that I no longer recall what, exactly, blew up), a manager in the office approached a case officer at his desk. The manager asked the case officer—at that point a 12-year veteran of the Agency's Counterterrorism Center—why he hadn't yet filled out a survey on Agency employee satisfaction.

I thought the case officer's head was going to explode. He managed to keep his cool just long enough to say to the manager, "The terrorists aren't filling out any fucking forms."

Then, he walked out.

And I thought: What if terrorists *did* have to fill out forms? That would be hilarious.

When I left the Agency, I pulled together the administrative ridiculousness I had experienced and witnessed myself, combined it with some pretty great anecdotes from friends and colleagues, and transposed that bureaucratic system on the terrorists. Indeed, what if terrorists had to fill out forms and go through the same bureaucratic rigmarole our Intelligence Community must go through?

And thus I began to write *Victor in the Rubble*, a satire of the CIA and the War on Terror.

The novel was my catharsis, my release from the whiplash incurred on the Agency in those tumultuous post-9/11 years. It hadn't taken long, after the initial shock of the attacks wore off, to fall into a rather mundane and bureaucratic approach to fighting terrorism. We increased the size of the Intelligence Community, but also increased process: inter-agency coordination, cross-agency cooperation, inter-office value-added up-ramping, to the point where we reached "over-strength." (This presumably meant we had too many people, as evidenced by the appearance of new and smaller cubicles in every inch of empty space at headquarters. I half-expected to find an office like that in the movie *Being John Malkovich*, where we would all have to hunch over to sit in our cubes.)

There were boxes to check. Cables to format. Lines of code to rewrite when the Directorate of Operations became the National Clandestine Service (nothing changed functionally, but the name change resulted in new letterhead, a new logo, and rewritten e-mail codes. It all had to be changed again a few years later, when Director John Brennan reverted the name back to the Directorate of Operations). We settled into a routine, seemingly thinking that as long as we were really busy, we were probably doing what needed to be done.

In the end, for all its smoke and mirrors, CIA is a lot like any other large organization.

I had seen officers deal with the stresses of the job and the inanities of the bureaucracy in different ways. Some withdrew into themselves. Others drank the Kool-Aid. Some switched to work on other topics, pleased not to have to perform traces on yet another person named Mohammed variant Mohamad variant Muhammed variant Muhamad.

I chose to write a satire about it.

The narrative of *Victor in the Rubble* pits a counterterrorism officer against a West African terrorist. While each tries to outsmart the other, their own organizations' respective bureaucracies keep getting in the way. They soon realize they actually have a common enemy: red tape.

There was certainly a precedent for using satire to deal with these issues. Matt Parker and Trey Stone set the tone (and a high bar) in 2004 with *Team America: World Police*, which used Fuck-Yeah puppets saving the mother-fucking day from terrorists (while simultaneously destroying everything around them). The satirical paper *The Onion* forayed into jihadi territory with its 2007 article "After 5 Years in U.S., Terrorist Cell Too Complacent to Carry Out Attack." The article outlined several reasons the terrorist cell decided it could wait to bring apocalyptic showers of fire to the infidels, including an unexpired free subscription to Netflix, and the fact that the attack was supposed to take place at 5 in the morning, but Starbucks doesn't open until 6.

Nowadays, satire as a means for coping with the bureaucracy of the military and intelligence industrial complex is everywhere. The *Duffel Blog* is written by military folks who make fun of their own bureaucracy and turf battles. (A favorite has the Coast Guard launching a GoFundMe campaign to help with its budget woes.) I've built up a portfolio of articles poking fun at the terrorists and our response, including a U.S. government plan to defeat terrorists by dropping on top of them all the reports we've written about how to defeat them.

Much like the antagonist terrorist in *Victor in the Rubble*, today's terrorists seem to be facing more bureaucratic hurdles, including tinkering with logos, and administering an increasing work force of faceless bureaucrats filling out forms. Let's hope ISIS and al-Qaeda, like so many large organizations before them, bureaucratize themselves to paralysis.

Alex Finley is a former officer of the CIA's Directorate of Operations, where she served in West Africa and Europe. Before becoming a bureaucrat living large off the system, she chased puffy white men around Washington, D.C. as a member of the wild dog pack better known as the Washington media elite. Her writing has appeared in Slate, Reductress, Funny or Die, Politico, *and other publications. She has spoken to C-SPAN's* Washington Journal, *CBC's* The National, *Sirius XM's* Yahoo! Politics, The Cipher Brief, *the Spy Museum's* SpyCast, *and numerous other media outlets. She is author of two satires of the U.S. Central Intelligence Agency:* Victor in the Rubble *and the sequel* Victor in the Jungle. *Follow her on Twitter:* @AlexZFinley

War Is (Funny as) Hell

By David Abrams

There's nothing funny about war.

Or is there?

Out of the horrible realities of the battlefield—the losses of limb and life, the trauma of watching a friend's life bleed away, the permanent wreckage of the soul—out of all that, is it possible to dredge up a laugh, or even a wry smile?

I think so. And what's more, I think we *need* to laugh at war. Soldiers do it all the time. They laugh during combat as a way to keep themselves and their sanity alive. Dirty jokes, insults, and sarcastic comments abound in the foxhole. To those who've never lain prone in a fighting position, or felt the hot burn of a bullet in the air around their heads, it might seem outrageous, asinine, or insensitive. For the ones whose boots are dug into the mud, however, laughter is essential.

I grew up mocking the military. It was a case of laughing *at* the Army, rather than *with* it. For the first eight years of my life, I lived in two small cities in Pennsylvania. In 4th grade, I moved to an even smaller town in Wyoming. Any military bases were miles away—sometimes, entire states. I don't recall ever seeing an actual person in uniform.

In truth, however, I saw them every day. They lived in black-and-white worlds, marched down grey streets, and sometimes their crispy-creased khakis were fuzzy around the edges. I'm talking, of course, about the television shows I drank down like milk back in the 1960s. In particular, *I Dream of Jeannie* and *Gomer Pyle, U.S.M.C.* These were my first role models: the wound-tight astronaut and U.S. Air Force Capt. Roger Nelson, played by Larry Hagman, who finds a genie in a bottle, and later tries to hide his wish-granting girlfriend from his superiors back at headquarters. There was also Pvt. Pyle, played by Jim Nabors, a sweet-natured and naive gas station attendant from *The Andy Griffith Show*'s town of Mayberry, who joins the U.S. Marines. There, he meets his nemesis, the slow-burn, veins-popping Gunnery Sgt. Vince Carter, played by Frank Sutton, who is also a member of the Wound-Tight Club.

I can still see myself sitting cross-legged in my Batman flannel pajamas on the floor in front of our family television, a floor-model Zenith ornately-clad in thick oak that must have weighed as much as our family sedan. I'd sit there watching slack-jawed country bumpkin Gomer frustrate the hell out of Sgt. Carter with his slow-as-syrup drawl, "Well, golll-ly, Sarge," and

179

I'd laugh and laugh and laugh. Those military leaders had a stick up their asses, and it was fun watching Gomer twist the stick with his bumbling innocence.

Those shows later included *M*A*S*H* and *Hogan's Heroes*, set in a World War II prisoner-of-war camp—a sitcom that never should have worked, but somehow did. You may think Cold War-era television was inordinately polite and patriotic, but with programs like *Gomer Pyle, U.S.M.C.* and *Hogan's Heroes*, it was also subversive. I didn't realize it at the time, but these shows set the stage for the way I always root for the underdog. The little guys (the privates) always got their way while the higher ranks (the officers) came off looking like fools.

When I joined the Army in 1988, I had no inkling of what military life would be like. None of my family members had ever served; my father, uncle, and grandfather—Baptist ministers, all of them—had deferments. I never played with G.I. Joe toys, I didn't read books about war heroes, and I couldn't even have told you the difference between Colonel Sanders and a colonel in the Army. When I entered basic training, I hoped I could pass myself off as a sweet-souled Gomer, and prayed my Sgt. Carter wouldn't be too rough on me.

That was my worldview of the military as my head was shaved and a new uniform was shoved into my arms: That this would be hard, but I could get by with a little laughter now and then. Standing in formation, at least I was smart enough to keep those chuckles inside, and to keep my lips pressed against the twitch of a grin.

The real basic training was nothing like Gomer's boot camp, of course. But, even in the hardest afternoons on the obstacle course, I consoled myself by thinking, *If Pyle could survive this, then I will, too.* Thankfully, none of my drill sergeants could see inside my head.

In my childhood sitcoms, discipline was turned upside-down, creating chaos. Out of that chaos, came comedy. I was determined to continue that tradition throughout my 20-year career with the Army. When the time came for me to deploy to the Middle East in 2005, I carried those jokes with me to Iraq. Literally.

The long packing list issued to me by my superiors in the 3rd Infantry Division included, at the end, "Personal Items." I knew right away what one of those things would be: *Catch-22* by Joseph Heller. My paperback copy was small enough to fit in a cargo pocket, and that's where it went, buttoned up for the journey into war.

Though I'd heard about the 1961 novel before, and had always intended to read it, I still hadn't cracked it open by the time I was packing my duffel bag. I decided there would never be a better time to read it. I liked the juxtaposition of starting a comical critique of war as I was on my way to a Forward Operating Base I imagined was populated with a cast of real-life

Col. Cathcarts, 1st Lt. Milo Minderbinders, and Maj. Major Majors (I wasn't too far off).

As the plane revved its engines and rumbled down the runway in Savannah, Ga., I turned to page 1. By the time we'd reached cruising altitude, Capt. John Yossarian was already naked. In his memorable act of civil disobedience, the bombardier shed his uniform and climbed a tree to watch Snowden's burial service. Snowden had been killed in the mission over Avignon and had bled all over Yossarian, and so the surviving bombardier swears he'll never wear another uniform again.

The bumbling Gomer trips, and the rebellious Yossarian strips. My war heroes, each of them.

I looked around the plane as we flew the 7,000 miles from Georgia to Iraq in the Continental Airlines 777 chartered by the 3rd Infantry Division. Like me, my fellow passengers wore desert-camouflage uniforms. I prayed to God none of them ever took the notion to disrobe and walk around camp naked. By the looks of it, however, there were no Yossarians among us. This was a deadly serious bunch of soldiers, fueled by U.S. President George W. Bush's rhetoric, and—for many of them—the memories of their first times through Iraq two years earlier. It was still Mission Yet to be Accomplished, but by God they were determined to "git 'er done." These were all go-with-the-grain troops.

I seemed to be the lone dissident on the plane. I was heading into combat for the first time and, to get myself in the right mindset, I was also reading *Catch-22*. I had planned it like this: Go to war, read the book which mocked war, survive the war through satire. In truth, Heller doesn't so much poke a satiric finger at war, as much as he does poke the men who make it. It's the war machine that comes under side-splitting scrutiny. The tangles of red tape, the complicated cogs of bureaucracy, the nonsensical rules carried out by battalions of buffoons. I was having deja vu back to my childhood sitcoms.

And now I was flying straight into the eye of that storm of red tape—an unnatural occurrence that, at its greatest failure, could cause my death. Did I want to get out combat duty? I'd be lying if I said "No." Was I about to take off my clothes, or wear a dress like *M*A*S*H*'s Cpl. Klinger? No. I would play the part of an obedient warrior—albeit an anxious one heading into the unknown—and follow orders.

But at the same time, I could be subversive in my own small way. I would read *Catch-22,* and I would not try to hide the cover. I lifted the paperback closer to my face, the blue cover with the dangling red soldier-puppet plain for all to see.

No one seemed to care. The other soldiers on the plane had retreated into the earphones connected to their iPods, their eyes closed to catch the 40 winks they'd have a hard time catching once in Baghdad. Or they sipped their watery Cokes, and watched the in-flight movie (*Meet the Fockers*). Or they stared at the headrest in front of them with glassy, distant eyes.

The inside of the plane had been festooned with red, white, and blue balloons, crepe paper, and drawings from elementary students wishing us the best of luck and to "come home soon after you kill the Iraqis."

It was Jan. 2, 2005 and if any of us had made a resolution beyond "I will come back with all four limbs attached … and maybe kill a few Iraqis along the way," we kept it to ourselves. The plane was quiet as a funeral parlor, until the assistant division commander for maneuver, shedding all military decorum, walked up and down the aisles wearing a cardboard party hat and blowing a noisemaker.

"Hap-peee New Year!" he cried.

Bits of parti-colored confetti flew through the air, settling on our shaved scalps. A few of us grinned out of awkward courtesy, and then went back to staring at the inscrutable pattern on the headrest.

I continued reading *Catch-22*:

> It was a vile and muddy war, and Yossarian could have lived without it—lived forever, perhaps. Only a fraction of his countrymen would give up their lives to win it, and it was not his ambition to be among them. To die or not to die, that was the question. … That men would die was a matter of necessity; *which* men would die, though, was a matter of circumstance and Yossarian was willing to be the victim of anything but circumstance. But that was war.

Was it? Was that the war I was flying toward? Months from now, would I be cradling a Snowden in my arms while he bled all over my uniform?

No. As it turned out, mine was not a vile and muddy war. Unlike most of the others on that chartered jet, I would spend 99.9 percent of my tour of duty safely ensconced in division headquarters on the Forward Operating Base, writing press releases that described the blood-soaked, death-drenched days of those patrolling the city outside the concertina wire. Mine was a war fought in cubicles, cooled by air-conditioners, and leavened with enough downtime so I could read books like *Catch-22*. I was a true "Fobbit," much like the characters I'd later write about in the novel by the same name, a book that opens with the following lines:

> They were Fobbits because, at the core, they were nothing but marshmallow. Crack open their chests and in the space where their hearts should be beating with a warrior's courage and selfless regard, you'd find a pale, gooey center. They cowered like rabbits in their cubicles, busied themselves with PowerPoint briefings to avoid the

hazard of Baghdad's bombs, and steadfastly clung white-knuckled to their desks at Forward Operating Base Triumph. If the FOB was a mother's skirt, then these soldiers were pressed hard against the pleats, too scared to venture beyond her grasp.

Supply clerks, motor pool mechanics, cooks, mail sorters, lawyers, trombone players, logisticians: Fobbits, one and all. They didn't give a shit about appearances. They were all about making it out of Iraq in one piece.

At the time, sitting on the plane, I had no way of knowing I faced a somewhat cushy future with "three hots and a cot." I didn't know if I should expect bullets or bubble baths. But I didn't really care. I'd think my way through this war on my own terms. Besides, marshmallow has always been one of my favorite flavors.

As I read *Catch-22*, war was still the great unknown, the ultimate Fear Factor in my future. Joseph Heller was painting a picture for me of a life filled with equal parts terror and absurdity. Oh boy. I could hardly wait. I didn't finish *Catch-22* during that plane ride. My mind was too knotted with fear and lack of sleep. And there was *Meet the Fockers*, after all. I got as far as The Soldier Who Saw Everything Twice, and decided to give it a rest, gently dog-earing the page. I would come back to Yossarian, Milo Minderbinder, Snowden, Col. Cathcart and Maj. Major Major Major many more times, as I waited in limbo at the division's way-station in Kuwait. Later, I would read another of the books I'd packed in my duffel bag for the deployment—*Don Quixote*—and I would have jumbled dreams in which Yossarian attacked windmills with a 10-foot lance.

Throughout my time in Baghdad, there were continual reminders I was living in a Heller of a war. Going back through my journal now, I read:

U.S. soldiers responded to an explosion in central Baghdad and discovered that two Iraqis had blown themselves up while constructing a car bomb. I banged out a quick, almost giddy press release with the headline "Two terrorists vie for Darwin Award." Col. K____ later said that was inappropriate and we changed it.

On another day, I received a casualty report for a soldier who passed out after being hit with a roadside bomb. The illiterate report-writer claimed the soldier suffered "a loss of conscience." I'm not even going to mention the long e-mail chains, in which generals and colonels issued guidance on which words we could and couldn't use to describe those we fought against. An entire week was consumed with the debate over the term "terrorists" versus "insurgents."

The comedy stew was already bubbling on the front burner in my writer's brain. Halfway through my tour of duty, I had enough material for three *Fobbit* novels. All I had to do was look around. By the end of my year in Iraq, I was convinced *Catch-22* should be mandatory reading for soldiers heading into combat. We need more Yossarians sitting in a tree, naked and cat-calling the bloated and pompous decision-makers: *Catch-22* is an owner's manual for How to Survive a War with Everything Intact—particularly your sense of humor.

Something shakes loose inside us when we laugh. Blood pressure drops, endorphins are released, your immune system gets a boost. There's a rubbery freedom, an unclenching of the jaw, and a willingness to be vulnerable. When writing *Fobbit*, I tried to take advantage of that vulnerability to make a point about the hardships of war. I thought, *If I can make them laugh, I can make them think.* When readers chuckled at one of my funny turns of phrase, I hoped, there would be a split-second breach of their defenses that would allow me to slip inside with a message: War is foul, war is folly, war is futile.

While writing *Fobbit*, I didn't shy away from grim realities. I mean, hell, on page 2 of the book, I wrote this sentence: "A soldier was vaporized when his patrol hit an Improvised Explosive Device, his flesh thrown into a nearby tree where it draped like Spanish moss." Humor on one page, horror on the next. I couldn't sustain that level of gore throughout the book—nor did I want to. But how could I write true scenes of war without losing readers who'd turn away in disgust? In the words of Donald O'Connor in *Singin' in the Rain*, "Make 'em laugh, make 'em laugh, make 'em laugh!" Or, as I wrote about my main character, a public affairs soldier who churns out reams of bland press releases in order to make the war more palatable: "Gooding's weapons were words, his sentences were missiles." I targeted soft, vulnerable spots in readers and pulled the trigger.

I made it through my war with all four limbs and my sense of humor intact. Sometimes, I think the only way I survived was by way of the laughter I drained from *Catch-22,* and the irony and sarcasm I tossed onto the pages of *Fobbit*. After all, if I didn't laugh, I'd cry. And if I cried, I may as well die.

David Abrams retired in 2008 after a 20-year career in the active-duty U.S. Army as a journalist. He was named the Department of Defense's Military Journalist of the Year in 1994. In 2005, deployed to Baghdad in support of Operation Iraqi Freedom. The journal he kept during that year formed the blueprint for the novel that would later become known as Fobbit. *Abrams' second novel,* Brave Deeds, *was published in 2017. It tells the story of six deployed soldiers who go AWOL in order to attend a memorial service for their squad leader. Abrams was born in Pennsylvania and grew up in Jackson, Wyoming. He holds an undergraduate degree in English from the University of Oregon, Eugene; and an MFA in Creative Writing from the University of Alaska-Fairbanks. He now lives in Butte, Mont. with his wife.*

How I Wrote "World War Z"

By Max Brooks

"How would I survive a real zombie attack?" That was the question that spawned my book, *World War Z: An Oral History of the Zombie War.* The key word in that question was "real" and it went back to my childhood hero, Tom Clancy.

Before Clancy's 1984 book *The Hunt for Red October*, military-espionage fiction rested on the altar of Ian Flemming's pseudo-macho, psycho-sexual, middle-aged male fantasies. Clancy smashed that and replaced it with the faith of facts. Reading his books—including titles such as *The Sum of All Fears* to *Debt of Honor*, as well as my personal favorite *Red Storm Rising*—I felt educated, as well as entertained.

Like Clancy, I felt that the real world was fascinating enough, and wanted to pattern my stories along those lines. So, when I attacked my childhood fear; zombies, with the question of how I would survive, the answer had to be 100 percent real.

My first book, *The Zombie Survival Guide,* was essentially a disaster preparedness manual. Like any actual disaster, the questions posed by zombies generated secondary and tertiary threats. Be it wars or earthquakes, most people don't die of direct violence. They die when that violence cuts their society lifeline. Hunger, thirst, disease, these are what kills most people in a crisis.

Part of my research came from living in Southern California my whole life, and preparing for the inevitable "Big One." Part of it came from my experiences camping in different environments (including a potentially disastrous adventure in Greenland). And part came from my very short but very intense stint in Army ROTC (ah, the joys of dehydration and the jam-prone M16).

Researching and writing the book taught me that surviving a zombie attack was really no different than surviving any other disaster. The threat might be fictional, but the solutions were not. That is why the *Zombie Survival Guide* mixes security (guns, walls, etc.) with sustainability (clean water, sewage treatment, etc.). That is the only way I could survive attack.

But what happens when "I" becomes "we"? What about large groups? Countries? The world?

Every zombie story I'd ever read never went beyond a small band of short-term survivors. Every now and then, books and movies would mention "the government." In his genre-defining movies, George Romero occasionally sprinkled his narratives with news bulletins. But for the most part, zombie stories ignored the big picture.

And "big picture" is the exactly what a zombie outbreak would be. We're not talking about one giant shark off the coast, or one psycho killer in a summer camp. We're talking about hordes—millions or even *billions* of flesh-eating automatons ravaging our planet. If those hordes were ever real, how would our planet survive?

Jumping from micro to macro, I went back to researching a credible scenario. (This took a lot more time than the first book!) I wanted the new story to be global, not just American. I wanted to try and counter what I consider to be our greatest cultural weakness: isolationism. I wanted to show that everything is connected, that overseas crises will inevitably reach our shores. I wanted to show how the economic, cultural, political, even environmental issues of today will one day be the military issues of tomorrow. I wanted to prove to my fellow isolationists that chanting "America First" only makes us the last to fall.

That is why every element in the story's compound disaster is based on actual events. I modeled my plague on the late 2002 outbreak in China of Severe Acute Respiratory Syndrome (SARS). The cultural dismissiveness of Americans in my fiction came from our societal responses to AIDS. The Israeli intel flexibility came from its near-extinction in the Yom Kippur War. And the U.S. Army's bloody rout at Yonkers came from the 1879 British massacre at Isandlwana.

The winners and losers of the story, the countries that survive or perish, were based on the genuine geopolitical strengths and weaknesses of the time. China's authoritarian state is the ultimate groupthink, for example, and gambles its entire survival on the decisions of an unchallengeable cabal. Japan still relies greatly on American protection, and would be vulnerable if that protection suddenly evaporated. As an island nation, Cuba has always prepared for invasion. The United States seems to always get sucker punched and yet, at least part of the time, demonstrates a flexibility and resilience unmatched anywhere else in the world.

Unlike my first book, a large chunk of research came from the library. I avoided the Internet. For some strange reason, I don't entirely trust it. Sometimes it helped to search on-line, like when I watched a laser demonstration video from the company that made lasers. (My conclusion: Lasers are *way* too inefficient for killing zombies). Most of the time however, I depended on printed pages. I should have bought stock in Amazon. Stuffed with books, maps, tech manuals, weapons schematics, and even copies of the Koran (if I'm gonna quote someone's holy scripture, I better get it exactly right), my Spartan studio office started to look a little suspicious.

I also consulted with experts. From medicine to intelligence, to academia, and to the military, I tried to match every faux interview in the book with a genuine human being. Sometimes, such as those regarding the effects of themobaric weapons, my sources would confirm my theories. Sometimes, such as the need for a credible catalyst for underground open-heart surgery, they'd send me back to square one.

In conducting those interviews as research, I came to realize that an oral history was the only way to tell the "big picture," multi-perspective story of an entire planet. Growing up, one of my favorite books was *The Good War* by Studs Terkel. His collection of interviews, from every country, from every walk of life, showed how World War II affected the entire world.

Once my manuscript was finished, once the book deal with Random House was made, I decided to hire a fact-checker just to make sure I'd done my homework. And I did, mostly. All the hard stuff was spot on; all the technology, geography and cultural references. What had I gotten wrong? The location of a sporting goods store, literally a few streets away from my office.

Oh, well, no one's perfect.

Max Brooks is a New York Times-bestselling author. Through books such as The Zombie Survival Guide, World War Z, *and* The Zombie Survival Guide: Recorded Attacks, *Brooks has explored issues of disaster preparedness, crisis management, and societal survival. Brooks is also the author of the historical non-fiction graphic novel* The Harlem Hellfighters, *illustrated by* Canaan White; *and is co-editor of the pop-culture inspired anthologies* Strategy Strikes Back: How Star Wars Explains Modern Military Conflict, *and* Winning Westeros: How Game of Thrones Explains Modern Military Conflict. *Brooks' new horror title,* Devolution: A Firsthand Account of the Rainier Sasquatch Massacre, *is forthcoming in spring 2020.*

Getting Lost On the Way to the Future

By P.W. Singer and August Cole

The two of us didn't meet until we were in our 30s, but we each grew up on similar diets of science fiction, techno-thrillers, and big sprawling novels. We'd prepare for summer vacation trips by getting a stack of books from the library, that might range from Tom Clancy's *Red Storm Rising* and Herman Wouk's *The Winds of War* to William Gibson's *Count Zero* and Ray Bradbury's *The Martian Chronicles*. A classic Sir Arthur Conan Doyle read on the beach might be followed by staying up late to cram in just one more chapter from Michael Crichton.

Perhaps influenced by this love of reading, each of us would go on to become professional writers: August as a journalist working the defense beats at places like *The Wall Street Journal*, and Peter writing non-fiction books on topics like private military contractors, drones, and cyber-security. It was this latter work that led to us first meeting and then becoming friends. August was exploring topics like the story of China hacking our fighter jet programs, and Peter was writing books on the ramifications of cyber-security becoming a new realm of battle.

When we decided to team up on a book exploring the future of war and technology, however, we kept returning to the spirits of our youthful summer reading. With *Ghost Fleet: A Novel of the Next World War*, we set out to write a book that wouldn't just peer into the potential future, but immerse readers in it.

The novel explores what might World War III actually be like. The idea that a Cold War between the great powers of the 21st century could ever turn hot is no mere fiction, but a real risk. After Russian land grabs in Ukraine, and cyber-meddling in U.S. politics, NATO remains on its highest alert since the 1980s. Meanwhile, China and the United States are engaged in a massive arms race, with the two working on a new generation of futuristic tech: robotics, electromagnetic railguns, artificial intelligence, and hypersonic weapons. On their own, these are remarkable breakthroughs. They become even more troubling after years of increasing confidence and bellicosity between nations moves out into the open. A Chinese regime newspaper, for example, once declared "war is inevitable" if the United States doesn't change its policies in the Pacific, while new U.S. defense strategy has identified Great Power conflict as a core risk to the nation.

The books we enjoyed most as entertainment shaped our approach, but also drove desire to tell a comprehensive story. Similar to the storytelling of

Red Storm Rising, *World War Z*, or *Game of Thrones*, the novel follows multiple characters and settings, rather than following one character on a single story thread. This allowed us to cover more ground, to play with more "what if's?," and even to treat the war itself like a character.

Fiction can reveal underlying uncomfortable truths, especially how a 21st century war between great powers would be different than earlier wars. Battles will take place not just on the land, but also at sea and air (where U.S. forces haven't had to face off against a peer power since 1945), and in two new domains: space and cyberspace. To tell the story of the war, we had to dance across domains well out of reach of any single character.

What made *Ghost Fleet* perhaps something different was a new kind of fusion. We experimented melding two classic book genres, the techno-thriller and the non-fiction book. In this way, the work emerged as a new kind of "novel," in which the story was backed by 400 factual endnotes. Every technology and trend in the book, no matter how science fiction-seeming, was drawn from the real world. The scenarios we hoped would thrill and chill were built on non-fiction research, including DARPA contracts and Pentagon wargame results. We mixed in real-world concerns regarding new Chinese drone prototypes, and news items about how U.S. weapons platforms have been hacked. We interviewed real people who would fight in such a war, from U.S. Navy destroyer captains and fighter pilots, to Chinese generals and Anonymous hackers. All this improved the realism of our story, but also literally let us get to know our characters.

Even the book title reflects this emphasis on realism. Yes, "Ghost Fleet" had a cool, ominous sound to it, but it is actually the real nickname of the National Defense Reserve Fleet that makes an appearance in the book. These are the mothballed Navy ships, stored in places like Suisun Bay near San Francisco—the Navy's version of the Air Force's "Boneyard" of retired planes kept in the desert. In our book, those dusty warplanes also got a chance to fight another day.

The spark was an actual policy question: Just why do we keep these old ships around? We connect that question to the larger issues of whether a world war could happen again. What kind of war could go badly enough that the United States would need to resurrect these old ships and planes? And then what would happen? Answering these questions led us down intriguing pathways often overlooked when planning for future conflict. For example, how would the out-of-date gear—and the retired sailors who operated them—relate (or not) to digital-age warships and sailors?

It was rewarding to see how people reacted to the project, which we feel proved that a mix of fiction and non-fiction can be both entertaining and helpful, promoting thought and discussion about the seemingly unthinkable. Our readers constantly contact us, telling how they see the story's fictional elements reflected in the real world. Soon after the book's release, they even began posting about "#GhostFleet moments of the day," a mantra that has filled the Twitter feeds of everybody from tech watchers and soldiers to members of Congress. It was and is uncanny for us, too.

We've been able to talk about the applied lessons from the novel with groups that range from the U.S. Naval War College to NATO allies, to the Defense Science Board to U.S. bases around the world. It may have an influence on future leaders, given that it has been named to many military reading lists, including those from Special Operations Command and Space Command, to those put out for their forces by the U.S. Marine Corps Commandant, Army Chief of Staff, and the Chief of Naval Operations. Those endorsements certainly helped expand the book's professional reach.

Perhaps most gratifying, however, was how many readers often told us how much they enjoyed our mix of realism crossed with imagination. Very often, our readers told us of how, once they started reading, they lost track of all time and place. This combination hits the mark of our own hopes. Maybe our book will help keep our story where it belongs, in the realm of fiction. Along the way, we're glad to have given people that same wonderful feeling we had on summer vacations some 30 years ago.

Peter Warren Singer is a strategist at New America, a think tank based in Washington, D.C. He has been named by the Smithsonian Institution as one of the nation's 100 leading innovators, by Defense News *as one of the 100 most influential people in defense issues, by* Foreign Policy *to their Top 100 Global Thinkers List, and as an official "Mad Scientist" for the U.S. Army's Training and Doctrine Command. With August Cole, he is the co-author of the best-seller* Ghost Fleet: A Novel of the Next World War, *and the forthcoming* Burn-In: A Novel of the Real Robotic Revolution *Singer is also author of several non-fiction books, including:* LikeWar: The Weaponization of Social Media; Corporate Warriors: The Rise of the Privatized Military Industry; Children at War; Wired for War: The Robotics Revolution and Conflict in the 21st Century; *and* Cybersecurity and Cyberwar: What Everyone Needs to Know. *Follow him on Twitter: @PeterWSinger*

August Cole is an author exploring the future of conflict through fiction and other forms of storytelling. His talks on the future of war as well as his workshops on how to write "FICINT" have taken him from speaking at the Nobel Institute in Oslo, to presenting at SXSW Interactive, to tackling the "Dirty Name" obstacle at Fort Benning, Ga. He is also a non-resident senior fellow at the Brent Scowcroft Center on International Security at the Atlantic Council. With P.W. Singer, he is the co-author of the best-seller Ghost Fleet: A Novel of the Next World War, *and the forthcoming* Burn-In: A Novel of the Real Robotic Revolution. *By writing stories that identify potential societal or strategic problems, August uses narrative to empower individuals and large*

organizations to prepare for an era of accelerating change. At the Atlantic Council, he directed the organization's Art of the Future Project, which explored creative and narrative works for insight into the future of conflict, from its inception in 2014 through 2017. A former journalist, from 2007 to 2010 August reported on the defense industry for The Wall Street Journal. *From 1998 to 2006, he worked as an editor and a reporter for* MarketWatch.com. *Follow him on Twitter: @August_Cole*

Three Lieutenants

By Roger Misso

The ship shuddered, and it woke her.

Climbing down from her bunk—top in a stack of three, affectionately referred to as "coffins" for their size—Lt. Erica Wood squinted into the dark, familiar red glow of nighttime lighting.

Something was not quite right.

As her microfiber-socked feet touched the ground, she took a moment to be sure of her balance. She was thankful for the ugly brown shag carpet she and her bunkmates had smuggled aboard just before getting underway. It added some character and much-needed warmth to an otherwise frigid, sterile dwelling.

Cautiously tiptoeing past the divider between bunks and the rest of the small, 98-square-foot room, her eyes finally focused on the source of her misgivings: the blue glow of a computer screen and the dimly-lit face of one of her roommates, Lt. James "Sluggo" Akaka.

"Sluggo," she whispered. No response.

"Sluggo!" this time a hiss, and a sharp crane of the neck from her target audience. "What the hell are you doing?"

"Oh hey, Chip," he answered sheepishly, addressing her by the abbreviated version of her callsign, "Chippy." "I'm sorry, was I being too loud? Did I wake you?"

"No. I felt a jolt and I—answer my question, what are you doing?"

"Probably just the cryo tanks. Me? I'm just finishing up some things."

"Some 'things'? Could you be any more evasive?"

James grimaced. "I'm finishing some research for an article I'm writing."

Erica's eyes rolled, a smirk spreading across her face. "Overachieving much? Did they move up FITREP season or something? You know they don't let boot pilots command starships."

"No, no," replied James. "I just care about this. And I'm really close."

Erica's smirk turned to a sad smile. She had heard this line before.

"Why do you do this to yourself?" she asked, lowering herself into a seat a few meters away. "What could you possibly hope to achieve with that computer as an unqualified Fike pilot?"

Erica was referring to the spacecraft they both piloted, the F/E-11C Star Cruiser, or "Fike" as it was known in the aviation vernacular. Assigned to the USS Enterprise (CVQ-105), the fifth carrier starship to employ the orbit-breaking Quantum Drive propulsion system, James and Erica were two of 16 pilots and 40 science officers assigned to the Black Star Lions of VFE-213. The "F" and "E" in both spacecraft and squadron designation stood for "Fighter" and "Exploration," respectively, referring to the plane's dual role as an offensive weapon and humankind's most expeditionary science tool.

In their typically chilly quarters, James waited a moment too long before answering. Erica took a long breath, mouth open about to speak, when James cut in—*sharply.*

"Because I'm tired, Chippy. I'm tired of the 9-to-5ers, the minimum-required-effort cowboys, the 'this is how I had it' brigade, the 'ego instead of improvement' corps. I'm tired of the FITREP darlings and the golden path wannabes. I'm tired."

"I joined the Space Corps to make space exploration better. I joined to work together with the best to go places and do things that no human beings had ever done before."

"But that's not the way it's gone, Chip. You and I have both felt that. From the first day of boot camp, that current of cynicism just washes over and takes over. We don't do things to get better. We do things to avoid looking bad."

"And so it goes at every rank, in every position, on every ship. We regress to the mean. We hide behind our billets. We cower at the specter that somebody might think we're inadequate."

"Well, that might be fine for some people, but it's not good enough for me. I want this service to be better. And I'm going to run headfirst into every brick wall I can find that deserves to come down. And I'm going to keep running into those walls, and recruit people who believe like I do to run into 'em alongside me. Because eventually, Chip, *those walls fall down.*"

James surprised himself with how out of breath he felt. Still, it was cathartic to get that off his chest. Erica, however, was having none of it.

"Look around you, Sluggo!" Erica, exasperated now, sat up straighter in her chair, hands waving. "You're on the greatest starship humankind has ever created! We're the most powerful force in the universe! That service you're talking about got us here, and it didn't get that way because a few junior officers had some Earth-shattering revelation. It's easy for you to throw rocks, but the reality is that you don't have the perspective of the senior officers or policymakers. If you want to effect change, you've got to sit down, shut up, and make command."

A stunned silence followed for a moment before Erica added, "I just don't like thinking of you like this. You're my friend. Why can't you go with the flow?"

Just then, the door cracked open. Lt. Kwame "Toto" N'danga slipped in quietly, not expecting to see his roommates awake and conversing at this hour.

"What is going on here?" he whispered, a look of bemused surprise on his face. "Are you two having a fight?"

Erica snorted. "Sluggo here is changing the universe."

Kwame's eyes lit up. "Schrodinger would say that our presence out here is changing the universe every second. So, really, our friend James is late to the party."

Erica, smiling momentarily at his Senegalese accent and propensity for nerdy physics jokes, interjected. "What I'm talking about is why he's always writing. Sitting there, not sleeping, never content. I'm your friend, Sluggo, but it really makes it look to other people like you think you're better than they are."

Before James could respond, Kwame raised a finger. "'If you wish to move mountains tomorrow, you must start by lifting stones today.'"

A befuddled silence fell over the room, so Kwame continued. "This is not about our friend James. It is about a person"—he looked back and forth between the two—"who believes so strongly in the identity of the whole that he forgets he is judged as an individual."

"What does that mean?" Erica asked, no longer confrontational but intrigued.

"Consider this," Kwame began. "How far have we come to be here? We are on a starship, orbiting the third planet of a star 12 million light years from our own. This ship is made with metals and powered by machines that our ancestors of stone and wood and steel could not possibly have dreamed of."

Kwame smiled, looked around the room, then back at his roommates. "And think of what we are doing right now. Did you know that our ancestors once segregated berthings by gender? They believed that it would be impossible for men and women to live and work together. But here we are."

"Did you know that our ancestors once thought space travel and exploration to be a waste of time? They believed they should mine and destroy their own home planet and pay homage to their imaginary borders instead of protecting it as the most precious home in the universe. But here we are."

"Kwame, what's your point?"

"How do you think we got here? It was not because humanity waited for one old person to bestow the knowledge and the right. Moses was a great man, but the change we need will not come down from a mountain on stone tablets."

"You think Sluggo ... is *Moses*?"

"No," chuckled Kwame. "But I think he is a good man. With a good heart. We should want that in our leaders. People who do not want the spotlight, but want to shine a light."

Erica's voice was barely above a whisper, her eyes lowered. "But how do you know? How does anybody ever know whether they're on the right path, or just shooting space dust?"

James silently closed his computer screen. Slowly rising from his seat, he motioned to Erica.

"C'mon, Chip. Let's head to Midrats. I'll buy you a beer and tell you all about it."

The stateroom door closed with a click behind three lieutenants, the air between them filled with laughter and hope. Their vessel, banking slightly to port, plied the silent depths around Tau Ceti. Beyond the star lay the future of humankind, yet unwritten.

Roger Misso is a candidate for congress in New York's 24th Congressional District (NY-24). He is a husband, father, and veteran—a former naval flight officer and victim advocate for survivors of sexual assault in the military. He is a graduate of the U.S. Naval Academy and the Harvard Kennedy School, co-host of the podcast 2 Vets Upstate, *and an officer in the U.S. Navy Reserve.*

Making Military History Relevant through Fiction

By Kiki Watkins

I didn't set out to be a military writer. There was foul weather in Richmond one day a few years back, and I had to get the kids out of the house. As admission to the Virginia Historical Society was free, I ended up traipsing with my children through an exhibition of Edwin Forbes' etchings, made while he was embedded as a war correspondent with the Union Army during the American Civil War. I paused several times to examine his depictions of various routine events in lives of soldiers—writing letters, for example, or preparing a meal. I became fascinated by the details marking these relatable activities, in a long-ago time and place near combat.

Then, I was dumbstruck by a singular work of art.

Forbes depicts the execution of five soldiers tried for desertion, convicted, and executed in rural Virginia. None of them spoke English. They spoke Hanoverian, Prussian, and Italian. The military had to import a Jewish rabbi and a Catholic priest, just so three of the men could have spiritual consolation. Yet somehow, the entire court martial occurred within three weeks in August 1863, all appeals exhausted.

Because it's my job to coordinate interpreters for cases in Virginia state courts, I began to guess how challenging it was to provide adequate language access for the accused. I set off to discover what led to the execution at Beverly's Ford, Va. On-line searches led me to purchase paper editions of journals, letters, more etchings, and regimental histories. I traveled to the National Archives, the Historical Society of Pennsylvania, and to Gettysburg National Military Park. I drove my family to the place of the trial and execution, as well as many other Civil War sites. After two years of research, I spent a year writing an historical fiction manuscript. I paid for professional feedback, begged everyone I knew to read it, gritted my teeth, and rewrote for another year. My manuscript, *Grasshoppers at Dusk*, was a semi-finalist for the 2018 Blue Mountain Novel Award, and a first-in-category winner for the 2017 Chanticleer Book Reviews Laramie Writing Award.

Here are some lessons I've learned about military research and writing:

Lesson No. 1: I've learned to go down rabbit holes. Union Army military records about the court martial at the center of my narrative are relatively comprehensive at the National Archives. Aside from official records, published information about many Civil War battles, the historical context of conflict, soldiers' daily experiences, and the motives of military leaders is fairly deep. Although it is tempting to rely on well-trodden works, research is exploration. No real explorer would travel only where an area was already fully reconnoitered. Researchers should be open to wherever their explorations take them.

In researching a history of the 118th Pennsylvania Volunteers, the regiment in which the court martial had been held, I read a letter relating the tale of a Union officer coming across a copy of *Ivanhoe* on the march to the Battle of Fredericksburg, eight months before the trial of the deserters. This work of historical fiction was published just a generation before the time period I was researching. The mention led me down an important rabbit hole. Rediscovering and re-reading *Ivanhoe* not only helped me understand historical fiction better, but also Robin Hood's highly evolved notion of justice echoed one real historical Union officer's altruistic commitment to do right regardless of the regimental rules. The character of Rebecca recalled for me the *belle juive* stereotype, and I began wonder about incorporating a similar trope within my story. I considered the value of books in that time period as entertainment, a common cultural narrative among certain officers, and an analogue to current popular communication and culture. I became more capable of developing a story that was complex and relevant. Had I dismissed re-reading *Ivanhoe* as unrelated to my research, my story could have suffered.

I investigated why desertions were common, how military justice and political leaders dealt with desertion, and also how conscripts and substitutes were enlisted, and the various attitudes toward these soldiers after joining their regiments. If I based my work only on the court martial and execution, I never would have answered the questions that originally sprang to mind when I first saw Forbes' etching, starting my quest. I wanted to know how the non-English-speaking deserters had gotten there; if they were aware of the legal requirements of enlistment, the crime of desertion, and the penalties thereof; and if they could meaningfully participate in their defense. Research helped me start the story where it really began, with a bounty broker on a ship full of new immigrants in New York Harbor, rather than in a field at Beverly's Ford, Virginia.

While meticulous research lends vibrancy to a story, however, it does not itself tell the story. Just because I learned military jargon, for example, didn't mean it was always effective to use it in dialogue. I had to love and leave other "rabbit holes," acknowledging that a writer may never know everything about a time period or situation. Standing in a bookshop, I read the back of a text about the visual language Southern women used to communicate using fans. As a linguist, I loved the idea, but I walked away. Today's readers don't need a lesson in Southern fan communications to understand a court martial. As I got farther along, compiled my notes, and organized my tale, I went on a "research diet." While creating my first draft I closed my web browser and eschewed all research, keeping a handwritten list of things I wanted to go back and explore. At that point in the writing process, more research would have gotten in the way.

Lesson No. 2: There is no one true account. I have come to accept pure historical accuracy may be unattainable. In the case of this court martial, there are many divergent records created by individuals whose accounts may be inaccurate or variously motivated. This was evident when I came across another etching of the execution, one created by another artist, A. R. Waud.

In Waud's imagery, it appears one of the deserters remains sitting after the firing squad's volley, rather than all men falling backward at once. The three spectators on the right are military men on horseback, rather than three civilians with a woman among them. Which artist was correct? Some newspaper accounts say there were 36 men on the firing squad—others, 50. Journal accounts and letters from witnesses to the execution provided several sets of facts. Accepting no version as entirely true allowed me to make the best decisions about what likely occurred. If I had immediately accepted the first etching as accurate and ignored the friction of conflicting reports, I would not have arrived at the most likely—but surprising—outcome of the execution.

Considering historical truths in this way also helped me confront unpleasant facts related to important historical figures' actions. For example, I read questions sent by Union Army generals to the Judge Advocate General's office, which seemed to seek to delay or halt the execution, and missives sent by a major within the regiment on the convicted deserters' behalf. It was jarring, then, to discover President Lincoln denied the men's appeal—seemingly after only cursory consideration.

To my way of thinking, an acknowledged legal thinker should have understood the limited access someone who did not speak English might have had at court martial. True facts do not exist in a vacuum, however, and an accurate written portrayal places truth within context. The desertion problem during the Civil War was something with which Lincoln grappled before and after this execution, and I have found nothing to document Lincoln was aware the men did not speak English. The commanding general, Maj. Gen. George Meade was eager to prove himself before Lincoln, who did not see Meade as particularly effective after the victory at Gettysburg. While it is true the president denied the appeal, he did so as a manager and not as a lawyer. He relied on Meade's best judgment.

Writing historical fiction has allowed me to employ inaccuracy to get main truths across. I deleted a captain who was a close witness to the court martial. I made several generals just one. I folded five separate courts martial into two. I swapped the nationality of deserters for plot. My own "truth" lacks accuracy in these ways, but the story can be better understood with simplified names and ranks, and less redundancy. Reading the transcriptions of the court martial, I could see the interpreters' misstatements as clearly as if I were there. I hired a translator to retranslate from Italian a letter found on one of the deserters, because I sensed there were errors. The correct translation I commissioned is better than the translation I found with the original court martial records. These errors aren't described in my manuscript. Because of the inaccuracies I knew how the interpreters and translator performed, and I was able to create for the reader the most likely characters providing language access at the court martial. As a former interpreter and translator, I can take the reader on reasonable leaps toward a fair perception of what happened, and carve out the story of events leading to the execution without letting true details confuse the audience.

Lesson No. 3: Believe in the message. It takes curiosity to learn about a different time and situation, discipline to complete a 95,000-word project, and humility to rewrite it after getting feedback. I have expended a great amount of resources—both time and money—to share the story of this court martial. It has not always been the easiest path. Still, I was taken by the notion I had when I first saw Edwin Forbes' etching: That a Civil War story is relatable to modern times and relevant to something I care about: cross-cultural communication.

I can close my eyes and remember the feel of the indentations on the papers where the deserters etched their signatures as part of the court martial record. These men existed. I believe their story means something. I felt the same way when I decided on my next project. My grandfather was in a U.S. Marine division and killed during World War II in the Pacific Theater, dying before seeing his only child. My father grew up, joined the Marines, and fought in Vietnam. Later, he headed a Japanese corporation. So I will research another military story from long ago, to share currently relevant information about how cultures interact.

Kiki Watkins served Virginia courts as a magistrate before becoming the manager of language-access services within the court system. Her historical fiction manuscript, Grasshoppers at Dusk, *was a semi-finalist for the 2018 Blue Mountain Novel Award, and a first-in-category winner for the 2017 Chanticleer Book Reviews Laramie Writing Award. It is a Civil War story about the court martial of five Union deserters who did not speak the English language. She lectures regularly on language access and cultural competency.*

The Warrior-Poet and an Unexpected Journey

By Colin D. Halloran

It seems that whenever I give a lecture about my work, I find myself telling the audience, "I have three distinct identities: veteran, writer, and veteran-writer." Not everything I write has to do with my military experience, and not all of my activities as a veteran have to do with my writing. But it is often this intersectional identity that people have come to ask me about.

So here I am, once again, speaking, writing—*thinking*—about what exactly it all means. To me, to my students, to my readers, to my work, and to my future as a writer. And it's this question about the future that seems to come up just as frequently when I am with other military writers. Do we continue on this path of "write what you know" at the risk of being pigeonholed, or do we step away from the subject which, for many of us, made us marketable in the first place?

With each of my poetry collections, I have taken a step away from my war; first, exploring it outright through a memoir-in-verse, then taking on its aftereffects through metaphor and persona, and, most recently, exploring war from an outsider's perspective by delving into the rise of ISIS and the global refugee crisis. But despite moving further from my own experience, the fact remains that war is still there, front and center. And there's that nagging fear again: Am I a writer? Or am I a war writer?

I always wanted to write, from the time my mother gave me my very first journal in the 2nd grade. Rather than get ready for school in the morning, I would sit dreamily on the warm bathroom radiator, watching winter unfold outside, transcribing it into terrible poetry about cardinals and squirrels and snow. But for every poem about animals I wrote in my blue hardcover poetry journal, I wrote a short memory of my deceased father in the mustard-yellow spiral-bound notebook I'd gotten at the suggestion of the family therapist. As much as I have always loved creating stories and converting my view of the world into words, for just as long I have used writing as a tool for processing loss, grief, and change.

In spite of this history, it somehow didn't immediately occur to me to use writing as a way of dealing with my war experience. Where I used to read novels as a means of escape in my youth, after war I used work to avoid confronting my struggles. I threw myself into school, overloading on courses, working 60 hours a week across multiple jobs. Anything to exhaust myself to the point of dreamless sleep. I found myself falling into that all-too-familiar trope: *I can't talk to anyone about this because how could they—civilians—possibly understand?*

Eventually my body capitulated to the exhaustion. I was sick, I was stuck, and it was unsustainable. I finally sought help. And it was there, sitting with my new therapist—a graduate student the same age as I—talking about something completely unrelated to the war, that those old journals reentered the conversation. Had I ever thought about writing about Afghanistan? I thought it was ludicrous; I was here because I couldn't sleep, but also couldn't function awake. I wasn't here because of Afghanistan. But she insisted I try, so I did.

Next thing I knew, I was living in England, writing poems, some of which were so important to get out of me that I was physically ill after getting the experience onto the page. Using England as a base, I bounced around Europe with a new small, dark-grey spiral-bound notebook that I bought for the sole purpose of rediscovering myself—my post-war self—for the first time. With each new table in each new bar in each new city, I uncovered a piece of myself by converting my war into words. I was a warrior-poet. And I realized the answer to that old question: *They can't possibly understand what it's like to go to war unless we tell them.*

Two years after returning from Europe, having nearly completed both my Master of Fine Arts degree and that first manuscript I'd begun abroad, I went to see the poet Yusef Komunyakaa. His collection of Vietnam War poetry, *Dien Cai Dau*, had been invaluable to me in my growth as a student of poetry, and as a veteran. I was eager for his new collection, *The Chameleon Couch*, and the new wisdom it would grant me. I reveled at the chance of meeting this titan of poetry, whose insights had helped me understand so much about myself, about the nature of war. The reading took place in a church at Wesleyan University, Middletown, Conn., which seemed just right for the occasion: somber, reflective, quiet. So many shadows.

I was not greeted with poems of war, however. Rather, I found myself dancing through poems of jazz music, of blues, of religious contemplation and racial tensions. Poems of identity. After the reading, I told Komunyakaa how much his work had meant to me, and asked what advice he may have for a young, veteran poet. He told me that he had written *Dien Cai Dau* because he had needed to, but that once that collection was complete, he never wanted to write about the war again. And that, with the exception of a single poem in 25 years, he had been able to. The war was something he experienced. It wasn't who he *was*.

I thanked him for his time, for his words, then drove home, unsure of what to make of the encounter. Once home, I turned to *The Chameleon Couch* in search of further clarity. His "Ode to the Chameleon," for example: "Little shape shifter, lingering / there on your quotidian twig / of indifference..." Was this what I must become? A shapeshifter, a keeper of camouflage drastically different than that which I wore in Afghanistan, in order to fit into this new daily monotony? I wanted to write broadly. I wanted to achieve what Komunyakaa had achieved, and to free my creative self from the confines of war. I kept reading. From "How It Is": "My muse is holding me prisoner. / She refuses to give back my shadow". The poet himself had told me he was no longer writing about war, yet here I was, not 20 minutes later, reading my war in all of his words.

This interaction with Komunyakaa and his words was essential. All art exists on multiple planes: the creator's, the consumer's, and, perhaps, some objective existence in-between. As creators, we give up control when we send our art into the world, and as consumers we apply our own needs to each piece we encounter. Komunyakka wasn't writing about his war anymore, but that didn't mean I couldn't apply his words to mine. That's the power of language. It is not only transformative in effect, but the language itself transforms with each new reader, each new reading. I found as much wisdom in the works of great war poets as I did in the darkness of Ted Hughes' *Crow* poems, and Charles Simic's meandering, yet somehow pointed, contemplations. But try as I might, my own writing remained firmly rooted in central Asia.

I remember so clearly the first poem I wrote that wasn't about my war experience. I was recovering from a serious knee surgery, reading Ron Padgett's poem "Method," when my muse finally set me free. It was so different than anything I'd previously written: a prose poem, scribbled furiously on the back of the bookstore receipt that was tucked inside the front cover. Its sole connection to the war was the surgery that eventually led to its writing. I hadn't yet finished my first manuscript. Rather than a betrayal, this new poem felt like a refreshing release—a glimpse into a future where I could just write, not write war. I hobbled back upstairs from that front porch, and immediately typed out this new me. It was published within six weeks. I felt validated, with a renewed confidence that perhaps I could avoid the narrow classification I feared.

And yet, I felt I needed to lean into my identity as a veteran-writer in order to really break into the published world. This, in spite of the seeming contradiction of the supposed conservative world of soldiering and the liberal realm of poetry. I believed in my ability when it came to craft, but there were definitely times I felt my content was holding me back, keeping me from getting published. War, while not my identity, was a brand—*my* brand. At least for now.

I continued to write both, not realizing I was starting my second book parallel to finishing my first. I continued to read books about war, but also delved into other topics, from science to the surrealist prose poems of Russell Edson, to Edgar Lee Masters' imagined epitaphs of Spoon River. I moved beyond poetry as well, reading memoirs and novels. Some of these regarded war, others went nowhere near the topic. I was reminded of my youth, escaping the tribulations of life in the pages of a novel. And I was brought back to my favorite place: J.R.R. Tolkien's Middle Earth.

Tolkien's work had a profound effect on me when I was younger, and I realized that it could again. Having taken a course in Tolkien Studies while in England, I had a renewed appreciation and understanding of the man, the scholar, and the writer. Here was someone who had written about his war *without* writing about his war. What began as a bedtime tale for his children, evolved into a world in which he could process his experiences outside the realities he'd experienced—and perhaps was still experiencing.

Taking a deep dive back into Tolkien, I realized just how many of his identities were present and interacting with each other in Middle Earth. There is no question that his experience in World War I impacted the narrative arc of the books, from the rising evil influence spreading across the idyllic Shire, to the sprawling industrial complex of Saruman mirroring the rapid development of new killing technologies. But alongside such elements was his skill as a philologist, evident in his creation of multiple original languages. His scholarly work on the study of ancient mythologies can be seen in his world-building, evident in *The Silmarillion* and the shorter tales, myths, and songs left behind in his copious notes.

Where most people saw a fantasy world, I saw an answer to the question of who I wanted to be as a writer. I saw that it was possible to write about the emotional landscape of my war, without writing about the physical landscape of my war. I saw that it was possible to engage other sides of my intellectual identity, and even merge them with the part that was processing my war experience.

Just as I am no longer the person I was before the war, I can no longer be the writer I was before the war. That doesn't mean, however, that I'm beholden to the war as a writer or a person. For too long, I ignored the effects Afghanistan had on me. I narrowly defined my existence as a person, confusing events with identity. It was through the exploration of words—both read and written—that I was able to break this cycle. Perhaps on some level, my war will always be present in my writing. Through experience and the work and encouragement of those who have come before me, however, I know that I have permission from myself to not have it there. And, perhaps more importantly, that it's OK if it is.

204

Colin D. Halloran served as U.S. Army infantry soldier in Afghanistan in 2006, and has since devoted himself to art and education. His award-winning debut poetry collection, Shortly Thereafter, *has been taught at universities and military institutions in the United States and abroad. His second poetry collection,* Icarian Flux, *was published in 2015. His essays have appeared in the anthologies* Proud to Be: Writing by American Warriors *and* Retire the Colors: Veterans & Civilians On Iraq & Afghanistan, *and his short-fiction was featured in the 2017 anthology* The Road Ahead: Fiction from the Forever War.

An Iraq War Veteran Reads the Iraq War

By Hugh Martin

> "Iraq is variegated, contradictory, endlessly confusing.
> Over the years its people have watched as others have sought
> to define them, creating images to be displayed beyond its borders."
> —Anthony Shadid,
> *Night Draws Near: Iraq's People in the Shadow of America's War* (p. 10)

It may not be surprising that I, along with the other soldiers in my platoon, didn't really consider the war outside of what happened to us directly. The suffering of Iraqis, the lives they were trying to live amidst the presence of us, our war, our occupation, was hardly ever our focus. Usually, we had so many of our own hardships to deal with that it was difficult to imagine much else beyond our daily tasks and missions: patrolling villages and towns populated with tens of thousands of people, training and working with Iraqi police and Iraqi soldiers with too few interpreters, raiding homes and farms late at night to arrest men or take weapons and bomb-making materials, standing all day outside pulling security for political meetings and city council meetings, too many Improvised Explosive Devices or IED-scares to count, indirect fire attacks at the base which were, thankfully for us and not so much for the insurgents, poorly aimed and unsuccessful. After so much time—12 years—has passed and I've developed more emotional distance from my time in Iraq in 2004, I've been able to, finally and fortunately, begin to study, as best as I can, the war through the eyes of Iraqis.

> There's a line from history that nearly everyone in Baghdad remembers: "Our armies do not come into your cities and lands as conquerors or enemies, but as liberators." The speaker was Major General Sir Stanley Maude, the British commander who in 1917 entered the capital to end Ottoman rule. (p. 47)

In *Night Draws Near*, Anthony Shadid, the Lebanese-American journalist, documents his time from March 2003-June 2004 living with and among Iraqis. His accounts overlap, somewhat, with my time in the country—roughly late February 2004-December 2004. While deployed as a 20-year-old specialist in the Army National Guard, I was aware of the British occupation after World War I, but I had never heard about this well-known line from Maude. I imagine most Americans have not. If Shadid emphasizes anything, it's how that the longer he stays in Iraq, the more complicated and complex the country and the war becomes. Before deploying, as a 19-year-old trying to understand the gravity of my situation, I started reading, when time permitted, about Islam, Iraqi history, Saddam Hussein and his family, among other things. I also asked my undergraduate advisor—I'd finished one semester of college at the time—for reading suggestions. She mentioned *Rabbit, Run; Portnoy's Complaint; A Farewell to Arms*. At the time, because my professor knew me well, all fit my interest as a young male drawn to masculine-driven realist fiction. Beyond literature, I also read the "news" obsessively. I began to read about the war with more intensity and attention because I knew I would, soon, be going to Iraq; somehow, as the deployment became more inevitable, each morning I'd consume every word in the newspaper—usually the Cleveland *Plain Dealer*, as my family still received daily copies back then—that dealt with any aspect of the war: bombings, militias, civilian deaths, insurgents, al-Qaeda, troop surges and reductions, IEDs.

> Shadid: "Some Iraqis foresaw the American invasion as a liberation." (p. 42)

> An Iraqi man says: "The American invasion has nothing to do with democracy and human rights ... it will bring more destruction, more civil war, and a nationalist war against American intervention in the internal affairs of Iraq." (p. 47)

> An Iraqi man says of Bush: "From the bottom of my heart, I really respect, I adore this man." (p. 150)

> Another Iraqi man: "It is basically an angry response to the events of September 11." (p. 47)

> After a bombing, an Iraqi man says in a hospital: "Our floors are covered with blood, the walls are splashed with blood ... they came to free us? This is freedom?" (p. 77)

Of course, Saddam is also mentioned, again and again, as justification for the invasion. If Shadid's book proves anything, it's how unclassifiable and complicated each Iraqi felt about the American invasion and presence. Shadid writes in the introduction: "There is a word in Arabic that I have heard uttered over and over in the city: *ghamidh*, meaning 'mysterious' or 'ambiguous.' If Baghdad's soul is loss, its mood always seemed to be *ghamidh*" (p. 10). Shadid argues that someone in his position, a journalist trying to "capture" the war, must "surrender to the ambiguities and embrace what is *ghamidh*" (p. 10). He later asserts what does seem to be the most effective way to present the war landscape: "Perhaps we simply tell stories" (p. 10).

Almost every day in Iraq I "left the wire," as we would say. We'd rumble out on our Humvees—I drove the last one in our small convoy of four—and do patrols, route clearances, and sometimes just drive around the hills or villages or towns doing "presence patrols." Every now and then, we'd stop for various reasons. I'd stand outside my Humvee where, unless we were in the middle of a desert field, Iraqis, usually young men or boys, would approach us and talk. To generalize, I'd say that any Iraqi approaching us had more positive feelings about our presence and what we were doing; so when they spoke to us, usually with broken English, they complimented what we were doing, thanked us, told us stories and stories about Saddam and the regime. Those who didn't want us there probably, I think, would not approach us. For much of Shadid's book, he does, remarkably and vividly, tell stories of the families dealing, on an intimate level, with the invasion, the bombing, and, later, the occupation.

> An Iraqi man says: "'I can't show my fear in front of my children ... if I'm afraid, they'll become afraid. Life's not comfortable,' he said, recalling the twenty missiles that had struck nearby the night before." (p. 64)

> After an American bombing, Shadid describes what a man says to him: "He simply turned to me and said matter-of-factly, 'Fuck all Americans.'" (p. 133)

As I worked on my second manuscript of poetry, tentatively titled *Service*, I attempted to write poems with a more expansive and wider range of personae. Specifically, I've wanted to write, I say with much humility, more *in* and *of* the Iraqi experience of the war. Previously, most of the voices I attempted to develop are centered around the soldier or veteran experience. I've wanted to create a more multi-vocal, polyphonic tapestry. I hope to provide a more-layered, multi-dimensional portrait of the war. I read accounts from Iraqis, journalists, and reached out to speak to Iraqis who might be willing to talk. I say this with no self-congratulation or nobility. My current position as a graduate student allows me to, luckily, simply explore and read what I want. Although I've worked over the past few years to discover first-person non-fiction accounts of war by non-soldiers, non-veterans, I've seen how very few there are. As I read Shadid's account of what Iraqis tell him leading up to and during the invasion, I also remember what people, in America, said to me:

"You see how they act over there—they're a bunch of animals."

"We should just bomb the whole place."

"They should be thankful we're going over there."

"We're just doing it for oil."

"Just like Vietnam."

Although it seems to be a well-worn, tidy cliché, I really didn't consider the political, social, historical, economic—to name a few—complexities involving my deployment to Iraq. All I knew was that I was going and I wanted to do everything in my power to come back. This was, usually, mixed with a feeling of vicious, nightmarish self-loathing and regret at joining: How did I get myself in this? After all, I signed on with the Army National Guard as an incoming high school senior, approximately four months before the terrorist attacks of 9/11. I remember practicing, in the barracks at Fort Bragg, N.C. disassembling my M16 and thinking, in terror, that if it took me just a second too long to complete my task, I might die. It never came to that, thankfully, but how was I to know?

One Iraqi man tells Shadid: "We have eleven thousand years of history ... I know it sounds facetious, but it gives you resilience." (p. 84)

A woman, Nadeen, says: "What gives them the right to change something that's not theirs in the first place? I don't like your house, so I'm going to bomb it and you can rebuild it again the way I want it ... what they're doing to us, they deserve to have done to them, their families, their children." (p. 87).

Shadid's account is one of the more startling and comprehensive among the many journalistic accounts of the invasion. His focus is solely on the Iraqis—those caught with the war, literally, in their backyards and front yards. Amidst the bombings, the destruction, the gradual and relentless movement of the war, life does, as much as it can, go on. Shadid writes: "Scenes from normal life persisted: young boys, their bodies dark and thin, swam in the muddy Tigris, while fishermen led their boats along the clumps of green reeds rising from the banks" (p. 54).

Alongside such innocent and bucolic scenes, however, Shadid describes plenty of gruesome moments. After a bomb during the invasion, Shadid writes, "Across the street the severed hand of a seventeen-year-old boy was tossed gracelessly in a pool of blood and mud" (p. 79). Much of the book is filled with this image: blood mixed with mud. There is also very much blood with water, oil, debris on the street; blood in various shades as it dries. Although we enter, as readers, the lives of Iraqis as they struggle through the invasion and the first months of the occupation, even Shadid can't come—like I want—to some plausible conclusion or closure: "Baghdad is a city of lanterns amid the blackouts," he writes. "A city of ghosts shadowed by fear, a city that is forsaken. The city I knew would always remain *ghamidha*" (p. 308).

Hugh Martin is an Iraq War veteran and the author of the poetry collections In Country *and* The Stick Soldiers. *He is the recipient of a Wallace Stegner Fellowship, and he was the inaugural winner of the* Iowa Review's *Jeff Sharlet Award for Veterans. His essays and poetry have appeared in various places, including* PBS Newshour, The New Yorker, *and* The New York Times. *He is currently completing a doctoral degree at Ohio University, Athens, Ohio.*

"Listen Up, Maggots! April is National Poetry Month!"

By Randy Brown

When packing for one of my first training experiences with the U.S. Army, back in the late 1980s, I knew that free time and footlocker space would be at a premium. I could live without luxuries like my Walkman cassette player for a few months. I also wanted to avoid too much gruff from drill sergeants. So I stuffed a paperback copy of Shakespeare's play "Henry V" into my left cargo pocket, wrapped in a plastic sandwich bag, as my sole entertainment.

If nothing else, I thought, I'd work on my memorization skills. ("Oh, for a muse of fire-guard duty …") Little did I realize that so much of my brain would already be filled, starting those summer months at Fort Knox, Ky., with the nursery verse of Uncle Sam. Training was full of poetry. Sometimes, it was profane. "This is my rifle, this is my gun!" Sometimes, it was pedagogical. "I will turn the tourniquet / to stop the flow / of the bright red blood." There were even times that it was nearly pathological. "What is the spirit of the bayonet?! / Kill! Kill! Kill!"

These basic phrases connected us new recruits to the yellow footprints of those who had stood here before—those who had marched in our boots, squared the same corners, weathered the same abuses. Every time we moved, we were serenaded by sergeants. Counting cadence, calling cadence, bemoaning that Jody was back home, dating our women, drinking our beer. We learned our lines, our ranks, our patches, our places as much by tribal storytelling as by reading the effing field manual. Even our soldier humor was hand-me-down wisdom, tossed off like singsong hand grenades. Phrases such as "Don't call me 'sir' / I work for a living!" and "You were bet-ter off when you left! / You're right!" became semi-automatic.

Nobody's quite sure why April got the nod as National Poetry Month. I like to think that it's because of that line from T.S. Eliot's "The Wasteland": "April is the cruelest month." Because that sounds like the Army. Besides, in springtime, the thoughts of every warrior-poet lightly turns to baseball; the showers that bring flowers ("If it ain't raining / it ain't training!"); and the start of fighting season in Afghanistan.

Poetry, I recognize, isn't every soldier's three cups of tea. Ever since I entertained my platoon mates with King Henry's inspiring St. Crispin's Day speech, however, I've enjoyed sneaking poetry into the conversation.

Perhaps more soldiers would appreciate poetry, were they to realize the inherent poetics of military life:

Every time you go to war, you are engaged in a battle for narrative. Every deployment—individually as a soldier, or collectively as an Army or nation—is a story. Every story has a beginning, middle, and end. Every story is subject to vision, and revision. History isn't always written by the victors, but it is re-written by poets. Treat them well. Otherwise, they will cut you.

Every time you eat soup with a knife, you are wielding a metaphor. Every "boots on the ground," every "line in the sand," every Hollywood-style named operation ("Desert Shield"! "Desert Storm"! "Enduring Freedom"!) is a metaphor that shapes our understanding of a war and its objectives. And, if you don't understand the dangerous end of a metaphor, you shouldn't be issued one.

(There's also a corollary, and a warning: As missions change, so do metaphors. In other words, when a politician trots out a new metaphor for an old war, you'd better check your six.)

Every poem is a fragment of intelligence, a piece in the puzzle. A poem can slow down time, to describe a moment in lush and flushed detail. It can transport the reader to a different time, a different battlefield. Most importantly, a poem can describe the experience of military life and death through someone else's eyes—a spouse, a villager, a soldier, a journalist. Poetry, in short, is a training opportunity for empathy.

Soldiers like to say that the enemy gets a vote, so it's worth noting that the enemy writes poetry, too. Like reading doctrine and monitoring propaganda, reading an enemy's verse reveals motivations and values. Sun Tzu writes:

> If you know the enemy and know yourself, you need not fear the result of a hundred battles. If you know yourself but not the enemy, for every victory gained you will also suffer a defeat. If you know neither the enemy nor yourself, you will succumb in every battle.

Every time you quote a master, from Sun Tzu to Schwarzkopf, you are delivering aphorism. I liken the aphorism—a quotable-quote or maxim—to be akin to concise forms of poetry, such as haiku. In fact, in my expansive view, I think aphorisms should count as poetry. In the world of word craft, it can take as much effort to hone an effective aphorism than it does to write a 1,000-word essay. Aphorisms are laser-guided missiles, rather than carpet bombs. We should all spend our words more wisely.

Reading a few lines connects us to the thin red line of soldiers past, present, and future. Poetry puts us in the boots of those who have served before, hooks our chutes to a larger history and experience of war. The likes of Shakespeare's "band of brothers" speech, John McRae's "In Flanders Fields," and Rudyard Kipling's poem "Tommy" continue to speak to the experiences and sentiments of modern soldiers.

I am happy to report that more-contemporary war poets have continued the march.

Here's a quick list to probe the front lines of modern war poetry: From World War II, seek out Henry Reed's "The Naming of Parts." For a jolt of Vietnam Era parody, read Alan Farrell's "The Blaming of Parts." From the Iraq War, Brian Turner's "Here, Bullet." In this tight shot group, modern soldiers will no doubt recognize themselves, their tools, and their times. Here is industrial-grade boredom, an assembly line of war, punctuated with humor and grit, gunpowder and lead.

Want more? Check out print and on-line literary offerings from Veterans Writing Project's *O-Dark-Thirty* literary journal; Military Experience & the Arts' twice-annual journal *As You Were*; the *Line of Advance* journal; and Southeast Missouri State University's *Proud to Be: Writing by American Warriors* annual anthology series.

Finally, you can buy an pocket anthology of poetry, such as the Everyman's Library Pocket Poets edition of *War Poems* from Knopf, or Ebury's *Heroes: 100 Poems from the New Generation of War Poets*. Stuff it in your left cargo pocket. Read a page a day as a secular devotional, a meditation on war. Or, pick a favorite poem, print it out, and post it on the wall of your fighting position or office cube. Read the same poem, over and over again, during the course of a few weeks. See how it changes. See how it changes in you.

Remember: April is National Poetry Month. And every time you read a war poem, an angel gets their Airborne wings.

Randy Brown embedded with his former Iowa Army National Guard unit as a civilian journalist in Afghanistan, May-June 2011. He authored the award-winning poetry collection Welcome to FOB Haiku: War Poems from Inside the Wire, *and has edited two books:* Reporting for Duty: U.S. Citizen-Soldier Journalism from the Afghan Surge, 2010-2011 *and* Why We Write: Craft Essays on Writing War. *He is the current poetry editor of the non-profit Military Experience & the Arts' literary journal* As You Were, *and is a board member of the Military Writers Guild. As "Charlie Sherpa," he blogs about civil-military topics at www.redbullrising.com; about 21st century war poetry at www.fobhaiku.com; and about military writing at www.aimingcircle.com. Follow him on Twitter: @FOB_Haiku*

"Reach for the Skies": Writing a Western Helped Me Face Down Rejection

By Kori Schake

I wasn't a good writer until I was nearly 50. I was too much worried about proving I knew what I was talking about, and too little worried about having something interesting to say. Because I've had an unusual career, hopscotching back and forth between policy jobs and being a schoolteacher, I've always doubted that I'm a respectable academic. Early on, I smothered my authentic voice to show I could ski the slalom of academic gates. It leadened my writing–even I was bored reading it. I could give interesting talks, but when I tried to translate the lectures into articles, they bogged down with the weight of my academic aspirations.

What made me a good writer, funnily enough, was writing a serial Western for a pal in military service. It was a dime novel, scribbled to give him something to take his mind off the demands on him, help him get to sleep. I'd write a short installment every week, just a few pages. The playfulness of the undertaking gave me license to just write without having to be impressive. Puzzling through the arc of the story was challenging, and letting the pungency of the characters drive plot lines and dialogue was all such fun that it let me hear my own voice as a writer. It also attuned me to the craft of telling a story well. When to give or withhold crucial information, for example, and what details anchor understanding. It sharpened my eye for when I was showing off, and disciplined me to delete the gratuitous.

I love the artist Chuck Close's insistence that "inspiration is for amateurs—the rest of us just show up and get to work." I pair that with Isabel Allende's reflection that "lots and lots of people are creative when they feel like it, but you are only going to become a professional if you do it when you don't feel like it. And that emotional waiver is why this is your work and not your hobby." Those two comments cement the professionalism of the undertaking, and help me concentrate on the craftsmanship of writing. You can't always wait for lightning to strike.

I enjoy the blocking and tackling of writing: Coming up with an argument, figuring out what would prove it right or wrong, arraying the information in a sequence that invites readers into an understanding, and finding memorable language to make the issue meaningful. If I structure an argument well, I can write easily; if I haven't successfully laid the foundation, I wander aimlessly and waste lots of time until I throw it out and start over. I also can't write until I have something to say. Which means that I can't write unless I'm reading. For my columns in *The Atlantic*, I need to be awash in current events and others' commentaries. That helps spark my thinking, because I'm reacting to events, navigating what I agree with and where I have different views than what are already on display. I read voraciously in order to write. Just as sharks need a constant streaming of water through their gills to breathe, I need a constant stream of information to write about current policy.

Because I am not expert on every subject, the same is true for my academic writing. I start out with a question I'm curious about, then start scouting answers. If it's been answered to my satisfaction by someone else, I savor their good work and find another subject.

My book *Safe Passage: The Transition from British to American Hegemony* started when I noted the recent popularity of topics regarding the possible "rise of China." I began thinking about hegemonic transition, and whether it could happen peacefully and what it might mean for the United States. It got me curious about what made for peaceful transitions between an established dominant power and a rising one.

It turns out there's only one peaceful hegemonic transition, and while that's a catastrophe for a political scientist (it's dodgy to identify patterns and extrapolate trends when n=1), it's a fun circumstance for an historian, because you can explore what made this example unique. Because I am poorly trained in several disciplines, I could choose to explore the subject as the latter, rather than the former.

Writing short pieces is a different process than writing longer formats. I find I write pretty naturally in 700-word arguments, accustomed as I now am to magazine columns. Long-form feature articles or books, however, require a different approach. I liken the difference to being a relief pitcher, as compared to being a starting pitcher on rotation.

Just like a starting pitcher needs the routine of throwing daily and working up to a game every five days, I find I need to be in the patterns that help me think and write clearly in longer forms: I need solitude and silence. I need to get up early to read the previous day's work and pick up the thread. I need research near at hand for patching holes. All of this helps work to a trajectory: a chapter every five days.

I write for five or six hours, until I either finish a substantial section or my concentration fails and I'm marooned. Having reached such a point, I'll go for a run, eat, laze around watching baseball, or read something unrelated to what I'm working on. All of these serve to refresh my mind. I start writing again the following morning.

As with short-form, architecture is important. When I'm writing a book, I break the subject down into discrete pieces that form building blocks.

That's the fun part, indulging the imaginary Prussian in myself to outline what needs to be said. The other really fun part is research. Writing a book is a fishing license to read and read and read, take notes, and then figure out where each piece of information best fits.

Because I'm always fearful I won't have enough to say in a book-length work, my early chapters are often padded with an adipose layer of unnecessary verbiage, which have to be liposuctioned after the first draft.

I try to write what I like to read; I hate reading books where writers just avalanche information down on my head, instead of curating it to only what is necessary to prove or disprove the argument.

I let myself write a first draft without editing, however, to focus on trying to wrestle the subject to the ground. For me, that's the hardest part: Getting from a sensible structure to translating the ideas into concrete words. That's the part I get paid for instead of doing it for free. It's arduous, I'm boring and terrible to be around because I'm walking around the house in my pajamas talking to myself, trying to conjure accurate and interesting ways to convey what is still taking shape in my head.

It's not a brief interlude, either—I typically spend about a third of the time of a book figuring out what question I'm trying to answer, a third doing research, and a third actually writing.

Editing is a chore for me, as it is for most writers. It feels profligate to erase things conjured from nothingness (one more reason to outline carefully, so that I don't dive down rabbit holes). More than that, reading back critically over my own writing is the time I am most skeptical of its value. I often feel like I'm looking at a cold soggy tangle of seaweed dredged up from the depths, and doubt the enterprise will be useful to anyone. Still, untangling and skeining the seaweed needs to be done, and it's my job. Again, it's why they pay me instead of me doing it for free.

Working with editors is, by comparison, a much easier process. I've never had an editor that hasn't added value to my work. Even when they (as Tod Lindberg did on *Safe Passage*) tell me it isn't adding up and I need to rethink how I'm approaching the problem. Getting criticism from such readers is much easier to handle because they give you concrete things to fix, which feels productive.

Once a given work is done, I tend to start liking it again. More importantly, I can allow myself to feel like a good writer. I was a student of Tom Schelling and he often told me there were only two kinds of dissertations: "perfect" and "finished." Because he knew I was a flight risk, he wanted mine finished rather than perfect. His encouragement to say what I learned and then to move on stays with me still.

My favorite solace when I'm writing is the house of adventure writer Jack London, nearby me in Glen Ellen, Calif. It's a museum of his life and his writing, and has right at the entrance a display of some of the ten thousand—*ten thousand!*—rejections he received from publishers. My favorite of these is from the *The Saturday Evening Post*, which declined a story from him in 1901. Editors wrote: "we have found the 'Sunlanders' a story of exceptional interest, and we should wish to give it a place in our columns were it not our policy to exclude the tragic from the magazine." What a gentle, gracious let down by the editors to remind him it wasn't about his talent, it was about fit with the brand of their magazine. Which is the final advice I would offer to writers, and to take also myself: rejection and tenacity are both integral parts of writing.

Kori Schake is the deputy director-general of the International Institute for Strategic Studies (IISS). She was a distinguished research fellow at the Hoover Institution and is the editor, with Jim Mattis, of the book Warriors and Citizens: American Views of Our Military. *Her history of the Anglo-American hegemonic transition is* Safe Passage: The Transition from British to American Hegemony. *She has served in various U.S. policy roles, including those at the National Security Council; at the Department of Defense for the Office of the Secretary of Defense and the Joint Chiefs of Staff; and the State Department for the Policy Planning Staff. During the 2008 presidential election, she was senior policy advisor on the McCain-Palin campaign.*

First, Write about a Barn

By Jerri Bell

September 2017, Amherst, Va.—I'm currently at the Virginia Center for the Creative Arts (VCCA) for two-and-a-half weeks courtesy of the National Endowment for the Arts (NEA), which kindly funded the visit fully and provided me with a $1,000 stipend through their scholarship program for artists who are military veterans. The VCCA houses a group of about 25 writers, artists, and composers for stays of up to a month, feeds us three squares a day, gives us studio space in a renovated barn or cottage, and then leaves us alone to work or socialize as we choose.

How am I using your tax dollars? I've been working from either 0600 or 0700 every morning until about midnight, with short breaks for an afternoon walk, meals, and perhaps for a pre-dinner happy hour involving wine from the local Food Lion. I'm doing my best to earn back your investment by writing—well, *trying* to write—something that's as good as I know how to make it.

One of conversational themes with other writers here is the challenge that many women face: of learning to believe in our right to create art, and to believe in the quality of the art that we create.

Many here can tell horror stories about times their work was derided, devalued, and dismissed. I had my creative writing ambitions shot down twice: Once, by a visiting writer at the college where I got my undergraduate degree in 1982; and again by a professor at another college, when I took her class while on shore duty in 1995.

In each case, I let discouragement, self-doubt, and a raging case of impostor syndrome deprive me of an art form I love. For a total of nearly a quarter-century. In those years, I did no serious creative writing. Made no effort to practice, or to improve my craft. I exercised no self-discipline, and didn't write anything creative regularly. I scribbled random journal entries or long e-mails if the spirit moved me, but otherwise set aside the cherished dream of writing a book. I'd had that dream since I was in the 4th grade.

Funny thing is, when it came to my serving on warships or to my work in U.S. naval intelligence, I'd never allow the naysayers to keep me down. I had no problem putting myself out there, demanding the opportunity to do jobs that I knew I could do well, and (at least after my first tour) insisting that I get appropriate recognition for having done them.

Military service boosted my confidence. I decided to use my G.I. Bill to pursue what I loved, even if it was completely impractical. I applied to the

Master of Arts in Writing program at Johns Hopkins, Baltimore, Md. and was accepted in 2005, three years before I retired from the U.S. Navy. By 2004, the Army and Marines were grinding themselves down with repeated deployments. Their support communities reached out to the Navy and Air Force with requests for "individual augmentees" to fill ground support billets in Iraq and Afghanistan. At first, these "IA" assignments were voluntary; sailors and airmen who believed in the fight, or wanted to do what they felt they'd been training for, jumped at the chance to deploy.

I had strong reservations about the wars in Iraq and Afghanistan, so when my commanding officer offered me the first shot at a plum IA assignment, I declined to volunteer. It was probably the first time in my entire 16-year career that I hadn't jumped at the chance to take on a challenging job—one that promised both excitement and great bullets on a fitness report.

Late in that year, however, naval intelligence was exhausting its pool of sailors motivated to go to the Middle East in a ground support job. The secretary of the Navy, or maybe it was the chief of naval operations, sent out a message that all personnel in certain specialties were immediately and indefinitely on 30-day stand-by to deploy to Iraq or Afghanistan. In other words: Update your wills, do the assigned on-line training modules, make sure that your affairs are in order and that your seabag is packed.

The following spring, I enrolled in a "craft of fiction" class at Johns Hopkins. To teach setting and mood, our instructor, Margaret Meyers, asked us to complete the "John Gardner Challenge," a prompt that is found in the author's 1983 book *The Art of Fiction*. It went something like:

> Consider the following as a possible exercise in description. Describe a barn as seen by a man whose son has just been killed in a war. Do not mention the son, or war, or death. It's an exercise that anyone can do, and one of the cool things that comes out of it is that every single person in a class will describe a different barn, from the point of view of a different man with a unique background, and the result will be something original and, usually, deeply unsettling to the writer.

I put everything I felt about the wars in Iraq and Afghanistan into that exercise. It wouldn't let me sleep at night. I kept going back to it. My mother-in-law read it and offered a 20-minute critique that ended with me half-shouting in exasperation, "Judy, there's no law against you writing your own barn. So if you think you can write a goddamn barn so much better than I can, I suggest that you sit down and start writing it already!"

The twinges of the old self-doubt and impostor syndrome began to resurface. If your family doesn't love your work, the critics sure as hell won't either. There was no going back, however. I couldn't *not* work on it. I brushed off my mother-in-law (though I never permitted her to read any of my work again). I allowed Iraq and Vietnam to creep onto the page, and the original paragraph morphed into a short story.

Although I didn't think I was ready to submit anything for publication, in a why-the-hell-not moment just after New Year's in 2007, I entered it in two categories in the West Virginia Writers annual competition. It took a first-place in "Appalachian Theme" and a second-place in "Emerging Writers." At the conference, the editor of a regional literary journal cornered me, asked me to send him the story, and requested the right of first refusal on it. So exciting! I'd arrived!

I did as he asked. The day I got home, I printed the story out on nice paper (this was before most journals were using Submittable), attached a self-addressed, stamped envelope, and mailed it off to Kentucky. And I waited. I was afraid to send a follow-up query, and believed that simultaneous submission to other journals was inappropriate when a respected editor had solicited my manuscript. I watched the mailbox for a full year, and never received either an acceptance or a rejection.

The story went out again to two other journals requesting "Appalachian" or "southern" fiction in 2009, as part of the thesis class requirement to submit finished work. Both journals declined to publish it. I'd made it to retirement in 2008 without being called up for one of those involuntary IA assignments, so I didn't feel that what I had to say about war much mattered to anyone. I figured there would be much more interest in the writing of the troops who'd deployed. After grad school, I decided I was done trying to write military stories. I filed the manuscript away, and forgot about it.

In 2013, I started editing for the Veterans Writing Project's literary journal *O-Dark-Thirty*. After editing for several months, I remembered my little barn story, and decided to try one more time to place it. I looked for a journal that seemed like a good fit, and fired it off to the journal *Stone Canoe*. They snapped it right up: It was published in 2014, nine years after I'd written the first draft.

When former U.S. Marine Tracy Crow and I were writing and editing the history/anthology hybrid *It's My Country Too: Women's Military Stories from the American Revolution to Afghanistan*, we were shocked to find out how women's stories about war, just like their contributions to the war effort, had been discredited and dismissed, or overlooked entirely. Very few women veterans of World War II wrote and published war memoirs before the 1990s, when the 50th anniversary of milestones like D-Day renewed American interest in that war and those who fought it. Most didn't believe that their contributions had been significant, or that anyone would be interested in what they had to say about how they'd done their little part for the national defense. Their families had to convince them that their efforts had mattered, and cajole them into writing things down so their stories would not be lost.

Knowing what I know now? I should have shotgunned my first story to every journal calling for submissions in the back pages of *Poets & Writers* magazine. I should have treated the submission and rejection process just like I treated the naysayers in the Navy: *Oh, yeah? Fuck you, I can so. I'm good enough, and you want me to do that job. You just don't know it yet.*

What would have happened if I'd treated my writing career the way I'd treated my military service? *Oh, yeah? Fuck you, I can so write. I'm good enough, I have something to say about the wars in Iraq and Afghanistan, and you want to listen. You just don't know it yet.* Maybe the story would have seen daylight in the first decade of the war. My story "Memorial Day" would hardly have revolutionized war writing, and it's certainly not the barn that I'd write if I wrote it now. But if I'd believed in myself more, and fought harder for the thing I had created, it might have found its way into print sooner. I might even have been able to say to my mother-in-law before she passed away, *See, Judy? That barn was just fine the way I wrote it.*

Jerri Bell is managing editor of O-Dark-Thirty, *the literary journal of the Washington, D.C.-based non-profit Veterans Writing Project. Bell retired from the U.S. Navy in 2008; her assignments included antisubmarine warfare in the Azores Islands, sea duty on USS Mount Whitney and HMS Sheffield, and attaché duty at the U.S. embassy in Moscow, Russia. Her fiction has been published in a variety of journals, and her non-fiction in journals and newspapers, including* The Washington Post; *her work has been twice nominated for a Pushcart Prize. She and former U.S. Marine Tracy Crow are the co-authors of* It's My Country Too: Women's Military Stories from the American Revolution to Afghanistan, *published in 2017.*

Babylon Revisited

By Thomas E. Ricks

As a young reporter in political Washington in the late 1980s, I noticed a type of person who thrived in the driven, transactional environment of the capital. These were people who somehow, as I thought of it, "enjoyed the game." I liked interviewing members of Congress and their staffers, who conveyed a sense of pleasure in the daily doings of the place.

I decided that theirs was the way to go, and also to maintain some perspective. For me, enjoying the game meant seeing the city's machinations as a grand Shakespearean show. That is, notice the character types. Enjoy the insiders' distinctive patois. Admire the deftness of the political tap dances. Step back and watch the daily pageant pass. It was often comedy, and sometimes tragedy, but it was almost always interesting.

This approach worked well for me for almost two decades. I scurried around Washington, from Capitol Hill to the Pentagon, from K Street expense account lunches to off-the-record dinners with powerful people, and from Hanoi to Rome to Riyadh and Seoul as I covered the travels of top officials. One bleary morning in Brussels, I marveled that, when my suitcase was delivered to my hotel room fresh from our U.S. Air Force flight, it had moved so fast from the military airport that the toothpaste was still cold from its time in the cargo hold.

I remember particular one day when we had lunch aboard an aircraft carrier in the hot Persian Gulf, listened to the defense secretary address some of the crew, and then helicoptered back to land, where we boarded a big Air Force jet for a flight to Moscow. Midway there, we were advised to go downstairs into the cargo hold, find our suitcases, and bundle up for the Moscow winter. On arrival late that night, we checked into a snazzy new hotel in Moscow where the American co-owner, we were told, had been shot on the front steps by his Russian partner.

It was after midnight and only the bar was still open for food, so I went there for some mushroom ravioli and a glass of red wine. Sitting next to me was a Russian man packing a pistol who identified himself as "investment banker." Given the rules of the game there, he might well have been. The next morning, we bussed out to a military deconstruction site. (This was back when the United States and Russia were cooperating on nuclear de-escalation.) We stood and waited for an hour or two in a tent pitched in the subzero Russian winter. The cold seeped into my bones, so much so that seemed to feel it linger in my marrow for weeks.

Even the boring times could be fun. I was once in Seoul to cover a fairly routine meeting between South Korean and American officials. Not much was going on, so while I waited for the concluding press conference, I sat in my 5-star hotel room, drank good tea, and finished writing a novel. This was life on a global carousel.

But early in the 21st century, around 2004, I stopped enjoying it all. Part of this was fatigue—I worked nonstop after 9/11 for months, perhaps years. But mainly I think it was the invasion of Iraq, and what followed there. The Iraq War broke my heart. I never thought my country would invade a country so recklessly, with so little understanding of the culture of the place or the politics of the region. Why did not we see that taking over Iraq and insisting on American-style voting inevitably would empower Iran? Plus, we went to war on false premises. Defense Secretary Donald Rumsfeld spoke of the unknowables. But I think that we didn't want to know what we should have known.

On top of that, I was powerfully disappointed by the U.S. military I saw in Iraq. I had covered it for years, both in Washington and on the ground in operations in Somalia, Haiti, Bosnia, and Afghanistan. I covered the armed forces objectively, but I generally had been impressed by the character and competence of our soldiers.

So, I wondered, how could our military then operate so clumsily, so counter-productively, and at times so cruelly, in Iraq? How could the Army that I had seen deal so well with the tortuous problems of the Balkans, operate so stupidly as to allow soldiers at the Abu Ghraib prison to taunt, torture, and humiliate their captives? Didn't American leaders see that this angered Iraqis and inflamed the insurgency? Most of all, the fact that something so wrong occurred showed how misbegotten the whole American enterprise in Iraq was.

In response to all that, I wrote the book *Fiasco,* about the first few years of our war in Iraq. Then, a couple of years later, out of a sense of obligation to stick to the story, I then wrote a sequel, *The Gamble,* about Gen. David Petraeus and the "surge" in Iraq in 2007. Finally, to answer my own lingering questions, I next wrote *The Generals,* examining the lack of accountability among senior Army officers.

But I was finished with Washington. I had seen too many people suffer in and from Iraq. I had lost friends. I saw good reporters struggle with depression, anxiety, and panic attacks. I felt some of this myself. My dreams were black, and I would awake covered in sweat. My family was unhappy. I was twisted by stress. In short, I no longer could see the capital's actions as a "game." Washington's actions had gotten hundreds of thousands of people killed and maimed. It made me sick, and worse, made me sad.

I didn't see it so clearly at the time, but I needed to leave Washington. I was done. My wife and I had vacationed in Maine for years, and I had gone there to finish writing books, doing the intense work of completing first drafts. She pointed out that I was spending so much time there that instead of renting, we could make a down payment on a house.

We soon learned we couldn't afford buying near Portland, or indeed anywhere within a weekend's drive of Boston. But there were lovely harbor towns farther up the coast. We bought on an island we liked, and settled in. We kept our house in Washington, and initially spent our winters there, heading south after Christmas.

The more time we spent in the new house, the more we liked it. And while in Washington, we always pined for Maine. One January, as we were packing up to leave Maine, we decided instead to spend the winter there, and see how it went.

We loved it. The summers are lovely, but there also is great beauty in the fall's sunsets, the winter's storms, and spring's mists. I've counted nine shades of green from a spot on one of my favorite walks — in lichen, two mosses, a fir, a spruce, some granite, two types of seaweed, and the translucent sea. I revel in the panorama of nature. Almost every day, I see a wild animal—fox, deer, seal, heron, eagle, osprey, and so on. I follow the phases of the moon, partly because the huge tides affect how I use my boat, but one side effect is that when I awake in the night I can tell roughly what time it is simply by judging the angle of the moon shadows. I don't have an alarm clock, I have chickadees and doves. In Washington, I felt every day was like climbing into the boxing ring for another few rounds. In Maine I look forward to my day with eagerness.

So, for the last several years, we've lived in Maine year-round. We enjoy the community here, especially in the winter, when many of our friends, preoccupied in the summer with taking care of visitors, or feeding or housing or teaching them, have time to socialize.

Then came Trump. Now, I feel like we got out just in time, before the slow-motion train crash began. Even from here, I find Trump disorienting and disgusting. I don't know how I would be able to stand being in the same city with him. It is a great time for journalism, but it wouldn't be for me. I admire people like Peter Baker, an old colleague now at *The New York Times*, for their stamina and persistence. I would not be able to do it.

In 2017, I flew down to Washington to be interviewed by C-SPAN's Brian Lamb about my book on Winston Churchill and George Orwell. As I walked around Capitol Hill, watching the conservatively attired young staffers hurry to and fro, planning their next moves, the thought occurred to me: "This is no longer my city." I didn't enjoy it at all. I wasn't just disoriented, I was alienated. I'd see the staffers chuckle as they walked and I would think, *What are you people doing? What events will break your hearts?*

I couldn't wait to get to the airport and head home.

Thomas E. Ricks covered the U.S. military for The Washington Post *from 2000 through 2008, and for* The Wall Street Journal *from 1982 to 1999. During his career, he covered military activities in Somalia, Haiti, Korea, Bosnia, Kosovo, Macedonia, Kuwait, Turkey, Afghanistan, and Iraq. He was part of a Wall Street Journal team that won a 2000 Pulitzer Prize for national reporting regarding 21st century challenges faced by the U.S. military, and part of a* Washington Post *team that won a 2002 Pulitzer Prize for reporting on the U.S. counteroffensive against terrorism. He is author of several non-fiction books, including* Churchill and Orwell: The Fight for Freedom; Fiasco: The American Military Adventure in Iraq, 2003 to 2005, *which was a finalist for a Pulitzer Prize;* The Gamble: General David Petraeus and the American Military Adventure in Iraq, 2006-2008; The Generals: American Military Command from World War II to Today; *and* Making the Corps. *In 2001, Ricks published* A Soldier's Duty, *a military thriller about two Pentagon aides-de-camp. He formerly wrote the* Best Defense *blog at* Foreign Policy *magazine, and* The Long March *blog at* Task & Purpose. *He lives happily in Maine. Follow him on Twitter: @TomRicks1*

Acknowledgements

Disclaimer: The views expressed herein by uniformed and civilian employees of government are their own and do not reflect the official positions or policies of their respective branches of service, agencies, or governments.

The editors wish to thank the members of the 2017-2018 board of directors of the Military Writers Guild, including Adin Dobkin, Carl Forsling, and Troy Mitchell, under whom this project was launched.

The editors also thank the members of the 2018-2019 board of directors of the Military Writers Guild, including Christopher G. Ingram, Gary M. Klein, and Pauline Shanks Kaurin, under whom this project was completed.

Robert L. Bateman's essay first appeared at *Esquire* Aug. 5, 2013.

Peter Van Buren's essay is excerpted from his 2012 memoir, *We Meant Well: How I Helped Lose the Battle for the Hearts and Minds of the Iraqi People*, and also appeared on *The American Conservative* Nov. 10, 2017.

Rachel Kambury's essay is adapted from a Dec. 5, 2016 post on *The Quivering Pen* blog.

Matthew Komatsu's essay appeared on *The New York Times'* blog *At War*, Sept. 12, 2014.

Steven L. Moore's essay previously appeared in the Spring 2017 issue of the on-line literary journal *Print-Oriented Bastards*.

Peter W. Singer and August Cole's essay originally appeared June 30, 2015 on John Scalzi's blog *Whatever*.

Hugh Martin's essay appeared on *Essay Daily* May 29 2017.

Randy Brown's essay appeared on the *Red Bull Rising* blog April 6, 2016.

Jerri Bell's essay is adapted from a Sept. 5, 2017 post on the blog *Presumption and Folly*.

Thomas E. Ricks' essay originally appeared Nov. 17, 2017 on *Foreign Policy* magazine's *Best Defense* blog.

Index

Marine Corps Gazette, 124

Newsweek, 22, 84

Official Karate, 95

Positive Living, 95

Publishers Weekly, 139

Reader's Digest, 95

Rolling Stone, 69

Soldier of Fortune, 95

Straight, 94

The American Conservative, 67, 227

The Lookout, 94

The Saturday Evening Post, 217

Time, 84

Vietnam Combat, 95

Mahan, Alfred Thayer, 35, 36, 37

Maine, 223

Marine Corps Heritage Foundation's
    James Webb award for fiction, 22

marksmanship, 62, 171

Marlantes, Karl, 173

Martin, Hugh, 227

Masters, Edgar Lee, 204

Mattis, Jim, 217

Maude, Stanley, 206

McCain IV, John "Jack", 3

McDermott, Tom, 2

McDonald, "Country Joe", 107

McNamara, Robert S., 107

McRae, John, 213

Meade, George, 199

medevac, 94

memoir, 67, 107

mentorship, 161

metaphor, 28, 86, 201, 212

Middle Earth, 204

Middletown, Conn., 202

military cartoonist, 245

Military Decision-Making Process
    (MDMP), 42

Military Experience & the Arts, 138,
    213, 245

military history, 36, 43, 55, 135, 153,
    154

Military Journalist of the Year, 184

military justice, 198

Military Occupational Specialties
    (MOS), 142

    11-Bravo, 143

    71-Quebec, 143

    71-Romeo, 143

Military Police, 1, 110

Military Reporters and Editors
    (MRE), 245

military spouses, 63

Military Writers Guild, 1, 9, 18, 38,
    40, 45, 88, 123, 125, 156, 158,
    159, 175, 213, 227, 244, 245

Military Writers Society of America
    (MWSA), 245

Mill, John Stuart, 91

Miller, Brenda, 103

Minneapolis, 145, 149

Minnesota, 145

Minnesota Humanities Center, 145

Mish, Jeanetta Calhoun, 108

Mississippi River, 145, 146, 149

Mitchell, Troy, 227

Modern War Institute at West Point,
    9, 16, 18, 123, 127, 128, 245

Monsarrat, Nicholas, 28

Moore, Steven L., 227

moral issues, 20

morality, 64, 89

Moscow, Russia, 221, 222

Movies

    Being John Malkovich, 177

    Dances with Wolves, 114

    Game of Thrones, 190

    Ghostbusters, 168

    Good Morning, Vietnam, 107, 140

    Hamburger Hill, 107

About the Military Writers Guild

The Military Writers Guild is a Texas-based 501(c)3 non-profit organization that serves a growing international membership of writers on military themes and topics.

Members include service members, civilians, and military veterans. They are writers of literary and genre fiction, creative non-fiction, essays and opinion, scholarship, policy and research papers, poetry, drama, and more.

In the words of 2018-2019 President Christopher G. Ingram, "Our guild seeks to build an inclusive community of practice that elevates the discourse in military writing through collaboration, and the promotion of our craft."

For more information about the Military Writers Guild, visit:

URL: www.militarywritersguild.org
Facebook: www.facebook.com/milwritersguild
Twitter: @MilWritersGuild

About the Editors

Randy Brown embedded with his former Iowa Army National Guard unit as a civilian journalist in Afghanistan, May-June 2011. He authored the 2015 poetry collection *Welcome to FOB Haiku: War Poems from Inside the Wire*, and edited the 2017 *Reporting for Duty: U.S. Citizen-Soldier Journalism from the Afghan Surge, 2010-2011*. His poetry and non-fiction have appeared widely, in such literary markets as *F(r)iction*; *So It Goes: the Literary Journal of the Kurt Vonnegut Library & Museum*; and the first eight volumes of the anthology series *Proud to Be: Writing by American Warriors*, published annually by Southeast Missouri State University Press. He is a three-time poetry finalist in the Col. Darron L. Wright Memorial Writing Award competition, administered by *Line of Advance*. Brown is the current poetry editor of the non-profit Military Experience & the Arts' literary journal *As You Were*, and a board member of the Military Writers Guild. He is a member of Military Reporters and Editors (MRE) and Military Writers Society of America (MWSA). As "Charlie Sherpa," he blogs about civil-military topics at www.redbullrising.com; 21st century war poetry at www.fobhaiku.com; and about military writing resources at www.aimingcircle.com. Follow him on Twitter: @FOB_Haiku

Steve Leonard is a former U.S. Army officer and senior military strategist, an award-winning faculty member at the University of Kansas School of Business, and the creative force behind the defense microblog *Doctrine Man!!* A career writer and speaker with a passion for developing and mentoring the next generation of thought leaders, he is a senior fellow at the Modern War Institute at West Point; the co-founder of the national security blog *Divergent Options*, and *The Smell of Victory* podcast; co-founder and board member of the Military Writers Guild; and a member of the editorial review board of the Arthur D. Simons Center's *InterAgency Journal (IAJ)*. Published extensively, his writing focuses on issues of foreign policy, national security, strategy and planning, leadership and leader development. He also occasionally writes fiction. An alumnus of the U.S. Army's School of Advanced Military Studies, he led the interagency team that authored the Army's first stability operations doctrine, spearheaded the reintroduction of operational art into capstone doctrine, and wrote the guiding principles for the Army Design Methodology. He is the author of five books, numerous professional articles, countless blog posts, and is a prolific military cartoonist. Follow him on Twitter: @Doctrine_Man

About the Cover Designer

Established by freelance designer Paul Hewitt, Battlefield Design was born out of a life-long fascination with military history. This passion, along with more than 25 years in graphic design, enables us to approach each task with a creative eye and an understanding of the subject to produce effective, eye-catching results.

We work in all areas of graphic design, including logos, branding, brochures, advertising and display graphics. What sets us apart is our work for military history publishers, film-makers, museums, and tour operators all over the world. We produce material including maps, tour guides, books, museum displays, and illustrations covering wars and conflicts throughout history.

For more information about Battlefield Design, visit:

URL: www.battlefield-design.co.uk
E-mail: info@battlefield-design.co.uk
Twitter: @BattlefieldGD

Did You Enjoy This Book?

Tell your friends and colleagues about it, or post your thoughts via social media sites, like Facebook and Twitter! On-line communities that serve military families, veterans, and service members are also ideal places to help spread the word about this book, and others like it!

You can also share a quick review on websites for other readers, such as Goodreads.com. Or offer a few of your impressions on bookseller websites, such as Amazon.com and BarnesandNoble.com!

Better yet, recommend the title to your favorite local librarian, book club leader, museum gift store manager, or independent bookseller! There is nothing more powerful in business of publishing than a shared review or recommendation from a friend.

We appreciate your support! We'll continue to look for new stories and voices to share with our readers. Keep in touch!

You can write us at:

Middle West Press LLC
P.O. Box 31099
Johnston, Iowa 50131-9428

Or visit: www.middlewestpress.com

Made in United States
North Haven, CT
13 September 2022

24055876R00155